All in War
with
Time

All in War
with
Time

Love Poetry of
Shakespeare, Donne, Jonson, Marvell

Anne Ferry

Harvard University Press
Cambridge, Massachusetts
and London, England
1975

Publication of this book has been
aided by a grant from the
Hyder Edward Rollins Fund

To Elizabeth and Stephen

Acknowledgments

Time to finish this book was provided by a sabbatical leave from Boston College and a fellowship from the John Simon Guggenheim Memorial Foundation, for which I am most grateful.

Many of its arguments originated in courses I taught at Harvard University from 1958 to 1966, and have since been developed, expanded, and revised in discussions with graduate students at Boston College. Our exchanges of interpretations have been a continual source of enrichment and encouragement; where I have borrowed ideas from those discussions I hope the other members will meet them in a new context with the same generous interest they have previously shown in this kind of exploration.

My husband, David Ferry, Sophie Chantal Hart Professor of English at Wellesley College, read and reread these essays and improved many interpretations of individual poems by his detailed comments. It was with him in mind as ideal reader that I wrote this book.

* * * *

I wish to acknowledge with thanks permission to quote Edmund Spenser, "The Minor Poems," edited by Charles Grosvenor Osgood and Henry Gibbons Lotspeich, in *The Works of Edmund Spenser*, edited by Edwin Greenlaw, Charles Grosvenor Osgood, Frederick Morgan Paddleford, and Ray Heffner (Baltimore, Md., The Johns Hopkins Press, 1947). Copyright 1947, The Johns Hopkins Press. I wish to acknowledge also permission to quote from *The Poems of Sir Philip Sidney*, edited by William A. Ringler, © 1962 by Oxford

Contents

All in War
with
Time

1

Shakespeare

The speaker in Shakespeare's Sonnet 15 declares himself to be "all in war with Time for loue of you," the friend whose precious quality he would preserve from mortality. Throughout the first one hundred and twenty-six poems in the collection we find sonnets concerned with this struggle.[1] The speaker varies in the attitudes he takes toward it, challenging or lamenting time's power, in tones arrogant or despairing, detached or resigned. His preoccupation with its destructiveness is evident from the first poem urging the young man to father a child, that his beauty might not "by time decease." Beginning with Sonnet 15, the lover who feels himself to be time's enemy is explicitly and repeatedly identified as an artist whose weapon in love's battle is his poetry.

The figure of the poet-lover dominates English lyrics during the later sixteenth century. Poets of this period, ultimately influenced by Petrarch but also by the French, characteristically introduce the lovers in their poems as poets, inspired to write or made tongue-tied by their feelings, eternizing, praising, persuading, complaining in verse, or comparing their beloveds to beauties celebrated in other poems. *Astrophil and Stella*, the earliest English sonnet sequence and of measureless influence, begins with three poems spoken by a lover struggling to find a literary language in which to write about his feelings, and throughout elaborates on the speaker's role as poet-lover. Following Sidney (and Petrarch), Spenser, Daniel, and Drayton, as well as many of their imitators, begin their sequences with poems explicitly "about" writing love poetry: Spenser's lover addresses his completed book of sonnets which he imagines the lady will read.

Shakespeare's collection (perhaps because it is a collection rather than a sequence[2]) does not begin with a lover who identifies himself explicitly as a poet, though he is pre-eminently an appreciator of beauty, but elsewhere it adopts all the conventional postures of the poet-lover; expands or alters them; even introduces the (perhaps autobiographical) motif of a rival who is also a poet.[3] Shakespeare's uses of the figure are distinctive because they are more pervasive and more various and therefore point us toward his most central concerns in the sonnets. The poet whose verse is love's weapon against time declares the nature of his own power in that struggle and so defines his conception of the nature and power of poetry.

The earliest declaration is Sonnet 15, which appears in the midst of the opening group of related sonnets where the speaker urges a young man to immortalize his beauty by reproducing it in a child.[4] Although connected to the poems in this group by images of time as the enemy of youthful beauty, this sonnet opens new interests which are pursued with many variations throughout the rest of Sonnets 1 to 126.

Sonnet 15 is the first to identify the lover explicitly as an artist, and the first of many to do so by adapting the convention of the eternizing conceit—"I ingraft you new"—immediately recognizable to readers of Italian, French, and English love sonnets as a metaphor for the poet's power to immortalize his beloved in verse.[5] Allusions to this convention occur more often in Shakespeare's than in any other group of English sonnets. His poet-lover, obsessed with the effects of time, refers to the traditional promise so often and with such variousness, so frequently asserts, questions, modifies, finally even attacks, ridicules, and condemns it, that its recurrent uses may be one of the principal reasons why readers tend to think of the speakers in these poems as one personality.[6] So much emphasis accumulates that Shakespeare's changing uses of the eternizing conceit can point to ways we may define his changing concerns about love and also about poetry in the sonnets.

In Sonnet 15 the poet's promise to preserve his beloved from time's decay, although he vows it in full and sad awareness of mutability, is finally asserted with a confidence supported by his ways of manipulating the language of the poem.[7] These devices are characteristic of a *kind* of poetry, found more often among the lower-numbered poems in the collection, which is designed to support the eternizing conceit, or the attitudes associated with its appearance. The assumptions implicit in this kind of sonnet are first consciously argued in Sonnet 15:

> When I consider euery thing that growes
> Holds in perfection but a little moment.
> That this huge stage presenteth nought but showes
> Whereon the Stars in secret influence comment.
> When I perceiue that men as plants increase,
> Cheared and checkt euen by the selfe-same skie:
> Vaunt in their youthfull sap, at height decrease,
> And were their braue state out of memory.
> Then the conceit of this inconstant stay,
> Sets you most rich in youth before my sight,
> Where wastfull time debateth with decay
> To change your day of youth to sullied night,
> > And all in war with Time for loue of you
> > As he takes from you, I ingraft you new.

The language is designed to persuade us, as well as the friend addressed directly in line 10, that an assertion may be true which we know to be contrary to fact. We know that all creatures in the temporal world must decline and eventually die as surely as we know that day must change to night and that seasons pass. The speaker even seems to insist on this knowledge, by his sadness in contemplating how brief and precarious is living "perfection," and by the way he ponders with lavish illustration the fate of "euery thing that growes." Yet the very language in which he dwells on the inevitable waste wrought in the much-loved world by time is his instrument for arguing and so promising his friend that he can defeat its universal power with his art.

The speaker's authority to challenge time is expressed most obviously by the detachment in his tone throughout most of the poem. We recognize it in the leisure he initially enjoys to "consider" and "perceiue," and in the generality and Latinate objectivity of his diction. We hear it in the ways his considerations seem to exclude him from the unconscious life of "euery thing that growes" or of "men as plants," toward whom he feels kindly pity for their vaunting in ignorance of their fate. We find it in his role as spectator which joins him in "secret" knowledge with the stars who also "comment" on the vast scenes presented for their entertainment by the ever-shifting "showes" of the mortal world. This tone of detached sympathy is itself achieved in contradiction of fact, for in fact the speaker as well as his friend belongs to the category "men," and so is subject to time. The authority expressed in his detachment must therefore depend on the ways in which his language manipulates the inescapable facts of temporal experience. The language of the sonnet itself must demonstrate, by it essential characteristics and their peculiar effects, the power of the poet at war with time.

It does so in part by making the passage of time a subject for contemplation while excluding its process, insofar as possible, from the language itself. There are no changes of tense in the poem. "When I consider" exists in the same expansive present with "euery thing that growes / Holds in perfection" and "Where wastfull time debateth" or "To change your day of youth." The prominent series, "When . . . When . . . Then," with which successive quatrains opens, is essentially not a temporal but a logical pattern. "When" and "Then" do not mark stages in a narrative of consecutive events but terms in a syllogism whose structure dictates the design of the poem.[8] Of course, in any argument there is a sense of advance or development, created by a sequence of logically connected points, as the speaker proceeds from one term to that which necessarily follows from it. Even more prominently, as this poet-lover unfolds his argument, his involvement grows, his feelings deepen and change, so that we hear a dramatic development as well as a sequential argument. Yet the ordering principle is different in kind and in its effects from that of a narrative recounting a temporal sequence of events whose succession is dictated by the order in which they happened. For it begins with the opening proposition and is

All in War with Time

derived from it, so that it seems to develop according to logical necessity. Within this order there are no references to single events, happening at specified moments in time, although the poet does speak of activities, his own or in the world he considers. In our experience outside of poems, actions are events which take place at particular times and in temporal sequence, but within the language of the sonnet all action is generalized and made to take place in the continuum of the argument. That is to say, the activities of "euery thing that growes," of "this huge stage," of "men as plants" are not presented as particular events in the speaker's remembered experience of individual times in his past, but as general illustrations of his major and minor premises. They point to his deduction, not by the inevitable passage of time, but by the direction of his own argument. In the language of the conclusion, it is not time which impels him to recognize how his meditation applies to his friend, but his own operations as observer and as poet:[9]

> Then the conceit of this inconstant stay,
> Sets you most rich in youth before my sight,
> Where wastfull time debateth with decay
> To change your day of youth to sullied night.

Here he perceives his friend's subjection to cruel changes, not because time has already wrought those changes and so forced his admission, but because his own verbal comparison has reminded him, as it actively "Sets . . . before my sight" the decline of "men as plants," that his friend will, like plants and men, cease to be. Yet even this painful recognition, forced upon him by the workings of his own comparison, does not ultimately destroy the speaker's control over his unfolding argument. That is, because the metaphorical action is performed by his own "conceit," it seems to operate according to philosophical or verbal laws rather than the cruel dictates of time. Because the act performed by his "conceit" is to set the youth before his "sight" like a scene on a stage or a subject of formal debate, both the friend and the speaker's "conceit" of his subjection to time seem of a different order from temporal experiences. They are like illustrations in an argument, which are also metaphors in a poem, existing outside of time within the verbal order that creates them.

The verbal order of Sonnet 15, which is in part logical and also, as we shall see more fully, metaphorical, is completed by the poet-lover's vaunting of his own power in the battle with time:

> And all in war with Time for loue of you
> As he takes from you, I ingraft you new.

This promise is made in the same present tense used by the poet all through the sonnet. It is designed to lift the destructive action of time, the poet's opposing action, and the fate of the friend out of temporal sequence and to incorporate them in the continuous present of the poem.

The conjunction "And" joins the couplet to the preceding quatrains as an additional conclusion of the syllogism: "When . . . When . . . Then . . . And." In this sequence "And" does not have primarily narrative suggestions of "then the next thing happens after" but has rather the meaning of "an additional conclusion is the following." The speaker therefore makes two deductions from his initial premises:

> When I see that every thing growing in the temporal world including "men as plants" must "decrease" and die,
> then I see you who belong to that category must "decrease" and die,
> and I renew you.

Acceptance of this second conclusion, as a possibility contrary to the facts of the timebound world, depends on the design of the poem, which is logical, we have seen, but also metaphorical.

In his last words, "I ingraft you new," the speaker identifies himself figuratively as a gardener, and his means of combating time as grafting.[10] This art he devotes to the preservation of his friend who, like a plant, is continually diminished by time. We are prepared to accept this claim by the ways in which the poet's metaphorical language all through the sonnet has directed us to think of time's power as it acts on vegetative life. To be sure, his first consideration—"euery thing that growes / Holds in perfection but a little moment"—applies to all living beings. It includes men as well as other natural creatures, but by using the verb "grows" to define the existence of "euery" undifferentiated "thing" he has already begun to speak of "men" as "plants." The second quatrain is therefore the minor premise of his syllogism and the extension of his metaphor. Here he calls attention to the comparison by explicitly naming its terms—"men as plants"—and then elaborating it by describing the flourishing and wilting of human and vegetative life in the same vocabulary. The working-out of the "conceit" points to the poet's means for rescuing his friend. Perceived in vegetative terms, his friend's "day of youth" is bound to "decrease" and die, but because he has been transformed into a plant, his existence in time, comparable with day and night, may be seen to belong to nature's cyclical pattern of decline and renewal—"As he takes from you, I ingraft you new"—and therefore like a plant he can escape individual mortality.

We are therefore able to accept the possibility of this second conclusion within the order created by the language of the poet, although our experience in the world outside the poem has taught us that man cannot be rescued from time's destruction by any human skill. Because the speaker's metaphor makes us perceive his friend as a plant, it makes possible the conclusion that like a plant his declines do not have the finality of human deaths and like a plant he can be renewed by grafting. The emphasis is less on the friend's power of survival, however, since as a plant he is made to seem fragile and helpless, than upon the speaker's manipulation of it by his ability to "ingraft." As a gardener he uses his knowledge and skill to make of a beautifully passive natural creature a new, more enduring creation, blooming as he has artfully designed within the whole order of his garden domain,

That life-giving knowledge and skill is shown in his capacity to "consider" the facts of experience in time, to transform them into the "conceit of this inconstant stay" (a phrase which, through the pun on "stay," itself seems to arrest the passage of time)[11] and so to create a nontemporal order, where sequence is ruled by philosophical necessity. The language of the poem is therefore a demonstration of what the couplet bravely claims, the poet's power through his art to combat destruction by time. It persuades us to accept the possibility of his final assertion contrary to fact, and to recognize his authority to assert it despite his own sad awareness of mutability. This authority is earned by his triumph over time, which he admits to achieve strictly within the design of the poem, his garden world. Although his assurance here is saved from complacency by his tender appreciation of his friend's "day of youth" and by his sorrow that time "takes from" that brief perfection, it allows the tone of detached sympathy with which he first considers the fate of "euery thing that growes" and the confidence with which he eventually engages the power of his art "all in war with Time."

That power is asserted in the final couplet of Sonnet 18 with more radiant assurance. Again we are persuaded to accept the possibility of the speaker's assertion contrary to fact by his manipulations of language, which are different in many details from those of Sonnet 15, but ultimately of the same kind. The poems are closely related not only by their common use of the metaphor of the lovely friend growing as a natural creature saved from time by the speaker's art; they are also alike in using this metaphor to define the poet-lover's conception of the nature and power of poetry itself.

The first line of Sonnet 18, by the use of "compare," identifies the speaker as a poet whose art is the creation of metaphor:[12]

Shall I compare thee to a Summers day?
Thou art more louely and more temperate:
Rough windes do shake the darling buds of Maie,
And Sommers lease hath all too short a date:

Sometime too hot the eye of heauen shines,
And often is his gold complexion dimm'd,
And euery faire from faire some-time declines,
By chance, or natures changing course vntrim'd:
But thy eternall Sommer shall not fade,
Nor loose possession of that faire thou ow'st,
Nor shall death brag thou wandr'st in his shade,
When in eternall lines to time thou grow'st,
   So long as men can breath or eyes can see,
   So long liues this, and this giues life to thee.

The opening question insists almost impudently that we attend to, and ultimately applaud, the speaker's verbal performance. Its effect is to call attention to the poet-lover's comparison even more emphatically than the prominent "When . . . When . . . Then" construction of Sonnet 15 makes the reader aware of the speaker's syllogistic argument. Both poems insist on their character as formal verbal arrangements in which details are selected by the writer according to his shaping conception. To be sure, this description could in some sense characterize any poem, but what is distinctive about the kind of poetry represented by these eternizing sonnets is the poet-lover's deliberate, self-conscious insistence on their special nature as artifacts, and the importance of that distinction to the central concerns of the poem. For by heightened emphasis on elaborately patterned manipulations of language they call attention to their own artistic control over observations of the mutable world. They point to the imposition of a formal pattern, such as a syllogism or a similitude, on the flux of feelings expressed in the lover's changing tones of voice.

In both Sonnets 15 and 18, details are taken from the speaker's habitual observations of the temporal world, particularly the unconscious life of vegetative things whose tender loveliness "declines," but in neither is there any reference to the particular moments when those observations were made or to impending events whose pressure forces him to draw on them now. The present tense in which activities in nature are all described is not located in any temporal continuum extending beyond the formal verbal order of the poem. The events on which the poet bases his observations—changes of weather, season, foliage—are not parts of a narrative account of his experiences as he remembers them to have happened at specific times, but demonstrations in his comparison arranged to support his conclusions. The poet seems to admit here, with conscious wit, the limitations of his metaphorical design—"Thou art more louely and more temperate"—and so to prove even more convincingly his control over the illustrative details he compares. For their sequence is from the beginning determined by the poet's extended metaphor, as he makes associations in the course of claiming to reject them. Within the sonnet, which is the promised comparison, the speaker is the ruler of sequence, even its originator.

It is the proud demonstration of this godlike power in the nontemporal order created by his language that prepares for his arrogant claim in the couplet:

So long as men can breath or eyes can see,
So long liues this, and this giues life to thee.

As in Sonnet 15, the poet-lover has transformed the timebound world, to which his friend belongs, into metaphors controlled by his power within the timeless present of his poem. He has made his own golden nature,[13] the "eternall Sommer" of his sonnet, ruled not by temporal but by poetic order where the only "time" is measure.[14] He has made his friend belong to that "eternall Sommer" by transforming him metaphorically into a "Summers day" whose "declines" all imply renewal. The poet here is therefore like the skillful gardener who engrafts anew, but his claims are far more extravagant. In this couplet the speaker boasts that, like God, his sonnet "giues life" by a power still more explicitly identified as the unique gift of a poet, a maker of metaphors which create a golden world matching the perfection of the lover's ideal.

In no other sonnet does the speaker quite equal the untroubled confidence, even cockiness, with which the poet-lover in Sonnet

18 boasts of his power in rivalry with death's "brag." Nowhere else are the signs of mutability so unthreatening as heaven's "gold complexion dimm'd," or the "declines" of nature so momentary and mild as of tender "buds" shaken by "windes" but not so roughly as to tear them from their boughs. Yet among approximately the first half of Sonnets 1 to 126 there are a number of other poems besides 18 and 15 where the poet-lover uses language in essentially the same ways, creates verbal constructs which work fundamentally by the same means, to pledge his art in the battle against time. It is these poems which can define most explicitly the kind of poetry represented by many of the lower-numbered sonnets in Shakespeare's collection.

In Sonnet 19, as in 15, the couplet asserts the poet's power to immortalize his love in contradiction of the fact which the speaker dwells on in the beginning of the poem, time's wanton destruction of everything in the "wide world." His means of making us accept the possibility of his claim are essentially the same as those of 15 and 18. For again his language transforms nature, where temporal sequence rules, into a verbal order created by the poet and governed by his aesthetic and moral judgments:

Deuouring time blunt thou the Lyons pawes,
And make the earth deuoure her owne sweet brood,
Plucke the keene teeth from the fierce Tygers yawes,
And burne the long liu'd Phænix in her blood,
Make glad and sorry seasons as thou fleet'st,
And do what ere thou wilt swift-footed time
To the wide world and all her fading sweets:
But I forbid thee one most hainous crime,
O carue not with thy howers my loues faire brow,
Nor draw noe lines there with thine antique pen,
Him in thy course vntainted doe allow,
For beauties patterne to succeding men.
    Yet doe thy worst ould Time dispight thy wrong,
    My loue shall in my verse euer liue young.

Again there are no references to particular moments past or future which would place the speaker's utterance of these lines in a sequence of experiences. Again changing time is excluded by the continuous present tense of the poem. Particular activities, although here far more painful to contemplate than the clouding of a "Summers day," are again generalized, even mythologized, so that what—in the world we know outside the poem—would be events happening at specific times here become terms in the poet's argument, illustrations chosen and arranged by him to represent his power in the world of the sonnet which he controls.

His command is asserted most obviously in the elaborately patterned and sustained series of imperatives he hurls at time, a device which works, like the opening announcement of the poet's comparison in Sonnet 18 and the syllogistic structure of 15, to impose a prominent rhetorical pattern on the poem, drawing attention to its development according to artistic plan. The speaker is again the designer of that pattern who determines what occurs within it. His commands, allowances, prohibitions dictate the activities of time, which his progression of epithets—"Deuouring time," "swift-footed time," the wittily contemptuous "ould Time"—attempts to cut down to a figure which it would be conceivable for a human being to dominate. The series of imperatives establishes a verbal order necessitated not by temporal sequence, which the language has excluded, but by the speaker's skillfully calculated choices.

These choices are expressions of his feelings as a lover—sorrow, pain, anger, desperation, outrage, defiance, scorn—but they are neither arbitrary nor formless, for they are the discriminations of a lover who is a poet, whose verse is the preserver of aesthetic and moral values embodied in his beloved:

But I forbid thee one most hainous crime,
O carue not with thy howers my loues faire brow,
Nor draw noe lines there with thine antique pen,
Him in thy course vntainted doe allow,
For beauties patterne to succeding men.

Because the poet-lover's language has created within the sonnet a verbal design ordered by his moral condemnation of time, it has made possible his final claim to preserve his love in the timeless world of his art:

> Yet doe thy worst ould Time dispight thy wrong,
> My loue shall in my verse euer liue young.

The degree of confidence we find in this promise depends on the mixture of desperation, bravado, righteous anger, and contempt we hear in the poet-lover's tone. But the nature of the assertion itself, and the devices of language designed to support it as a possibility, resemble the claims for the nature and power of poetry in Sonnets 15 and 18. The parallel of "My loue," referring at once to his feeling and his beloved, with "my verse" gives final emphasis to the argument that the poet has transformed temporal nature into a new creation. Its conclusion is that his friend has been lifted out of the "wide world and all her fading sweets," whose passing the speaker mourns, to become a metaphor, "beauties patterne," itself almost a synonym for the art which created it.

In Sonnet 65 the poet-lover's devices for combating time in one sense remind us of Sonnet 15 (and in a similar way also resemble another eternizing poem, Sonnet 60).[15] For the poem opens with a series of large considerations by the speaker of processes in nature, which he sets down, initially in philosophical generalizations, as illustrations for his observation of all that "time decayes":

> Since brasse, nor stone, nor earth, nor boundlesse sea,
> But sad mortallity ore-swaies their power,
> How with this rage shall beautie hold a plea,
> Whose action is no stronger then a flower?
> O how shall summers hunny breath hold out,
> Against the wrackfull siedge of battring dayes,
> When rocks impregnable are not so stoute,
> Nor gates of steele so strong but time decayes?
> O fearefull meditation, where alack,
> Shall times best Iewell from times chest lie hid?

> Or what strong hand can hold his swift foote back,
> Or who his spoile of beautie can forbid?
>> O none, vnlesse this miracle haue might,
>> That in black inck my loue may still shine bright.

Here he dwells on the inescapable fact of mortality in examples mounting painfully to what seems almost an explicit denial of the power defiantly claimed by the poet-lover in 19:

> Or what strong hand can hold his swift foote back,
> Or who his spoile of beautie can forbid?

There is a rising intensity in successive quatrains here (stronger than in the parallel intensifications in 15 and 60). His questions become less general and philosophical, seeming to imply growing fear of time's power over "beautie" more immediately dear to him than a flower or summer. The piling-on of questions in lines 9 to 12 makes his tone more urgent, as if his own observations have made him feel more helpless. Yet while the questions come more swiftly and more intensely, they also contain the possibility of answers perhaps more favorable to the speaker in his desperate contest with time. The saving actions posed in these lines—protecting some precious object, preventing an escape, prohibiting vandalism—in opposition to time (here in the sestet, as in Sonnet 19, reduced in stature by personifications as an immoral figure, a miser, a thief, a vandal) are human actions. They are therefore conceivably within the capacity of a man who, like the poet-lover, speaks with the authority of true aesthetic and moral judgments.

These questions, then, work in ways similar to the syllogistic conjunctions of Sonnet 15. They are part of an argument shaped by the speaker to make inevitable conclusions in support of his powers. We are made aware that the first twelve lines are a sequence of rhetorical questions (resembling in arrangement the series of imperatives in 19). We discover that even the first two quatrains which seem to evoke answers bitterly admitting the enemy's victory, can also be seen in the retrospect provided by the shape of the whole argument, to hint at other at least conceivable answers more favorable to the speaker. That is, if the questions in lines 9 to 12 imply even the frail possibility that the poet-lover's "strong hand" can hold back escaping time, that his voice can "forbid" not merely futiley the vandalism of beauty, then they make possible earlier answers that the beauty of a flower or of "summers hunny breath," although in fact fragile, passive, without physical "power," can also be seen to perform its own metaphorical "action" in war with time.

Here again the prominent rhetorical pattern calls attention to the poet-lover's creation of an order operating according to its own laws and controlled by him, not his wanton enemy, time. This seems to be emphasized precisely at the moment when he sounds most nearly defeated by his observations: "O fearefull meditation." The sense of lost control in such an exclamation is lessened—although the tone expresses his inescapable grief, dismay, even fear—by the poet's choice of the word "meditation" to describe his reflections. For "meditation" is the name of a formal genre of spiritual exercise with a defined intention and organization. His previous thoughts as "meditation," however fearful, do not ultimately break down his argument but point toward its inevitable development and conclusion.[16] By using that term for his reflections on time's destructive power (as in Sonnet 15 when the speaker refers to his "conceit" and endows it with shaping activity), he again exercises his own opposing power to give a controlled order to the facts of temporal experience in the verbal design of his poem. He again calls attention to the imposition of a formal pattern intended to lift his "loue," his feeling as well as his friend, out of the flux of experience to which his mounting fears belong, and to keep it beautifully "still" in his poem.

This demonstration prepares for the alternative to "sad mortallity" posed in the couplet:

O none, vnlesse this miracle haue might,
That in black inck my loue may still shine bright.

Here he calls his weapon against time a "miracle," by which he clearly does not mean to claim that God will intervene in his contest. "*This* miracle" refers to the last line of his poem. "That in black inck my loue may still shine bright" is a "miracle" because it is paradoxical, like the "action" of a flower or the strength of "summers hunny breath." A paradox is a verbal expression of the miraculous because it bears witness to a truth in contradiction of the facts of the natural world. For a flower is frail and passive, and yet its loveliness has a kind of "power" to oppose what is ugly and lawless; while a poem consists of words inscribed by ink on paper yet it does not. Like a miracle, a paradox operates according to its own laws, which transcend the limits of our experience in time. It therefore transforms that experience into a new order where the changing matter of the mortal world becomes "still," a word whose multiple meanings of "even yet," "continual," "motionless" (like the pun on "stay" in Sonnet 15), work in the last line toward arresting time's passage. The effect of the paradox is to diminish the pained uncertainty of "O none, *vnless*" or "my loue *may still* shine bright." For according to the formulation of "none, vnlesse," if the second claim is possible, it allows the possibility of the first, so that if the paradox is conceivable that "in black inck" the poet's "loue may still shine"—and it does so if the feelings in the sonnet are convincing to readers of all times—then it is possible to "hold . . . back" and "forbid" destruction by time. The peculiar logic of the paradox itself therefore touchingly strengthens the hope that the poet's feeling and his friend will, like his sonnet, escape "sad mortallity."

The last line of Sonnet 65 is here called a "miracle." As a verbal ordering of possibilities in contradiction of the facts of the physical universe this paradoxical line defines the nature of the sonnet as a whole, and the others like it, in which the speaker claims to give "life" to a poetic world matching his ideal as a lover, where beauty shines forever "bright" or, in the similar paradox concluding Sonnet 63, blooms eternally as metaphors in his verse:

> His beautie shall in these blacke lines be seene,
> And they shall liue, and he in them still greene.

The claims made by the speakers in these sonnets—15, 18, 19, 55, 60, 63, 65—although they vary in scope and confidence, are all for the ideal beauty of the youthful friend, for the lover's appreciation of the ideal, but above all for the poet's power to create verbal constructs which may alter the laws of nature, arrest change, exclude "Deuouring time," and so preserve the ideal eternally, a power which is, by metaphorical definition, not natural or human or even prophetic but miraculous.[17] The language designed to support these claims is best suited to generalize and to idealize, to discover the endlessly recurring patterns in our passing world, and to celebrate what is permanently worthy.

These eternizing sonnets define a kind of poetic language that also characterizes many others among approximately the first half of Sonnets 1 to 126. They have in common with the poems discussed a speaker, often identified as a lover writing a poem, who manipulates language in such ways that it calls attention to its creation of a nontemporal order where sequence is ruled by verbal necessity rather than by time. With such devices as loudly explicit rhetorical and logical schemes, by continuous use of the present tense, by generalized language which avoids reference to particular occasions, by elaborate metaphorical patterns, puns, paradoxes, the speaker insists on the special character of his language to transform experience into a unique and permanent order distinct from our life in the timebound world.

Among obvious examples of such manipulating of verbal devices is Sonnet 12, "When I doe count the clock that tels the time," which, like 15, consists of a sequence of generalized observations of nature's fragile beauties, here images associated with pastoral poetry, that "die as fast as they see others grow." Arranging these illustrations in a "When . . . When . . . Then" argument, the poet draws a conclusion closely parallel in construction to the eternizing couplets of Sonnets 15 and 60:

And nothing gainst Times sieth can make defence
Saue breed to braue him, when he takes thee hence.

Variations on this syllogistic pattern are Sonnet 29, "When in disgrace with Fortune and mens eyes,"[18] and Sonnet 30, where references to changes in time are oddly combined with a continuous present tense to emphasize the speaker's control over the very experiences he seems helplessly to lament:

When to the Sessions of sweet silent thought,
I sommon vp remembrance of things past,
I sigh the lacke of many a thing I sought,
And with old woes new waile my deare times waste:
Then can I drowne an eye (vn-vs'd to flow)
For precious friends hid in deaths dateles night,
And weepe a fresh loues long since canceld woe,
And mone th'expence of many a vannisht sight.
Then can I greeue at greeuances fore-gon,
And heauily from woe to woe tell ore
The sad account of fore-bemoned mone,
Which I new pay as if not payd before.
    But if the while I thinke on thee (deare friend)
    All losses are restord, and sorrowes end.

This sonnet seems on first reading to be "about" the speaker's helplessness to escape time's power because those painful "losses" which he suffered in the past are recreated in the present whenever he remembers them and force him to feel grief, from which only thoughts of his friend can relieve him. The speaker's powerlessness is belied, however, by his conscious manipulations of language, which are not here specifically identified as the gift of a poet, but which are of the same kind as the devices associated with eternizing power in the sonnets discussed, and which have the same effect of demonstrating the speaker's control over the flux of experience and feeling in preparation for his assertion of that control in the couplet.

All in War with Time

The most obvious of such devices is the prominent and orderly structure of the sonnet. Again the organization is a logical argument—"When . . . When . . . When . . . But if"—which has the effect of making the speaker's conclusion, and the relief it affords, seem inevitable. Within this argument there are here many mentions of different times—"past," "old," "new," "long since," "fore-gon," "fore-bemoned," "new," "before"—but they are incorporated into the continuous present tense of the verbs. Only "sought" is in the past tense, but because it comes in a subordinate clause it has almost the descriptive effect of an adjective, like the past participles "hid," "canceld," "payd." Although the present in which the speaker utters this poem is placed in some relation to "things past" by that and similar references to prior times, the remembered experiences are all generalized so that they become categories of "woe" rather than particular memories. As categories they are illustrations in an argument, deliberately chosen to lead to its conclusion, rather than events that force themselves on his memory. This effect is achieved by the generality of the language and by the fact that the categories are listed as a series of nouns. To illustrate, the second quatrain could be roughly paraphrased: "Then I weep unaccustomed tears because I grieved when my best friends died and because I recall how I suffered when I was unhappy in love and because I moan that I once paid a painful price for what is no longer mine." The paraphrase is in a form we might call narrative because it describes particular and consecutive events, because the verbs which define them to be events have not been eliminated as they have been from the speaker's list of "woes." This exclusion of changing time from his language is a further sign of his present control. "Remembrance of things past" does not rule him but answers when he chooses to "sommon." The tears which he is now "vn-vs'd" to weeping do not drown him, for "Then can I drowne an eye" implies that the power of choice is his, and implies also that if he chooses to weep it is for the unaccustomed pleasure of such indulgence. This reading is supported by the almost comic effect of alliteration in "with old woes new waile my deare times waste" and especially in the third quatrain:

> Then can I greeue at greeuances fore-gon,
> And heauily from woe to woe tell ore
> The sad account of fore-bemoned mone,
> Which I new pay as if not payd before.

If this absurd play on melancholic o sounds were not sufficient evidence of the speaker's control, his capacity to describe himself telling over his "woes" as a miser might count his money shows him so free from past sufferings that he can both indulge in the memory of them and joke about doing so. His awareness of the love he now enjoys has from the beginning filled the "Sessions of sweet silent thought" (making his professions of grief seem somewhat false or complacent as the elegiac tone of the eternizing sonnets does not). These "Sessions" are held in the court where time's lawless deeds are reviewed, judged, and brought to a stop:

> But if the while I thinke on thee (deare friend)
> All losses are restord, and sorrowes end.

This conclusion is achieved in the court of law which is his mind and in the sonnet which recreates its workings by conscious manipulations of language that transform the "waste" of temporal experience into the just and permanent order of the poem. It has an effect, comparable to a promise concluding an eternizing sonnet, of asserting the control over the flux of experience demonstrated in the speaker's manipulation of language within the design of the poem.

A different shaping principle, but one which has a fundamentally similar function, is used by the speaker in Sonnet 7, who identifies himself implicitly as a poet by his art of formal comparison. Like Sonnet 18, in which the speaker's ability to "compare" demonstrates his eternizing art, the poem *is* the speaker's extended metaphor:

> Loe in the Orient when the gracious light,
> Lifts vp his burning head, each vnder eye

Doth homage to his new appearing sight,
Seruing with lookes his sacred maiesty,
And hauing climb'd the steepe vp heauenly hill,
Resembling strong youth in his middle age,
Yet mortall lookes adore his beauty still,
Attending on his goulden pilgrimage:
But when from high-most pich with wery car,
Like feeble age he reeleth from the day,
The eyes (fore dutious) now conuerted are
From his low tract and looke another way:
 So thou, thy selfe out-going in thy noon:
 Vnlok'd on diest vnlesse thou get a sonne.

Perhaps even more obviously than in any of the poems we have discussed, the speaker here calls attention to poetic devices which are intended to arrest the processes of nature out of which he constructs his metaphor. Here are prominently displayed a structured comparison—"Loe . . . So"—calling attention to the imposition of a formal design, the generalizing diction (here as in Sonnet 19 even mythologizing), the continuous present tense, devices which characterize the kind of poem previously defined. Even the final pun has effects noticed before. For the pointed identification of "sonne" with the sun attempts to identify the friend's act of generation with the cyclical returns of nature (a device which seems forced here since he has previously described the sun in terms largely ignoring its renewals). The last line points to the way the poet's metaphorical language about time's passage can rescue the friend from it by likening him to the sun now perceived as perpetually returning. The couplet, somewhat arbitrarily here, eternizes the friend by this transformation, comparable in function to the conceit of the youth as a plant or a "Summers day," in a process resembling the parallel creative act of physical generation by which the speaker says the friend should perpetuate himself.

Most prominent, even mechanically so, of the types of verbal constructs characteristic of this kind of poetry among the lower-numbered sonnets are the elaborately patterned word-

plays learned from Petrarch, perhaps, or Sidney.[19] Examples are
the designs created by the balanced and sustained repetitions of
groups like "eye . . . heart . . . art" in Sonnet 24 and "eye . . .
heart . . . sight . . . part" in 46 and 47, of "all . . . loue" in 40 or
"loose . . . losse . . . loosing" in 42. Somewhat more successful
are Sonnets 27 and 43, in which modified patterns of such
word-play are combined with variants of the "When . . . Then"
structure found in many poems among approximately the first
half of Sonnets 1 to 126. Sonnet 43, based on the convention of
the beloved's appearance to the lover in a dream, builds a
sequence of paradoxes derived from the opening line, "When
most I winke then doe mine eyes best see." This series of
variations on "darkely bright" and "bright in darke" oxymorons
leads to a conclusion, itself paradoxical, asserting the power of
the friend's ideal beauty to alter the temporal pattern of "dayes"
and "nights" as they are arrested in the unvarying present of the
poem itself:

> All dayes are nights to see till I see thee,
> And nights bright daies when dreams do shew thee me.

Sonnet 27, in similar fashion, generalizes the conventional situation of the sleepless lover to illustrate the miraculous power of
the friend's beauty, which can alter temporal nature as his own
poetic language transforms it by the paradoxical force of his
metaphor:

> Saue that my soules imaginary sight
> Presents their shaddoe to my sightles view,
> Which like a iewell (hunge in gastly night)
> Makes blacke night beautious, and her old face new.

These assumptions, and the language designed to support them,
resemble in kind, though often not in quality, the poetry of the
eternizing sonnets, for whose concerns that language is best
suited.

The devices of language, the kinds of verbal constructs we
have defined, and the effects they create, characterize many

among approximately the first half of the sonnets numbered from 1 to 126.[20] These poems, whether or not they explicitly challenge time's destructiveness, define their art by its power to transform the shifting scenes of this "huge" world into an order miraculously preserved from impermanence. They therefore depend on a language which is assertive and controlled, richly figurative, consciously literary, designed to emphasize the shape of the poem as a distinct artifact. It is a language perfectly adjusted to the demands of a sonnet in which the poet-lover struggles to exert his power "all in war with Time."

Sonnet 64 would epitomize this kind of poetry if it ended the way other sonnets which it initially resembles would lead the reader to expect:

When I haue seene by times fell hand defaced
The rich proud cost of outworne buried age,
When sometime loftie towers I see downe rased,
And brasse eternall slaue to mortall rage.
When I haue seene the hungry Ocean gaine
Aduantage on the Kingdome of the shoare,
And the firme soile win of the watry maine,
Increasing store with losse, and losse with store.
When I haue seene such interchange of state,
Or state it selfe confounded, to decay,
Ruine hath taught me thus to ruminate
That Time will come and take my loue away.
　　This thought is as a death which cannot choose
　　But weepe to haue, that which it feares to loose.

The first ten lines are in many ways like previously discussed eternizing sonnets, especially recalling 15, 60, and 65 by the poet-lover's ordered series of observations of proud things subject to destruction by "times fell hand."[21] We recognize the speaker's tone of detachment becoming increasingly elegiac as the illustrations of "mortall rage" grow more threatening to him. Again his arrangement of examples is designed to illustrate a formal argument in which the measured repetitions of "When" mark an essentially logical rather than a narrative sequence. For the development does not depend on successive occasions "When" the speaker experienced first one and then after another incident in time, but on examples of mutability arranged in an increasingly inclusive series, culminating in a summary of "such interchange" as had been illustrated in the preceding quatrains. The reader therefore predicts the inevitable development of this argument toward a conclusion which, in other sonnets built on the pattern apparently recognizable here, is an assertion of the poet-lover's power in seeming contradiction of the inescapable facts lamented by him in the opening of the poem.

These resemblances make the violation of that pattern in the closing lines of Sonnet 64 more pointed and more shocking. Following the last and most inclusive illustration of temporal decay—"When I haue seene such interchange of state, / Or state it selfe confounded, to decay"—we predict that the speaker will "Then" admit time's threat to vulnerable life much nearer and more precious to him than "outworne buried age" or the "watry maine." We expect him to recognize the bitter application of his argument to his "loue" as the supreme illustration of mortal beauty, but finally to challenge that threat. We are prepared to hear him assert his control by concluding: and yet the miraculous power of my art transforms my love into a metaphor preserved in the permanently ordered world of my poem.

Contrary to these expectations, in Sonnet 64 the application of the speaker's observations to his "loue" forces from him the painful acknowledgment of his own helplessness:

Ruine hath taught me thus to ruminate
That Time will come and take my loue away.
This thought is as death which cannot choose
But weepe to haue, that which it feares to loose.

Where we expect an assertion of his power to conclude the speaker's argument we hear his bitter capitulation to "Ruine," a word given special emphasis by its position at the beginning of the line, by its trochaic accent in a poem whose other initial syllables are all unaccented, and by its echo in "ruminate."

"Ruine hath taught me thus to ruminate" expresses a bitterness directed not only against time but against the speaker himself. Its pompously abstract diction and inflated solemnity of sound contrast with the simplicity of the next line:[22]

> Ruine hath taught me thus to ruminate
> That Time will come and take my loue away.

The speaker seems to mock himself for the detachment with which he felt free to "ruminate" at a privileged distance from time's destructiveness. He seems to turn against the leisured observations of his poem, which has achieved its control by describing only impersonal categories of "losse." He calls in question the authority of his orderly argument and his consciously literary language. The argument breaks down, the artistry is stripped away by the simple obviousness of the fact "That Time will come and take my loue away."

It is not the action of his own "conceit" here, as in Sonnet 15, which brings about the application of his argument to his "loue," but "Ruine," whose teachings destroy his poetic power:

> This thought is as a death which cannot choose
> But weepe to haue, that which it feares to loose.

The couplet, with "This thought," reflects explicitly on what precedes it in the poem, as "such interchange" refers to the examples given in the two preceding quatrains. There are similar uses of "reflexive references" in the couplets of 63, "these blacke lines . . . they shall liue," and Sonnet 55, "You liue in this," and Sonnet 18, "So long liues this, and this giues life." In these eternizing sonnets the effect of referring to the poem itself as an existing entity to which the pronoun points is to heighten the awareness of the sonnet as a created work with an existence of its own, distinct from the natural world which it has transformed by its ordering power.[23] But in Sonnet 64 the speaker denies that art. "This thought" has no life to confer. It has no power to escape time by creating an eternally present world in the sonnet because "Ruine" has destroyed the literary order which the poet had tried to impose on the changing universe through his generalizations about it in the first ten lines. They belong to the past (marked by a shift in tense not found in the otherwise similar structures of Sonnets 15, 60, and 65), which has no power over the poet-lover's present suffering, altered as he has been by the "Ruine" of his "loue" and of his belief in poetry's miraculous power to immortalize it. Now he can only "weepe," a formless expression of feeling utterly different in nature from the "eternall lines" of poetry, which points to a difference in kind between Sonnet 64 and the poems from whose pattern it so markedly deviates.

In Sonnet 64 the poet-lover parodies a design characteristic of Shakespeare's eternizing verse, and so mocks his own lofty poetic generalizing for its failure to dispel his realistic fears as a lover. His inability to create a verbal order that allows the possibility of preserving his "loue" from "Ruine" is here a failure of rhetoric overpowered by fact and also by feeling. Not the value of the speaker's "loue"—his friend or his appreciation of his friend—but the validity of his language is called in question by the way this sonnet deviates from the pattern it seems to predict. It expresses disbelief in the miraculous power of poetry triumphantly asserted in Sonnet 18, at least hoped for as a possibility in 15, 19, 55, 60, 63, and 65.

In other sonnets which, like 64, allude to eternizing verse by violating its conventions, this distrust of poetic power is mingled with feelings revealingly different in kind from those expressed by the poet-lover in sonnets which do promise to rescue the friend from mortality. These poems can point to changing attitudes toward love and also toward art in Shakespeare's sonnet collection, and ultimately define a different *kind* of poem from those previously discussed as characteristic of many among approximately the first half of Sonnets 1 to 126.[24]

The speaker in Sonnet 54 seems closest to the poet-lovers in Sonnets 15 and 18 because he builds a literary comparison leading to a couplet asserting his skill as an artist—here a distiller of perfume—to transform into permanent "truth" the loveliness of his friend perceived as a rose which must otherwise partake of the "sweet deaths" of fading things:

> And so of you, beautious and louely youth,
> When that shall vade, my verse distils your truth.

This promise sounds like the claim of the skillful gardener in Sonnet 15 to "ingraft" his love into an endlessly renewed creation, or of the artist in 18 who predicts an "eternall Sommer" for his friend "When in eternall lines to time thou grow'st." The couplet of Sonnet 54 could be the conclusion of such a tenderly appreciative tribute to the youth's beauty, vulnerable to time but made to transcend it in art.[25] Yet this couplet is prepared for by lines which make the reader hear it very differently from the poetic promises it resembles:

> Oh how much more doth beautie beautious seeme,
> By that sweet ornament which truth doth giue,
> The Rose lookes faire, but fairer we it deeme
> For that sweet odor, which doth in it liue:
> The Canker bloomes haue full as deepe a die,
> As the perfumed tincture of the Roses,
> Hang on such thornes, and play as wantonly,
> When sommers breath their masked buds discloses:
> But for their virtue only is their show,
> They liue vnwoo'd, and vnrespected fade,
> Die to themselues. Sweet Roses doe not so,
> Of their sweet deathes, are sweetest odors made:
>> And so of you, beautious and louely youth,
>> When that shall vade, my verse distils your truth.

The poem seems to be cast in the graceful form of a compliment, built out of perhaps the most familiar of all comparisons, of a "louely youth" to roses, which look and smell "sweet" and with which literature has traditionally associated the pastoral qualities of fragility, harmlessness, innocence. The relationship between these conventionally pretty terms is complicated in the very first lines, however, by the way they introduce a distinction, not usually implied by the comparison, betwen "beautie" and "truth." We assume that the poet will use this distinction to enhance his compliment by attributing both kinds of "virtue" to his friend, as he does in the last line of Sonnet 14: "Thy end is Truthes and Beauties doome and date." This would make the opening lines an exclamation over his remarkable worth:

Oh how much more doth beautie beautious seeme,
By that sweet ornament which truth doth giue.

But the possibility of reading this exclamation as simply appreciative is prevented from the beginning by the disquieting notion in the first line of a beauty which may merely "beautious seeme." This suggestion of false appearance is then strengthened when the opposite of such beauty is defined in the second line with sharper cynicism. There the alternative beauty to that which merely *seems* is not one which truly is by nature "beautious," but rather is a beauty which the "ornament" of "truth" can make "more . . . beautious seeme" than it actually is in its unadorned state. The uncomfortable possibility of error, misleading appearance, deception, is therefore attached to both "beautie" and "truth" by the prominent verb "seeme," given special emphasis through its position and its ryhme with the equally ambiguous "deeme" (also implying false evaluation as in 96 and 121), and by the metaphor of "ornament." This could have the innocent meaning it bears in Sonnet 1, where the friend is the "worlds fresh ornament," but was often associated with "faulse Art," especially cosmetic, as in Sonnet 68.[26] The comparison which follows cannot therefore take the form of a simple contrast between what merely seems and what truly is "faire" (a word which sonneteers conventionally use to stress the *identity* of physical beauty and inward virtue here separated).[27] Nor does the wording of the speaker's comparison ultimately support such a simple distinction, although at first it may seem to do so, perhaps chiefly by its pretty conventionality:

> The Rose lookes faire, but fairer we it deeme
> For that sweet odor, which doth in it liue.

The parallels with the first lines—"more . . . beautious: fairer," "sweet ornament: sweet odor"—neatly sort out the terms. We connect the rose which both looks and smells "sweet" with "beautie" adorned with "truth," and both, by complimentary implication, with the "beautious and louely youth." What follows logically should be the contrasting term, paired to "beautie" without the "sweet ornament" of "truth," and the "Canker bloomes" seem to fullfil the logic of this set of paired opposites. The speaker uses "Canker bloomes" to represent flowers which only "show" like "Sweet Roses" but do not share their scent and so when they die cannot provide the kind of petals from which perfume may be distilled. Yet the poet's language about the flowers is as cynical as his initial distinction between the two kinds of beauty which merely "seeme":

> The Canker bloomes haue full as deepe a die,
> As the perfumed tincture of the Roses,
> Hang on such thornes, and play as wantonly,
> When sommers breath their masked buds discloses:
> But for their virtue only is their show,
> They liue vnwoo'd, and vnrespected fade,
> Die to themselues. Sweet Roses doe not so.

The very choice of "Canker bloomes," whether they are meant to be wild dog roses or roses eaten out by worms, called "Canker vice" in Sonnet 70, introduces the notion of nature common and tainted, an altogether different view from the sense of nature's limits in previously discussed eternizing poems, and others sharing their kind of language among the lower-numbered sonnets.[28] Those consider "euery thing that growes" to be all the more precious because impermanent. The "darling buds of

Maie" in Sonnet 18 are shaken, in 1 "beauties *Rose*" will "decease," in 12 the "violet" is "past prime," but none is vulgar or eaten out with corruption. What is still more pointed a change, the language here which attributes vicious qualities to nature applies not only to "Canker bloomes" but to roses. For both kinds of flowers share "full as deepe a *die*," a word for color implying artificiality, even vulgarity and guilty staining.[29] They "Hang on such *thornes*," a conventional reminder of imperfection attached to beautiful, seemingly harmless creatures, or of conflict and danger in the natural world.[30] They "play as *wantonly*," an adverb which in Shakespeare's time retained the innocent meaning of "sportively," but which was also used as equivalent to "lasciviously" and "cruelly." Even their unopened "buds" are made to seem vicious or at least suspect by the sinister beauty of "masked," with its suggestions of disguise, perhaps (following "wantonly") specifically for sexual intrigue, and of deception, such as the speaker broadly hints in Sonnet 70, "If some suspect of ill maskt not thy show."[31]

These suggestions are then confirmed by the ways in which the speaker distinguishes "Canker bloomes" from roses:

> They liue vnwoo'd, and vnrespected fade,
> Die to themselues. Sweet Roses doe not so.

He uses here the conventional language of the *carpe diem* or *carpe florem* poem, in which the poet-lover mingles compliments on youthful beauty with threats of the impending ugliness of old age in persuading the lady to accept his sexual invitation. A paradigm of that convention is Samuel Daniel's Sonnet 39 from *Delia*, obviously related to Shakespeare's Sonnet 54:[32]

> Looke Delia how w'esteeme the halfe blowne Rose,
>> The image of thy blush and Sommers honor:
>> Whilst yet her tender bud doth undisclose
>> That full of beauty, time bestowes vpon her.
> No sooner spreads her glory in the ayre,
>> But straight her wide blowne pomp comes to decline:

> She then is scornd that late adornd the Fayre;
> So fade the Roses of those cheeks of thine.
> No Aprill can reuiue thy withered flowres,
>   Whose springing grace adorns thy glory now:
>   Swift speedy Time, feathred with flying houres,
>   Dissolues the beauty of the fairest brow.
> Then do not thou such treasure wast in vaine,
> But loue now whilst thou maist be lou'd againe.

The resemblance sharpens our sense of how corrupt are Shakespeare's "Sweet Roses"—as well as his "Canker bloomes"—their "buds" not "tender" but "masked," while also making us aware of the viciousness (much harsher and coarser than the elegant worldliness of Daniel's would-be seducer) with which his poet-lover phrases the distinction between them and "Canker bloomes." These "Die to themselues," an expression which in this context cannot escape brutal suggestions from the common, punning sense of "to die" meaning "to reach sexual climax." "Sweet Roses," by contrast, are wooed and respected and "Die," not to themselves but to others. The distinction seems to favor the roses, to be sure, yet not in the most flattering way. For while it implies some kind of generosity in them by contrast with the self-loving cankers, the terms of contrast are not between "aboundance" and "famine," as in Sonnet 1, or expressed in images of "husbandry" as opposed to barrenness which occur often in the other sonnets urging the young man to marry. Here the distinction is merely of onanism from copulation rather than from life-giving procreation. The roses differ from "Canker bloomes" in that they are sexually active, promiscuous, perhaps even publicly or notoriously so, for "Of their sweet deathes, are sweetest odors made." Yet these "odors" are generally diffused, not lovingly bestowed upon a woman chosen to bear a child, as the speaker urges the friend to use his living sweetness in Sonnet 6:

> Then let not winters wragged hand deface,
> In thee thy summer ere thou be distil'd:

Make sweet some viall; treasure thou some place,
With beauties treasure ere it be selfe kil'd.

The sexual innuendo in the seeming praise of "sweet deathes" is
pointed by contrast also with the couplet of Sonnet 5, where the
distillation of perfume is a metaphor for creating a child in
whom the friend's true worth will survive:

But flowers distil'd though they with winter meete,
Leese but their show, their substance still liues sweet.

In Sonnet 54 the distinction between roses and "Canker
bloomes" is not that only one of them "liues," but that they prefer different ways to "Die" (that word being given extra
emphasis as the irregularly accented foot at the beginning of the
line). They have different tastes in ways to achieve sexual grati-
fication. With this preparation, the seemingly complimentary
promise of the couplet is also recognizable as a disguised insult
to the youth by the poet-lover:

And so of you, beautious and louely youth,
When that shall vade, my verse distils your truth.

The "truth" that his poem will perpetuate cannot here be inward
beauty hidden beneath "show," because none is ascribed to the
"Sweet Roses," by contrast with the flowers of Sonnet 5, whose
"show," threatened by "neuer resting time" but not by
corruption, is contrasted with their enduring "substance."[33]
Here the roses have no "substance." Their only "virtue," in addition to "show," is their capacity for "sweet deathes" which perhaps constitutes the "truth" the poet will publish. That is, he will
tell eternally, as he tells in this poem, the "truth" about his
friend's promiscuous nature, a reading supported by the present
tense of "distils." It is also possible to interpret the "truth" he will
perpetuate in art as the "sweet ornament which truth doth giue,"
by which reading the lover's poetry adorns the friend with
greater beauty than is his in his unornamented—unflat-
tered—state. The speaker's art "distils" a beautiful odor out of
impure matter. He creates perfume, which, we are reminded, is a

cosmetic used to enhance the body's seductiveness or to hide its dirty smells.[34] He writes a poem which seems to compliment the "beautious and louely youth" with a comparison so"sweet"—the repetition of that word is itself cloying here—that it becomes a "perfumed tincture" disguising what is beautiful but malodorous.

Like Sonnet 64, this poem is a parody of eternizing verse. Yet rather than showing the inadequacy of rhetoric to triumph over time by imposing its own order upon fact and feeling, it here demonstrates the power of rhetoric which has been perverted for calculated effects. For in Sonnet 54 the language of eternizing verse is cynically adjusted to expose "truth" in a world of natural and human beings whose "virtue only is their show." This is a very different world from the one whose "fading sweets" are at once celebrated and lamented in the sonnets previously discussed. The vocabulary in Sonnet 54 attaching a vulgar, tainted, and deceiving beauty to the friend, seen as the creature of a nature hiding within itself commonness and corruption, is different from the poet-lover's ways of talking in those other sonnets. It is a vocabulary scarcely used before Sonnet 54 but pervasive in approximately the second half of Sonnets 1 to 126, and frequently present there in poems which, like Sonnet 54, parody the conventions of eternizing verse. In these sonnets the lover's recognition of vileness in his friend makes impossible any genuine claim to rescue him from time's power by creating a poetic world matching the perfection of an ideal "loue." His parodic manipulations of the conventional promise to use his art "in war with Time" therefore define his conception of the nature and power of poetry in new ways.

There are other sonnets of the same kind as 54 which seem to be cast in the form of a compliment building toward a promise to preserve the friend's true worth from time's destruction by celebrating it eternally in verse. They adjust the conventions of this type of poetry so slightly that they seem almost calculated to deceive. The friend could accept them as tributes almost without uneasiness, as if they were genuine examples of the kind of sonnet they parody.

The poet-lover in Sonnet 101, for example, prepares for the conventional promise of the couplet by urging his silent Muse to praise his friend:

> for't lies in thee,
> To make him much out-liue a gilded tombe:
> And to be praised of ages yet to be.

The reminder of Sonnet 55:

> Not marble, nor the giulded monument,
> Of Princes shall out-liue this powrefull rime . . .

with the sweeping grandeur of "ages yet to be," predisposes the reader to accept the concluding promise without suspicion:

> Then do thy office Muse, I teach thee how,
> To make him seeme long hence, as he showes now.

Yet Sonnet 54 and the many others which share its vocabulary teach caution about the implications of "showes" and "seeme," and the whole of Sonnet 101 reread in the light of this warning confirms such suspicion:[35]

> Oh truant Muse what shalbe thy amends,
> For thy neglect of truth in beauty di'd?
> Both truth and beauty on my loue depends:
> So dost thou too, and therein dignifi'd:
> Make answere Muse, wilt thou not haply saie,
> Truth needs no collour with his collour fixt,
> Beautie no pensell, beauties truth to lay:
> But best is best, if neuer intermixt.
> Because he needs no praise, wilt thou be dumb?
> Excuse not silence so, for't lies in thee,
> To make him much out-liue a gilded tombe:
> And to be praisd of ages yet to be.
>   Then do thy office Muse, I teach thee how,
>   To make him seeme long hence, as he showes now.

The line "Both truth and beauty on my loue depends" sounds like hyperbolic compliment, but the previous distinction between "truth" and "beauty," making the latter a dye which changes the color of the former, questions (as in Sonnet 54) the purity of both qualities. To attach them to "my loue" is less than flattery if "my loue" means "my loved friend." Or if "my loue" means "my feeling for my friend," then to say "Both truth and beauty on my loue depends" is to claim for the poet-lover the power to attach these qualities to the friend who would otherwise lack them. Then "Because he needs no praise," which is certainly complimentary, can also suggest less flattering possibilities that the friend has already received more "praise" than is good for him (the explicit accusation of Sonnet 84), or than he actually deserves (as Sonnet 69 most strongly hints). The use of "showes" supports this reading: the friend's "truth" is in "beauty di'd," again with implications of an artificial stain, so that it "showes" itself with a deceiving loveliness. The poet's "office" is to match artifice to that deception, to apply "collour"—of dye and of rhetoric—to perpetuate the false seeming of his friend.[36]

The implications for a definition, or redefinition, of the nature and power of poetry in such parodies of eternizing verse are still clearer in Sonnet 100. Here again the adjustments of the conventions are so slight that the friend could almost accept as genuine tribute the poet-lover's promise to act on his behalf in opposition to time's destructive power:

Giue my loue fame faster then time wasts life,
So thou preuenst his sieth, and crooked knife.

Yet as it is prepared for in the development of the sonnet, these lines are closer to insult and to threat than to praise, and make a very different claim for the poet-lover's power "in war with Time":

Where art thou Muse that thou forgetst so long,
To speak of that which giues thee all thy might?

Spendst thou thy furie on some worthlesse songe,
Darkning thy powre to lend base subiects light.
Return forgetfull Muse, and straight redeeme,
In gentle numbers time so idely spent,
Sing to the eare that doth thy laies esteeme,
And giues thy pen both skill and argument.
Rise resty Muse, my loues sweet face suruay,
If time haue any wrincle grauen there,
If any, be a *Satire* to decay,
And make times spoiles dispised euery where.
　　Giue my loue fame faster then time wasts life,
　　So thou preuenst his sieth, and crooked knife.

As in Sonnet 101, the seeming compliment here is in the form of chastisement to the poet-lover's Muse for not celebrating its true subject. The command "Rise resty Muse, my loues sweet face suruay" makes the friend's unspoiled beauty seem to be the proper "argument" for the poet to write about, and so perpetuate. Yet in the lines which follow, the imperatives "be a *Satire* to decay, / And make times spoiles dispised euery where" have already accepted the possiblity (so defiantly forbidden in Sonnet 19) that time has begun to engrave wrinkles on the friend's beautiful face. In so doing they make the Muse's proper poem a "Satire" (not "gentle numbers") whose subject is "times spoiles."[37] Rather than rescuing the friend from "decay," the poem will publish its destruction of his lovely appearance. The brutality of the promise is heightened by the redundancy of "sieth, and crooked knife," both of which can carve up a face more murderously than, for instance, in Sonnet 19 an "antique pen" might "draw" on a "faire brow," or in Sonnet 60 time "delues the paralels in beauties brow" as an engraver draws a picture. Recalling in form the last line of Sonnet 15—"As he takes from you, I ingraft you new"— the poet's promise is again to oppose destruction by time with the continuous counteraction of his art, but by adjusting the nature of his claims—"Giue my loue fame faster then time wasts life"—he points out how limited is the power of poetry: "fame" does not renew wasted "life." Not asserting "this giues life to thee," or "My loue shall in my verse euer liue young," or "You liue in this," he says only of his Muse, "So thou preuenst his sieth, and crooked knife."[38] The verb "prevent" could be used in this period with its modern meaning of "hinder" or "defeat," but in the light of the previous admission that "time wasts life," here "preuenst" must have the now obsolete but then current meanings of "outstrip" or "act before."

Among such possibilities, none claims for the poet's art the miraculous power to create an ideal world in which his "loue may still shine bright." On the contrary, the speaker hints at a very diffferent conception of the power of poetry when he chastises his Muse for abusing it, in lines which recall in cynical form that metaphor of illumination in the couplet of Sonnet 65:[39]

Spendst thou thy furie on some worthlesse songe,
Darkning thy powre to lend base subiects light.

He may be scolding his Muse for corrupting poetry's power to "lend . . . light" by employing it for "base" rather than worthy "subiects." He may also be attacking it for dimming its "powre" which *is* the "powre to lend base subiects light" by expending it on other matter than the decay of his friend's beauty. The cynicism in this definition of the Muse's "powre" matches the definition of its "office" in the sonnet that follows, "To make him seeme long hence, as he showes now," or the equation of art with perfume in Sonnet 54. It also calls in question the poet-lover's gift to his friend of the "fame" promised in the couplet, which may be as falsifying as the loan of "light" to "base subiects" or, by implication, the promise of immortality to what is already decaying.

These sonnets define art in ways which accord with their own uses of parody. For they compare poetry to a process such as distillation, and therefore attribute to it a kind of power which has ironically conflicting possibilities. On the one hand, poetry has the power to distill the "truth" about its subject, which is to extract its hidden essence, to expose what lies beneath its false surfaces. On the other hand, verse which "distils" its subject has the power to refine away its impurities and therefore to alter its actual mixed and imperfect state. The art of poetry is therefore essentially ironic, for while it sees through the "showes" of this deceptive world, it also creates a new appearance that enhances its false seeming. These ironically conflicting effects are at work in Sonnets 54, 100, 101, and others of the same kind, where exposures of "truth" are deceptively phrased as compliments which tell and conceal simultaneously.

Most explicitly Sonnet 114 defines the workings of such poetry by comparing it to the art of "Alcumie" that is ultimately "flattery":

> Or whether doth my minde being crown'd with you
> Drinke vp the monarks plague this flattery?
> Or whether shall I say mine eie saith true,
> And that your loue taught it this *Alcumie*?
> To make of monsters, and things indigest,
> Such cherubines as your sweet selfe resemble,
> Creating euery bad a perfect best
> As fast as obiects to his beames assemble:
> Oh tis the first, tis flatry in my seeing,
> And my great minde most kingly drinkes it vp,
> Mine eie well knowes what with his gust is greeing,
> And to his pallat doth prepare the cup.
>   If it be poison'd, tis the lesser sinne,
>   That mine eye loues it and doth first beginne.

Here the poet's claim to transform imperfect nature by the idealizing power of his art, "Creating euery bad a perfect best," is frankly matched to the deceiving loveliness of the friend:

> To make of monsters, and things indigest,
> Such cherubines as your sweet selfe resemble.

And both are likened to the vain and greedy arts of "Alcumie" and especially "flattery," which transform base matter by means that are far from miraculous and that claim no power "in war with Time."

Such definitions of the poet-lover's art explain the workings of sonnets which seem to adopt the conventions of verse dedicated to perpetuating worth, while adjusting them in such ways that they expose false worth. By these manipulations of language the poems adapt themselves to the kind of world they ultimately portray, a world in which the deceptively fair friend is representative of nature hiding within itself commonness, corruption, even monstrous deformity.[40] For the poems themselves are in a sense deceptive. They are calculated by the poet-lover, using the skills of the perfumer, the alchemist, the flatterer; applying the colors of the dyer and the rhetorician, to seem like compliments within which are hidden insulting judgments of his friend's true nature, threats to expose him perpetually in verse, and reminders that whatever the poet-lover chooses to write, the friend's "beautious and louely youth" will fade, and all that will remain is an odor extracted from dead matter.

These sonnets therefore only pretend to transform temporal experience into a distinct poetic world matching the perfection of an ideal love, while exposing the truth about the actual world in which the poet and the friend now live. They are therefore different in kind from the poems previously discussed as characteristic of approximately the first half of Sonnets 1 to 126, a difference which can be more fully illustrated by Sonnet 104, yet another parody of eternizing verse:

> To me faire friend you neuer can be old,
> For as you were when first your eye I eyde,
> Such seemes your beautie still: Three Winters colde,
> Haue from the forrests shooke three summers pride,
> Three beautious springs to yellow *Autumne* turn'd,
> In processe of the seasons haue I seene,
> Three Aprill perfumes in three hot Iunes burn'd,
> Since first I saw you fresh which yet are greene.
> Ah yet doth beauty like a Dyall hand,
> Steale from his figure, and no pace perceiu'd,
> So your sweete hew, which me thinkes still doth stand

Hath motion, and mine eye may be deceaued.
For feare of which, heare this thou age vnbred,
Ere you were borne was beauties summer dead.

The first seemingly tender assurance that, to the speaker, the friend is exempt from time's passage introduces lines recalling previously discussed eternizing sonnets by arranging in an elaborately patterned sequence a series of observations of proud things in the natural world diminished by the "processe of the seasons." The shape of this sequence predicts a conclusion in which the poet-lover will dedicate his art to rescuing his friend from that "processe," and the couplet echoes such a conventional assertion. It grandly claims for the poet-lover's voice the power to force on generations yet unborn the perpetually renewed image of his friend, metaphorically transformed into "beauties summer." But this echo of the language of Shakespeare's eternizing sonnets slightly alters the conventions with effects which are painful, and which are made the more brutal by our awareness from the first line that the poet-lover is speaking these cruelties directly to his friend.

If the poet-lover's final pronouncement were phrased in some more strictly conventional form, such as "Ere you were born did beauty's summer live," it would be possible for the friend to accept it as genuine tribute to his beauty in art dedicated to perpetuate it. As the poet chooses to state his promise, however, the word "dead" rings out with frightening finality. Far from reassuring his friend that he will rescue him from time's power, the speaker exults in reminding him of his mortality, and of poetry's powerlessness to rescue him from it.

For the parodic form of the couplet has effects similar to the violations of conventional language in the conclusion of Sonnet 64, because it denies the miraculous art of the speaker's literary language to alter the facts of temporal experience. That is to say, the lover as poet describes his friend in a metaphor, "beauties summer," which according to the workings of language in Shakespeare's eternizing sonnets should place him within the endless cycle of nature's lovely renewals, permanently transformed in the "eternall Sommer" of the poem. Yet here the poet-lover uses the metaphor in such a way as to emphasize its inadequacy, or rather its ineffectuality, as a mere figure of speech, as simply a flattering way of talking, by declaring "beauties summer" to be "dead" in the final sense in which men but not summers die. The poet-lover's language, instead of miraculously transforming the "faire friend" into a metaphor existing eternally in the nontemporal order of the poem, merely describes him by a complimentary comparison which claims no power to alter the fact of his subjection to time. The poet can compare the friend to "beauties summer," but his way of doing so demonstrates that the art of comparison can have no divine or magical force to metamorphose him into a new and timeless creation, as Sonnets 15 or 18 or 65 claim. It has only the power to draw likenesses between things which the facts of experience either support or prove untrue, as they support the resemblance of the friend's beauty to summer's fleeting "pride"—significantly the only quality attached to summer here, by contrast with the lovingly detailed description in Sonnet 18—but not to its renewals.

In this poem, then, as in Sonnet 64, the facts of the temporal world have power to contradict feeling. But here the speaker's recognition of this control by time does not, as it does in 64, lead to his painful discovery of the inefficacy of his own verbal power, because he is using that very knowledge, shaping his art ultimately to expose the realities of experience in time rather than to recreate them in an idealized literary form. His means of exposure is his parodic language which, while seeming to assure immortality for his friend, actually reminds him that he lives in a world where all things are inevitably destroyed by time.

For although the opening promise, "To me faire friend you neuer can be old," sounds at first genuinely tender and reassuring, its implied contrast between how the friend appears "To me" and to the objective observer is itself unsettling.[41] Its loving concern is made further suspect not only by the couplet but by the whole of the sonnet in which no expression of tenderness is altogether free of threat:

For as you were when first your eye I eyde,
Such seemes your beautie still: Three Winters colde,
Haue from the forrests shooke three summers pride,
Three beautious springs to yellow *Autumne* turn'd,
In processe of the seasons haue I seene,
Three Aprill perfumes in three hot Iunes burn'd,
Since first I saw you fresh which yet are greene.

To a friend looking for reassurance that his beauty is not fading, these lavish, even redundant reminders of time's passage are unkind, and their brutality is made to seem intentional by the insistent repetitions of "first" and "three." The speaker here is deliberately summoning up and counting "things past," but in doing so he makes no effort to establish verbal control over them by generalizing at a distance from time's destructive power or excluding its effects from the world of the poem by the devices of language characteristic of the eternizing sonnets. Here his enumerations of the "processe of the seasons" are different in kind from the generalizations about natural declines in Sonnets 15 or 60 or 65, not only because less lovingly detailed but also because they are actually not presented as examples arranged to illustrate an argument but as memories of events—three specific Aprils followed by three particular Junes—recounted in narrative form. Because they are such references to specific times—April three years ago or two or last April—rather than metaphors existing in the "eternall Sommer" of the sonnet, they are not representations of nature's endless renewals but recollections of individual periods of time that will never come again. The poet-lover's metaphorical inclusion of his friend in this sequence, "Since first I saw you fresh which yet are greene," instead of rescuing him from time's power, actually includes him in a list of specific beauties diminished and never to be renewed. His "pride" will be shaken from him like last summer's leaves;

his "fresh" beauty will disappear like the blooming fragrance of last April. Furthermore, the metaphorical inclusion of the friend's beauty in a list of natural things seen to have diminished or disappeared implies that the process of decay is already at work: "greene" is not quite "fresh," as the green foliage of "hot" summer loses the tenderness of spring, loses especially its "perfumes," so possibly becoming stale or rank (like the plants in those sonnets sharing the cynical vocabulary of 54 rather than like the "darling buds of Maie" in 18 or "summers hunny breath" in 65).[42]

The subtle meanness—especially after the tender opening sentiment—of these reminders in the first eight lines that the friend's fairness is subject to sequential, not cyclical, time depends on the closeness of the language to the conventions of eternizing verse which it parodies. In line 9 the lover becomes more overtly threatening. He is not remembering past events here but deliberately exercising the poet's power to make metaphors. Here he uses it in a calculated way to construct a comparison whose working-out leads inexorably, even mechanically (like the similar metaphor of the "dyals shady stealth" in Sonnet 77), to the conclusion that the friend's beauty is decaying. The elegiac tone does not mitigate the brutality of this conclusion:

Ah yet doth beauty like a Dyall hand,
Steale from his figure, and no pace perceiu'd,
So your sweete hew, which me thinkes still doth stand
Hath motion, and mine eye may be deceaued.

The unquestioned assertion (among so many expressions of doubt) that beauty does operate "like a Dyall hand" eliminates the possibility that the poet's "eye may" or may not "be deceaued" in thinking his friend unchanged by the years. Because dials do in fact measure time's passage by physical laws and because the eye by its nature functions the way it does, "mine eye may be deceaued" simply recognizes that it is capable of being mistaken. This strengthens the doubt raised by "me thinkes still doth stand," while the repeated pun on "still" here points to similar doubts hinted earlier by "Such seemes your beautie still." Therefore beauty perhaps only "seemes . . . still" and the "eye may be deceaued" but what is certain is that time continues to pass and that its passing inevitably destroys. This is the conclusion of the poet-lover's argument, and it is the one thing of permanence allowed by the language of the poem.

Because the rest of the sonnet is spoken to the friend, as we are reminded by the recurrence of direct address in line 11, we are aware that the final pronouncement to posterity is also said for him to hear. The poet-lover's statement of it and the friend's reception of the declaration are aspects of an incident, an episode in their relationship being acted out in the present which is in a temporal continuum with the remembered past. The sonnet is a statement made at a particular time, occasioned by previous events and predicting others to come. Its language is not designed, like Shakespeare's eternizing verse, to support the possibility of the poet-lover's claims to rescue his friend from mortality. It is made instead to insist on time's inescapable power which his own "feare," but more especially his friend's self-loving "pride," has failed to perceive in the delusive shows of feeling and of poetry.

By parodying eternizing verse, Sonnet 104 exposes its conventions as deceptions: the deluding contrivance of metaphors describing the "processe of the seasons" as cyclical but not sequential, and the flattering falsity of the poet's promise to use the miraculous power of such metaphors to fix his friend forever within the "eternall Sommer" of his sonnet. By addressing directly to his friend a poem which so nearly imitates conventional eternizing sonnets, the poet-lover defines such verse as a form of flattery shaped to the emotional demands of people like the "faire friend," whose "pride" makes them accept false assurances—mirrored in their glass and in poetic praise—of their immortality.[43] At the same time, his own parodic language, seeming to imitate such flattery, actually insists that beauty, love, even poetry, belong to the timebound world in which the friend lives and the poet writes about him.

This is the weary burden of Sonnet 108, a poem fundamentally of the same kind as 104 and the other parodies of eternizing verse, distinct from the kind frequently found among approximately the first half of sonnets 1 to 126. To elaborate the differences we may contrast sonnets 108 and 38, which share the conventional notion of the beautiful friend as inspirer of the poet-lover's verse. Sonnet 38 opens with a rhetorical question as enthusiastically complimentary in tone as its implied answer:

How can my Muse want subiect to inuent
While thou dost breath that poor'st into my verse,
Thine owne sweet argument, to excellent,
For euery vulgar paper to rehearse:
Oh giue thy selfe the thankes if ought in me,
Worthy perusal stand against thy sight,
For who's so dumbe that cannot write to thee,
When thou thy selfe dost giue inuention light?
Be thou the tenth Muse, ten times more in worth
Then those old nine which rimers inuocate,
And he that calls on thee, let him bring forth
Eternal numbers to out-liue long date.
    If my slight Muse doe please these curious daies,
    The paine be mine, but thine shal be the praise.

The language of the sonnet itself is designed, by devices found to be typical of many among the first half of the collection, to represent "Eternal numbers to out-liue long date" in celebrating the "sweet argument" of the poet's ideal love. By so doing it claims, with a confidence not dimmed by conventionally polite demurrals, the miraculous power to lift his "Muse"—at once his friend and the poem to which the friend gives "light"—out of time's passage.

In Sonnet 108, by contrast, every detail of the poet-lover's language, from his opening rhetorical question implying a tired negative response, communicates to his "sweet boy" a burdened sense of passing time and approaching old age:

What's in the braine that Inck may character,
Which hath not figur'd to thee my true spirit,
What's new to speake, what now to register,
That may expresse my loue, or thy deare merit?
Nothing sweet boy, but yet like prayers diuine,
I must each day say ore the very same,
Counting no old thing old, thou mine, I thine,
Euen as when first I hallowed thy faire name.
So that eternall loue in loues fresh case,
Waighes not the dust and iniury of age,
Nor giues to necessary wrinckles place,
But makes antiquitie for aye his page,
    Finding the first conceit of loue there bred,
    Where time and outward forme would shew it dead.

The speaker here does not represent his poem as "Eternal numbers" but as the latest repetition of the same "old thing" that he has been "Counting" and recounting "each day" until "now" since that time in the seemingly distant past "when first I hallowed thy faire name." All these references to specific times, as in Sonnet 104, insist on the sequential time scheme of human experience, the friend's as well as the speaker's, and therefore remind the "sweet boy," no longer so young a boy as when "first" the poet praised him,[44] of his inability to escape the "dust and iniury of age" with its "necessary wrinckles." These references are given special insistence by the speaker's use here of a deliberately unevocative, literal vocabulary: "dust and iniury" or "necessary wrinckles" have a dry, factual specificity very different from the hyperbolic metaphors of sonnets like 38. In the context of this mundane vocabulary, the echo of the Lord's prayer—"Euen as when first I hallowed thy faire name"—undercuts the elevating convention that the friend is divinely inspiring to the poet with the more cynical implication that he exacts daily praises which must be wearily repeated by his worshipper.

After such preparation, the poet-lover's claims to counter the power of time scarcely pretend conviction. In this couplet he does not extend the personification of time, which could reduce it to a figure whom the poet might hope to dominate (as in Sonnets 19 and 65), but drops his personification and merely names time matter-of-factly as a nonhuman, physical force. His "conceit" therefore does not even attempt to assert his power as poet to counter that force:[45]

> So that eternall loue in loues fresh case,
> Waighes not the dust and iniury of age,
> Nor giues to necessary wrinckles place,
> But makes antiquitie for aye his page,
>> Finding the first conceit of loue there bred,
>> Where time and outward forme would shew it dead.

Whether we read "loues fresh case" as an "outward cover" or a "legal plea," we hear little "fresh" vigor in the speaker's tone. If we understand "But makes antiquitie for aye his page" to mean "gains permanent mastery over his servant, time" or "takes the past to write upon perpetually," it is bluntly obvious that both senses of the metaphor depend on deliberate denials of "necessary" facts—"Waighes not . . . Nor giues . . . place"—and therefore point out the weakness of the poet's final "conceit of loue" as an empty figurative claim, like the calculatedly powerless metaphor of "beauties summer" in the last line of Sonnet 104, to rescue from time's injurious course his once "fresh" feeling, his now aging "sweet boy," his no longer "new" verse.

The poet-lover's urge to educate his friend in the fact of his mortality, if not to threaten and punish him with it, is thinly disguised in such sonnets as 54, 100, 101, 104, 107, 108, 114, which by their parodic style expose the claims of eternizing verse as flattering lies. In Sonnet 122 the speaker does make such a promise in the opening quatrain to preserve his friend "Beyond all date euen to eternity" but then, with a brutality which seems perhaps not altogether within Shakespeare's control, he strips the mask from his feelings and withdraws that promise, denying to his friend the possibility of any survival, even in memory:

> Thy guift, thy tables, are within my braine
> Full characterd with lasting memory,
> Which shall aboue that idle rancke remaine
> Beyond all date euen to eternity.

Or at the least, so long as braine and heart
Haue facultie by nature to subsist,
Til each to raz'd obliuion yeeld his part
Of thee, thy record neuer can be mist:
That poore retention could not so much hold,
Nor need I tallies thy deare loue to skore,
Therefore to giue them from me was I bold,
To trust those tables that receaue thee more,
    To keepe an adiunckt to remember thee,
    Were to import forgetfulnesse in mee.

The hyperboles of the first quatrain, which sound like the promises of eternizing verse, are destroyed by the dry, bare specificity—"at the least"—of the next four lines, which make "braine" and "heart" sound like literal, physiological terms, not conventional synechdoches for the roles of poet and lover as, for example, they are used by Sidney in the first sonnet of *Astrophil and Stella* to represent alternative sources of poetic invention.[46] These lines make inevitable the time when the speaker will die, when each organ of his body will "yeeld his part / Of thee" and the friend's "record" will cease to exist. What the speaker promises is not to perpetuate his friend "to eternity" in art, but to "skore" his "deare loue"—"deare" meaning (as in Sonnet 87) both "cherished" and "costly" or "expensive"—like a financial "record" in his memory until his own death, when the friend will cease to be remembered and so, like all things in nature, will "to raz'd obliuion yeeld."

Again in Sonnet 123 the reader's expectations about the conventions of eternizing verse are violated by parodic adjustments of language leading to the speaker's calculated omission of the predicted claim to immortalize his friend's worth. Here the imitation of the poet-lover of Shakespeare's eternizing sonnets is worked out in the speaker's personification of time as a vain boaster whose power he defies in the poem, itself a "vow" to his enemy to defeat that power "dispight thy syeth and thee." Such detailed resemblances make very pointed his avoidance of the promise to immortalize his friend, his omission of any mention whatever of his poetry, or even of his love except by vague suggestion in the first and last lines:

No! Time, thou shalt not bost that I doe change,
Thy pyramids buylt vp with newer might
To me are nothing nouell, nothing strange,
They are but dressings of a former sight:
Our dates are breefe, and therefor we admire,
What thou dost foyst vpon vs that is ould,
And rather make them borne to our desire,
Then thinke that we before haue heard them tould:
Thy registers and thee I both defie,
Not wondring at the present, nor the past,
For thy records, and what we see doth lye,
Made more or les by thy continuall hast:
    This I doe vow and this shall euer be,
    I will be true dispight thy syeth and thee.

The speaker seems to go through many of the motions that characterize eternizing sonnets, but without the slightest conviction. He contemplates large examples of the workings of time but they evoke no sense of wonder and rarity—"nothing nouell, nothing strange"—or noble loss. The things of this world are old, stale, and deceptive—"but dressings of a former sight"—and "Time" is a cheat who "dost foyst vpon vs" false goods, who basely caters "to our desire," whose "registers" and "records" of such shoddy transactions "lye." The speaker's tone as he contemplates the fraudulent operations of time is not elegiac but weary, his detachment indifferent rather than philosophic—"Not wondring at the present, nor the past"—his defiance unheroic, knowing, empty. He makes no claims to have found an embodiment of the ideal worth preserving from time's "continuall hast" (a pun which seems to have effects the reverse of "inconstant stay" in Sonnet 15 because it tends to speed rather than arrest time's motion). He has no art to pit against time's power, and indeed his style here is as deliberately unevocative, as scrupulously mean as the speaker's language in 108, 122, or, we shall see, in 83. He makes no claims for himself as a poet or for his verse as a weapon "in war with Time," but pledges only to be "true" to some undefined object, to remain unchanged in a state of feeling which seems weary and willed—"I will bĕ trúe"—to which he stubbornly adheres in a world that offers neither permanence nor worth to warrant "true" devotion.[47]

In Sonnet 123 the poet-lover's disbelief in the immortalizing power of art to create a permanently ordered world matching an ideal love is expressed by his pointed avoidance of such claims. This calculated silence, used with variations in a number of other poems, is actually discussed and with heavy irony defended in Sonnet 83, where the speaker defines promises to "giue life" as the "barren tender of a Poets debt," exacted by the friend in "praise" of his "faire eyes":[48]

> I neuer saw that you did painting need,
> And therefore to your faire no painting set,
> I found (or thought I found) you did exceed,
> The barren tender of a Poets debt:
> And therefore haue I slept in your report,
> That you your selfe being extant well might show,
> How farre a moderne quill doth come to short,
> Speaking of worth, what worth in you doth grow,
> This silence for my sinne you did impute,
> Which shall be most my glory being dombe,
> For I impaire not beautie being mute,
> When others would giue life, and bring a tombe.
>   There liues more life in one of your faire eyes,
>   Then both your Poets can in praise deuise.

The speaker's unwillingness to "deuise" flattering poems, which he likens to the cosmetic art of "painting," was expressed in the past by his refusal to promise immortality, "being mute, / When others would giue life, and bring a tombe." It is also embodied in the manner he chooses now to break his "silence," which is different in kind from the language used so often in the lower-numbered sonnets to support the poet-lover's eternizing claims, or the attitudes toward love and poetry associated with them. An example is Sonnet 17 which, like 83, contains the conventional argument that the beauty of the friend's eyes exceeds the poet's art, but which nevertheless concludes with a promise to perpetuate his loveliness in verse as it would also be recreated in a child:

Who will beleeue my verse in time to come
If it were fild with your most high deserts?
Though yet heauen knowes it is but as a tombe
Which hides your life, and shewes not halfe your parts:
If I could write the beauty of your eyes,
And in fresh numbers number all your graces,
The age to come would say this Poet lies,
Such heauenly touches nere toucht earthly faces.
So should my papers (yellowed with their age)
Be scorn'd, like old men of lesse truth then tongue,
And your true rights to be termd a Poets rage,
And stretched miter of an Antique song.
  But were some childe of yours aliue that time,
  You should liue twise in it, and in my rime.

By contrast, in the closing lines of Sonnet 83 the speaker withholds such reassurance, turning compliment into threat: "There liues more life in one of your faire eyes" than in all the contrivances of poets, which are powerless to extend that "life" when time inevitably takes it from you, as it has already begun to take your fairness since that period in the past when "I neuer saw" what it is now possible to see (because my feeling and your face have altered). For at the present time when I am breaking "silence" to write this poem I see that you may "painting need," perhaps always needed it although I then "thought" you did not, need cosmetics to enhance your "beautie" and false "praise" to reassure you that "worth in you doth grow" perpetually and will never fade.

The poem itself, like Sonnets 104 and 108, is at once an account of a relationship changing in the course of time and a statement spoken at a particular stage in the sequence of experiences which compose the relationship. It places itself in that continuum by references to specific occasions prior to the moment when the poet-lover makes this defense of his behavior—"This silence for my sinne you did impute"—and to past states of feeling which in the intervening time have altered, or which he reflects on in the present from a new perspective—"I found (or thought I found)." Its structure seems therefore to be chiefly narrative rather than logical or rhetorical: the speaker appears to be describing a sequence of events as they happened in time rather than arranging a series of illustrations in which sequence is dictated by the shape of his argument. This narrative is made to seem factually descriptive, unlike the imagined "age to come" in Sonnet 17, by rejecting its generalized, figurative, and hyperbolic style for a dry, literal, specific vocabulary like the language of Sonnets 122 and 123.

In approximately the second half of Sonnets 1 to 126 there are many which parody Shakespeare's eternizing verse, and by so doing define very differently the nature of the poet's art, as well as the lover's feelings. In other sonnets the speaker comments on the conventions of eternizing poetry explicitly by withholding its claim to miraculous power, implicitly in avoiding devices of language designed to support that claim by transforming experience into a poetic ordering distinct from the timebound world. These poems employ language in ways virtually never used among the first half of Sonnets 1 to 126, but consistently found in the second half, and in poems which are not explicitly concerned with the poet-lover's "war with Time."

Sonnet 29 uses the language we have seen to be best suited for generalizing and idealizing, for celebrating the permanence of the poet-lover's "state," assured by his appreciation of the friend's "sweet loue," amid the seeming flux of experience:

When in disgrace with Fortune and mens eyes,
I all alone beweepe my out-cast state,
And trouble deafe heauen with my bootlesse cries,
And looke vpon my selfe and curse my fate.
Wishing me like to one more rich in hope,

Featur'd like him, like him with friends possest,
Desiring this mans art, and that mans skope,
With what I most inioy contented least,
Yet in these thoughts my selfe almost despising,
Haplye I thinke on thee, and then my state,
(Like to the Larke at breake of daye arising)
From sullen earth sings himns at Heauens gate,
    For thy sweet loue remembred such welth brings,
    That then I skorne to change my state with Kings.

Every device of language is shaped to assert that moments of change which we experience as if "Haplye" or "by accident" are then "happily," meaning both "fortunately" and "joyfully," transformed by the poet's argument—"When . . . then . . . then"—which, although it records an experience in time with a suggestion of narrative sequence, generalizes it in a perpetual present. The poet also compares it to the timeless recurrences of nature—"Like to the Larke at breake of daye arising"—because it celebrates the permanence of the speaker's fidelity to his ideal "loue." The sonnet therefore insists on its distinct identity as a work of art, different in its essential nature from the changes and contradictions of temporal experience, which it has miraculously transformed into "himns at Heauens gate." By this insistence on itself as a poem it evokes awareness of an audience of readers more extensive than simply the friend (here not directly addressed until line 10), and by such means strengthens its claims to generality and also to permanence, since the continuous present of the sonnet is eternally present to all readers at all times, past and to come.

Sonnet 120, which is also concerned with changes wrought in the speaker's feelings by thoughts of his friend, uses a language altogether different in kind and therefore in its effects:

That you were once vnkind be-friends mee now,
And for that sorrow, which I then didde feele,
Needes must I vnder my transgression bow,
Vnlesse my Nerues were brasse or hammered steele.
For if you were by my vnkindnesse shaken

As I by yours, y'haue past a hell of Time,
And I a tyrant haue no leasure taken
To waigh how once I suffered in your crime.
O that our night of wo might haue remembred
My deepest sence, how hard true sorrow hits,
And soone to you, as you to me then tendred
The humble salue, which wounded bosomes fits!
  But that your trespasse now becomes a fee,
  Mine ransoms yours, and yours must ransome mee.

The language here is not designed to make us feel that we are members of a general public of readers addressed in a sonnet shaped by the poet's rhetorical argument. We are instead put in the position of an eavesdropper overhearing part of a private conversation about a series of episodes involving the speaker and the listener. This effect is achieved partly by the prosaic, nonfigurative style that sounds more like speech than verse, and also by its use to refer to particular though unexplained incidents, not the conventional, representative occasions of Petrarchan poetry (such as the sleepless nights of Sonnet 27 or the metaphorical war of eye and heart in 46 or the journey in 50), but specified situations: "you were once vnkind," "I then didde feele," "once I suffered," "our night of wo." The sense of the poem being spoken to someone as we listen is increased by the prominent references to "now," in the first line and in the couplet, in contrast to "once" (lines 1 and 8) and "then" (lines 2 and 11), and especially by the references to the continuum between "then" and "now":

For if you were by my vnkindnesse shaken
As I by yours, y'haue past a hell of Time,
And I a tyrant haue no leasure taken
To waigh how once I suffered in your crime.

The sonnet also creates the illusion that it is not a poem but part of a conversation because the speaker's language conveys a very different sense of the listener's presence than in sonnets like 29, where he is placed as a theme for the poet-lover to "thinke on," and as he is "remembred" in the generalized term "thy sweet loue," and in the literary association with nature's renewals, "Like to the Larke at breake of daye arising." Here the listener is simply addressed as "you." He is not transformed by a comparison—a plant, a "Summers day," a "Iewell," "beauties patterne"—controlled within the "eternall lines" of a poem, but remains a specific person, neither metaphorical nor representative, to whom the speaker anxiously addresses some advice which he hopes the friend "now" hearing it will follow in the future.

Instead of claiming to transform its matter into a poetic ordering essentially different from temporal experience, this poem and others of its kind among approximately the second half of Sonnets 1 to 126 presents itself as a moment in time as well as a reflection on other such moments. Its speaker is not identified as an artist; his language is not literary in any conventional sense and makes no references to itself as "these lines" or "black inck." His speech asserts no powers except perhaps of persuasion—"yours *must* ransom me." It derives no grandeur, generality, or permanence from resembling itself to the large cycles of nature, for the natural world seems exhausted or inaccessible as a source for comparisons, except the negative and mechanical "Vnlesse my Nerues were brasse or hammered steele."[49] Certainly it claims nothing miraculous about itself or about the emotions that inspire it, for the Christian language used here to talk about feelings is explicitly emptied of religious meanings, and so confined to mundane human and social situations, even cynically perverted since the biblical term for transgression, "trespasse," is reduced to a financial equivalent when it "now becomes a fee."

This sonnet is therefore altogether different from poems of the sort represented by Sonnet 29, which uses language characteristic of eternizing verse, but of the same kind as those in approximately the second half of Sonnets 1 to 126, which define themselves by their violations of eternizing conventions. These pointedly omit claims to the miraculous power of transformation, but compare their workings to such processes as distillation, which is physical, even mechanical. Like the other crafts-men to whom the poet is compared in these sonnets—the cosmetician, the dyer, the alchemist, the rhetorician—the dis-tiller of perfumes operates with human skills on the matter of this world and with effects that are designed to be felt in society. This suggests a further difference between them and the first kind of poem, where the setting which the poet's art transforms to match his love is characteristically the pastoral "world and all her fading sweets." There the friend and the poet-lover exist against a natural background which is personifiable but not cynically socialized. By contrast, in many sonnets in approx-imately the second half of the collection, the speaker and the young man live in a human society which is linked to the natural world chiefly in sharing with it vulgarity, corruption, and deceit.[50] The language of these poems is the language of such a depraved society, and compares its effects to the fraudulent and seductive arts of adornment and flattery.

In approximately the first half of Sonnets 1 to 126, the claims of eternizing verse and the manipulations of language designed to support those claims are the poet-lover's means of defining his own power to rescue his love from destruction by time, and so defining the miraculous nature and power of poetry. The speaker in the second half of the collection does not demonstrate his different sense of his power as a poet by avoiding the con-ventional promise to eternize his love in art, but more character-istically by parodying, attacking, ridiculing, condemning, or so pointedly withholding the promise, that even its absence is a self-conscious device for expressing his concerns about love and about poetry.

The presence of so many sonnets which reduce the claims of eternizing verse to veiled admonition, insult, and threat suggests that its metaphors were charged for Shakespeare with very personal feelings of an intensity, even bitterness, difficult to control. The figure of the poet-lover in approximately the second half of Sonnets 1 to 126 appears to be obsessed with this convention: it seems to represent or embody for him the fraudulent shows of the world which his poems are designed at once to imitate and to expose.

The source of this obsession is explored in Sonnet 126, occurring last in this part of the collection,[51] which begins with yet another series of seeming compliments to the "louely Boy":

O thou my louely Boy who in thy power,
Doest hould times fickle glasse, his sickle, hower:
Who hast by wayning growne, and therein shou'st,
Thy louers withering, as thy sweet selfe grow'st.
If Nature (soueraine misteres ouer wrack)
As thou goest onwards still will plucke thee backe,
She keepes thee to this purpose, that her skill
May time disgrace, and wretched mynuit kill.
Yet feare her O thou minnion of her pleasure,
She may detaine, but not still keepe her tresure!
Her *Audite* (though delayd) answer'd must be,
And her *Quietus* is to render thee.
   (   )
   (   )

In lines 1 to 8, as in so many of the first sonnets in the collection, the friend's "sweet selfe" is perceived as a plant partaking—"by wayning growne"—of nature's cycles and so rescued from the universal "wrack" of time. Here, however, the comparison does not attach to the friend the pastoral associations of fragility, passivity, and innocence, such as describe the beauty of Sonnet 65, "Whose action is not stronger then a flower." Here the friend is a figure of "power" which actively, even aggressively "goest onwards," sustaining and nourishing itself like a carnivorous plant or a parasite:

Who hast by wayning growne, and therein shou'st
Thy louers withering, as thy sweet selfe grow'st.

This attributes sexual promiscuity—with "louers"—to the friend, like the "Sweet Roses" of Sonnet 54, even a rapacity which is cruelly perverse, for there is a brutal suggestion that the friend rejuvenates himself by using or using up his numerous "louers." In the same way that the metaphor of the friend as a lovely plant is corrupted here, the familiar praise of him as the supreme illustration of mortal beauty is made vicious when the poet-lover calls him nature's "minnion." For although this word could mean "darling" (like the innocently "darling buds of Maie" in Sonnet 18), it could also mean "paramour," "slave," "servile creature," "one who owes everything to the patron's favor and is willing to purchase it by base compliances."[52] The phrase "minnion of her pleasure" therefore accuses the "louely Boy" of submission to the demands of his "soueraine misteres." The speaker attacks him for prostituting himself to nature to insure that she will "still keepe" him beautifully young. He then reminds the friend with undisguised hostility that neither his own capacity to see himself unchanged in "times fickle glasse" nor nature's "skill" in opposing "time," as if she had the power of eternizing art, can do what the poet-lover pointedly refuses to do: to promise him the immortality he has sold himself to gain. Where the opening compliments would predict some form of eternizing conceit in the conclusion, the speaker delivers a naked threat:

> Yet feare her O thou minnion of her pleasure,
> She may detaine, but not still keepe her tresure!
> Her *Audite* (though delayd) answer'd must be,
> And her *Quietus* is to render thee.

The vengeful satisfaction in his tone is not disguised here by the parodic uses of language which earlier in the poem thinly veil his resentment, contempt, even horror, for the "louely Boy" who is no longer quite a "Boy," but whose beauty is monstrously untouched by time and feeling that have left their mark on those who love him.[53]

The quality of the speaker's own feeling in this last poem of the group can be measured by contrasting it with Sonnet 3:

> Looke in thy glasse and tell the face thou vewest,

Now is the time that face should forme an other,
Whose fresh repaire if now thou not renewest,
Thou doo'st beguile the world, vnblesse some mother.
For where is she so faire whose vn-eard wombe
Disdaines the tillage of thy husbandry?
Or who is he so fond will be the tombe,
Of his selfe loue to stop posterity?
Thou art thy mothers glasse and she in thee
Calls backe the louely Aprill of her prime,
So thou through windowes of thine age shalt see,
Dispight of wrinkles this thy goulden time.
   But if thou liue remembred not to be,
   Die single and thine Image dies with thee.

While idealizing the friend's "fresh" beauty, again perceived in uniquely close association with growing things of nature, the speaker here also teases and even chides him for qualities un-mentioned in sonnets promising to immortalize an ideal love: his readiness to look in the "glasse," his "selfe loue," which is "fond" also in the sense of "foolish" or "self-defeating," his indulgence in seductive games to "beguile the world." Yet these criticisms seem gentle by contrast with the savage scorn of the speaker in Sonnet 126, and they are much softened by the tenderly loving tone of lines 9 to 12 and by the association throughout of the friend's beauty with a pastoral nature "fresh," fallow, and "goulden," implying both "precious" and "unfallen," rather than with a nature likened to a courtly "misteres" with a taste for perverse "pleasure." Furthermore, although in the couplet of Sonnet 3 the speaker seems to withhold the conventional promise to immortalize his friend's "Image" in art, he has actually perpet-uated it already in the poem by manipulating language in ways characteristic of eternizing verse. For he has transformed him into a poetic figure of speech in which past and future are miraculously present in "this . . . goulden time," a metaphor for the mythical quality of the friend's beauty and the miraculous power of the poet's lines where, as in the "eternall lines" of Sonnet 18, the only "time" is measure:

Thou art thy mothers glasse and she in thee
Calls backe the louely Aprill of her prime,
So thou through windowes of thine age shalt see,
Dispight of wrinkles this thy goulden time.

The poem therefore perpetuates his "Image" by a creation parallel to generation, insuring that its hyperboles will make the friend's face forever "live remembred," whether or not he accepts the witty chiding of the couplet. Although the sonnet is cast as persuasion or advice, it is also a poem in praise of the young man's beauty, which the poet-lover values as dearly as the young Narcissus he addresses. If the friend is affectionately criticized, it is for keeping to himself the treasure of his "goulden" loveliness, not for too highly valuing it or for prostituting it to insure its perpetuation.

By contrast, Sonnet 126 is an attack on the friend's "power" to "hould" before himself the signs of his unchanging beauty in "times fickle glasse," to "hould" off his "sickle, hower." It condemns his sense of himself as a uniquely privileged "tresure" who, like a plant, belongs to a world apart from that of "withering" humanity. It therefore criticizes him for conceiving of himself in metaphors like those used to praise the friend by the poet-lover in the eternizing sonnets and for seeming to achieve, by the "power" of his untouchable beauty, the triumph over time there claimed as the unique "might" of the poet's art.

The speaker's obsession with this kind of "power," and the poetic conventions which express it, seems to derive here, as in many sonnets among the second half of the collection, from his recognition that his friend imagines himself in what the poet considers to be the flattering conceits of eternizing verse because his mirror shows a beauty which perversely, unnaturally, inhumanly—if not miraculously—triumphs over time. His own verse is intended, like the "booke" presented by the poet to the friend and made the occasion of Sonnet 77, to record the fact of his mortality:

All in War with Time

Thy glasse will shew thee how thy beauties were,
Thy dyall how thy pretious mynuits waste,
The vacant leaues thy mindes imprint will beare,
And of this booke, this learning maist thou taste.
The wrinckles which thy glasse will truly show,
Of mouthed graues will giue thee memorie,
Thou by thy dyals shady stealth maist know,
Times theeuish progresse to eternitie.
Looke what thy memorie cannot containe,
Commit to these waste blanks, and thou shalt finde
Those children nurst, deliuered from thy braine,
To take a new acquaintance of thy minde.
    These offices, so oft as thou wilt looke,
    Shall profit thee, and much inrich thy booke.

This sonnet, like 126, is itself a "glasse" which "will truly show" what the friend disguises by his belief in his beauty's "power" to immortalize. Its brutality is revealed through the metaphors derived from the impartial operatons of physical objects which demonstrate irrefutably "Times theeuish progresse to eternitie." They are chosen to "profit" the friend in knowledge of precisely those facts which eternizing verse claims miraculously to transform.

Like many other poems among approximately the second half of Sonnets 1 to 126, these assign to poetry a mission, to which the poet-lover seems dedicated with vindictive and not always controlled passion, of denouncing the "power" of that beauty and destroying the claims of eternizing poetry to match it by its own miraculous language. His role as poet is to expose the ugliness and inefficacy of such unnatural forms of "power" by truth-telling art. His is not designed to rescue his "loue" from mortality by combating it with the weapon of his verse, but to incorporate into poetry the processes of mutability, so that it may teach the aging "Boy" how he shares with the poet-lover the pain of our inevitable defeat "in war with Time."

2

Donne

In Donne's *Songs and Sonets,* as in Shakespeare's sonnets, we meet a speaker who is "all in war with Time" to preserve his love in a world threatened by change and loss. In some of Donne's finest lyrics the speaker pits himself against mortality as vehemently as Shakespeare's in his challenges to "times fell hand," but he does so in ways which seem intended to distinguish the nature of his defiance from that of other poets. Donne's choice of such means for defining his own concerns is characteristic: throughout his poetry, by echoing, imitating, parodying, transforming recognizable poetic styles and conventions, he habitually sets off the special nature of his own poems.

"The Good-morrow," which readers since the seventeenth century have traditionally met as the first poem in the *Songs and Sonets,*[1] ends with a tentative promise that defies the inescapable end of temporal experience:

> What ever dyes, was not mixt equally;
> If our two loves be one, or, thou and I
> Love so alike, that none doe slacken, none can die.

A poem concluding with a hope that the lovers whose experience it celebrates will be exempt from mortality inevitably recalls the claims of the sonneteers to preserve their beloveds from the effects of time. These ·promises are most familiar to us in Shakespeare's sonnets, where they occur more often than in those of any other English poet, but they pervade the love poetry of the period in which Donne began to write the *Songs and Sonets.* He and all other readers of that voluminous literature were familiar with many poems ending in variations of the eternizing conceit. Spenser's *Amoretti* 75:[2]

> my verse your vertues rare shall eternize,
> and in the heuens wryte your glorious name.
> Where whenas death shall all the world subdew,
> our love shall liue, and later life renew.

Or Daniel's *Delia* 45:

> That Grace which doth more then in woman thee,
> Liues in my lines, and must eternall bee.

Or Drayton's *Idea* 6:[3]

> So shalt thou flye above the vulgar Throng,
> Still to survive in my imortall Song.

Or Shakespeare's triumphant Sonnet 18:

> So long as men can breath or eyes can see,
> So long liues this, and this giues life to thee.

In three of Donne's own poems, "The Canonization," "The Relique," and "The Anniversarie," he plays with the notion of a speaker presenting future ages with a written record of his love surviving beyond the mortal span of the lovers. "The Good-morrow," too, by its ending invites the reader to consider it in relation to other poems using the eternizing convention, and when it is set in this context, we can isolate the way in which Donne's poem differentiates itself.

The tentativeness of his speaker's promise is not its distinguishing feature. For although a kind of exuberant self-confidence is associated with this convention,[4] the sonneteers are rarely so radiantly assertive as the poet-lover in Shakespeare's Sonnet 18, who challenges death's "brag" with his own boast of the godlike power of his art to give "life" itself. More often, as even the few quoted examples illustrate, the poet promises to rescue only some special quality of the beloved—virtue, grace, truth, beauty, love, worth, or name—from the fate of all mortal creatures. Such variations on the conceit among the sonnets of this period are numberless; Donne's transformation of it does not differentiate itself either by the extent of his speaker's claims or the degree of his assurance.

The most important difference between the ending of "The Good-morrow" and the eternizing sonnets is that Donne's challenge to mortality is not spoken by a poet. This does not mean only that the lines do not sound literary in any conventional sense, although the special quality of the diction at the end of the poem (quite different from the equally unliterary speech at the beginning of the first stanza) is essential to the way we read the final lines. Unlike Shakespeare's poet-lover, Donne's speaker does not claim that he and his love may escape mortality by the power of his art or in his verse. Nor does he identify himself as a poet; he is not writing to his beloved but lying in bed talking to her. When in his speech he introduces the hope of immortality, it is not in an assertion of the miraculous power of his poetry to transform temporal experience, but in a proposition, apparently a generally accepted formula, about the laws of nature: "What ever dyes, was not mixt equally."

His defiance of mortality in language which is pointedly not a poet's metaphor for his art directs our reading of "The Good-morrow" in ways which can help also to define the distinctive nature of other poems in the *Songs and Sonets*. The relation of this poem to the conventions of eternizing verse, and the attitudes expressed in that relation, are revealing of ways in which Donne's imagination works, in poems representing his deepest concerns and highest achievement.

Throughout the collection of *Songs and Sonets* there are very few poems in which the speaker identifies himself as a poet. Again I do not mean simply to repeat the familiar observation that Donne's idiom is often a colloquial spoken language foreign to the literariness of much sixteenth-century love poetry (although this diction is of course the chief instrument for seducing us into imagining that we are listening to a speaking voice instead of reading poems). The point here is that there are very few poems in which the speaker is presented as a man in love who is a poet writing about his feelings in verse—remarkably few for a group of love lyrics begun during the 1590s. For the conventions of language in sixteenth-century love poetry are so largely dictated by the figure of the poet-lover that Donne's *Songs and Sonets*, richly related to that language, by characteristically avoiding the conventional role of the speaker make a departure with large implications for the kinds of poems he intended them to be. [5]

Donne plays with the convention of the poet-lover in "The

Indifferent," in which the opening of the last stanza, "*Venus heard me sigh this song*," underlines that the attack on constancy which precedes it is the complaint of an anti-Petrarchan poet-lover. In "The Triple Foole" he mocks and wittily rejects the conventional plight of the lover who publishes his feelings in verse, or the poet who suffers the "paines" of love. In "The Will" the speaker bequeathes, with intentional inappropriateness, "To Nature, all that I in Ryme have writ," espousing silence and death "To'invent, and practise" a poet's revenge for "neglect" by the lady whose "beauties" will then be buried uncelebrated. In "Loves Growth" the conventional figure is lightly dismissed as a posturing theoretician:[6]

> Love's not so pure, and abstract, as they use
> To say, which have no Mistresse but their Muse,
> But as all else, being elemented too,
> Love sometimes would contemplate, sometimes do.

In the other *Songs and Sonets* the lover who identifies himself as a poet is virtually excluded, with the exceptions, to be discussed, of "The Anniversarie," "The Relique," and "The Canonization." While some of Donne's speakers compose letters as part of the "stocks intire"[7]—with sighs, tears, oaths, and hearts—used by the stylish lover to bargain for the lady's "rewards," like the speaker in "The Good-morrow" they omit references to themselves as poets or to their words as "black inck," "these lines," "Eternal numbers," or "my imortall Song."

Donne also avoids many of the conventional motifs which interested sonneteers: the lover who writes to entertain or seduce the lady;[8] who composes his poem because he cannot sleep; who apologizes in verse for the inadequacy of his art; who sings praises of his mistress in comparison with ladies in other poems; who promises to eternize her in his immortal lines. Among the conventions which most often interested Donne, which seem to have provided the opportunity for the exercise of his fullest powers, are those traditional to the aubade and the valediction: the situation of the lover, after a night of joy with his mistress, greeting the dawn which has awakened them, and of the lover bidding farewell to his mistress before sorrowfully parting from her.[9] Donne's use of these situations in a number of the *Songs and Sonets,* and in ones which most readers find to be among his finest achievements, suggests that they provided opportunities for poems of a kind not so readily offered by conventions in which the lover is represented as a poet concerned with giving distinct literary shape to his expressions of feeling.

The title of "The Good-morrow" predicts a poem in which a man, with his mistress beside him, greets the morning light as it shines into their bedroom.[10] References to the "roome" in stanza two and to the lovers' faces closely reflected in each other's eyes in stanza three insist on the physical presence or actuality of the situation in which we hear the speaker's voice. By contrast, for example, with Shakespeare's Sonnet 7,[11] "Loe in the Orient when the gracious light, / Lifts vp his burning head," in which sunrise is generalized as a category of nature's activities and then transformed by explicit poetic comparison—"So thou, thy selfe out-going in thy noon"—into a metaphor for a kind of human condition. The poet-lover, whose authority seems to derive from this capacity to generalize and compare, instructs the friend and also the reader (commanded to attend with the biblical "Loe"), by this literary similitude.

In "The Good-morrow," by contrast, the sun rising is particular and immediate, and does not cease to be literally present when the lover makes metaphorical use of it in speaking intimately to his mistress:

> The Good-morrow
>
> I wonder by my troth, what thou, and I
>   Did, till we lov'd? were we not wean'd till then?
> But suck'd on countrey pleasures, childishly?
>   Or snorted we i'the seaven sleepers den?
> 'Twas so; But this, all pleasures fancies bee.
> If ever any beauty I did see,
> Which I desir'd, and got, 'twas but a dreame of thee.
>
>   And now good morrow to our waking soules,

Which watch not one another out of feare;
For love, all love of other sights controules,
    And makes one little roome, an every where.
Let sea-discoverers to new worlds have gone,
Let Maps to others, worlds on worlds have showne,
Let us possesse our world, each hath one, and is one.

My face in thine eye, thine in mine appeares,
    And true plaine hearts doe in the faces rest,
Where can we finde two better hemispheares
    Without sharpe North, without declining West?
What ever dyes, was not mixt equally;
If our two loves be one, or, thou and I
Love so alike, that none doe slacken, none can die.

In the first stanza the speaker makes no reference to the physical details of his situation. Yet we know that he is a successful
lover by his opening exclamation, by the contrast of "this" with
all previous "pleasures," pàrticularly those beauties which he
"desir'd, and got" in the past, and by his freedom to amuse the
lady with such sexual boasting or with his wittily unglamorous
pictures of having "suck'd" and "snorted" among crude
"countrey pleasures" until enlightened by those, richer and more
sophisticated, which they now share.

In this opening stanza the speaker defines his relationship with
the woman by contrasting their present with past experience.
These contrasts express delighted self-assurance: he feels that
they have outgrown "childishly" undiscriminating affairs, have
wakened from dreaming unconsciousness to sophisticated adult
experience, in which the ideal has become fully actual: "If ever
any beauty I did see . . . 'twas but a dreame of thee." Yet this
triumphant definition of the lovers' achievement places it in
time. It is reached through a temporal process which they have
experienced, although perhaps unknowingly, like the legendary
youths who slept away more than a hundred years,[12] by contrast, for example, with the literary "pleasures" which Marlowe's
"Passionate Shepherd" paints to "move" with "delight" the
"mind" of his "love":[13]

Come live with me, and be my love,
And we will all the pleasures prove
That valleys, groves, hills and fields,
Woods. or steepy mountain yields.
       . . .
The shepherd swains shall dance and sing
For thy delight each May-morning.
If these delights thy mind may move,
Then live with me, and be my love.

Marlowe's pastoral ideal is not achieved through growth in time. His speaker makes no reference to previous experiences which he and the lady have passed beyond, or to any actual, physical present which they share. They exist entirely in the generalized, metaphorical landscape of the poem which is eternally present—"For thy delight each May-morning"—to the imagination capable of appreciating its unchanging perfections.

The ideal "pleasures" celebrated by Donne's lover in the first stanza of "The Good-morrow," on the contrary, exist in his actual experiences of the previous night, in his awareness of them at the present which is not a timeless condition in a poem but a specified period in the lifetime of the lovers, even a particular morning. This they have reached in time's passage, leaving behind other moments, other experiences, themselves actual but now remembered in the present as if they were pastoral or mythological "fancies."

This ideal has been achieved in time, but not fully consciously or intentionally, for there is mystery as well as delight in the lover's "wonder" at the distance between their now fully wakened maturity and their unaware past. He understands their feelings without being able to trace or explain the changes wrought in them by the course of time. He therefore celebrates the present realization of his ideal, while acknowledging that it grew without his design. He cannot claim to have the control over it that Shakespeare's eternizing poet-lover exerts when he evokes an "eternall Sommer" created by his own arrangement of images in the timeless order of his poem. For unlike a literary creation, a relationship reached through the process of time must in growing be subject to its changes. Because it flourishes in time, it must be vulnerable to decline and loss as well as capable of growth. Having achieved such a love, to preserve it in its present perfection the speaker must therefore establish his power over the effects of time.

Apparently the dawning light as it wakes the lovers reminds the speaker of their vulnerability to change, for in the second stanza he begins his effort to assert his authority over the flux of experience. He then does so by adapting, in his own manner of speaking, the aubade convention of hailing the dawning light, as, for example, Shakespeare's Romeo greets it:[14]

> Look, love, what envious streaks
> Do lace the severing clouds in yonder East.
> Night's candles are burnt out, and jocund day
> Stands tiptoe on the misty mountain tops.

The less reverent, less elevated language of Donne's lover is in itself part of his attempt to assert his freedom from dominance by the coming day:

> And now good morrow to our waking soules,
> 　Which watch not one another out of feare;
> For love, all love of other sights controules,
> 　And makes one little roome, an every where.
> Let sea-discoverers to new worlds have gone,
> Let Maps to others, worlds on worlds have showne,
> Let us possesse our world, each hath one, and is one.

The lover's exuberant greeting seems to welcome the morning as a fitting complement to their feelings, not as a hostile intruder, like Romeo's "envious" day, who would interfere with their "pleasures." His easy acceptance of it is a way of showing that it poses no threat to their love. The day has, his tone implies, come to say in unison with him its personal "good morrow" to the lovers' "waking soules." It has come as if allowed only when the speaker is ready and has decorously summoned it with "And now," meaning "now that I have finished what I wanted first to say" and "now that we are prepared for delighted consciousness."

The lover's grand manner of speaking—his radiant greeting, his large generalizing about "love," his lordly dismissals in "Let sea-discoverers . . . Let Maps," his godlike *fiat*, "Let us"—are designed to support his assertions of power over the flow of experience. These "soules," he claims, unlike less conscious lovers, "watch not one another out of feare." What the causes of their fears might be is undefined, which tends to intensify their ominousness, but implied by the lines which follow, apparently as explanation:

> For love, all love of other sights controules,
> And makes one little roome, an every where.

What he argues that they need not "feare" is "love of other sights" than those beautifully revealed by the light now shining upon their bed, for their perfectly aware feeling for each other, he claims, "controules" their other feelings,[15] not by eliminating but by including them, by bringing them to enrich their appreciation of each other so that the "one little roome" which contains their love holds all the novelty that discoverers find in "new worlds," all the diversity shown by maps of "worlds on worlds." Yet because their mutual awareness "controules" the "world" they "possesse," it has the design and completeness of a created object: it "makes one little roome, an every where."

This large, philosophical definition of the way love "controules" experience, given special prominence at the precise center of the poem, sounds like a description of an eternizing poet's power to transform fact into metaphor, to create out of the limits of experience in time a generalized ideal existing in a distinct world impervious to change and loss. The speaker in "The Good-morrow" then seems to demonstrate that art by turning the lovers into a "world, each hath one, and is one," and from that metaphor deriving the further comparison of their images reflected in each other's eyes to "better hemispheares" which, like the pastoral nature in Marlowe's song, exist beyond reach of time and season, "Without sharpe North, without declining West," and so escape mortality.[16]

Yet the speaker, in these efforts to rescue love from mutability, never identifies himself as a writer exercising his verbal art *in a poem*. He is a man trying to give shape to moments in time as he experiences them, so that his interpretation becomes part of the experience itself rather than existing independently as a permanent literary record of passing minutes. His ideal only flourishes in the "little roome" on this "good morrow." The reflected images of the lovers' faces in which he finds "better hemispheares," are actual "sights" described by the speaker as they are revealed in the dawning light (and therefore in a sense dependent on its continuance). Although his descriptions of them are elaborate and figurative, they are derivations from the facts of his immediate situation, not metaphorical inventions to illustrate a poet-lover's argument, as they are, for example, in a poem like Shakespeare's Sonnet 24:[17]

> For through the Painter must you see his skill,
> To finde where your true Image pictur'd lies,
> Which in my bosomes shop is hanging stil,
> That hath his windowes glazed with thine eyes:
> Now see what good-turnes eyes for eies haue done,
> Mine eyes haue drawne thy shape, and thine for me
> Are windowes to my breast, where-through the Sun
> Delights to peepe, to gaze therein on thee.

Because his ideal exists in time, not in the "eternall lines" of verse, if Donne's speaker makes any claim to preserve his love in its present perfection from "declining," an eventuality which his use of that word shows his "feare," he cannot do so by immortalizing it in the perpetual "May-morning" or "eternall Sommer" of a poem.

To emphasize this difference in kind between the conclusion of "The Good-morrow" and the eternizing convention as the sonneteers used it, when at this point Donne's speaker introduces the possibility of escape from mortality for their love, he abandons his own metaphor of a "world" from which he has excluded mutability. That is, he does not extend his comparison to a logical conclusion derived from its terms in contradiction of the facts of the physical world. In this way he differs from the poet-lover in Shakespeare's Sonnet 18, for example, who derives the promise to immortalize his love by art—"When in eternall lines to time grow'st"—as the conclusion to the conceit of the friend perceived as "eternall Sommer." Rather than extending the possibilities of an ideal "world" in which fact is transformed into metaphor, Donne's speaker in "The Good-morrow" drops the metaphors and also the rhetoric of the first two and a half stanzas in the final three lines. When readers of eternizing sonnets would expect to hear the hyperboles of a poet-lover vowing to defeat time with his art, Donne's speaker cites from scholastic philosophy an impersonal formula for natural laws of survival: "What ever dyes, was not mixt equally."[18] Creatures in the temporal world can, according to this proposition, escape mortality only if they exist as a simple substance or as a compound composed of elements mixed in perfect proportion. This statement is altogether different in kind and in its implications from "When in eternall lines to time thou grow'st." The speaker is not creating a conceit but reciting a generally recognized proposition. He is not deducing a conclusion from the terms of an argument he has invented, but applying to the particular experiences of himself and his love an accepted formula for the workings of physical objects. He is not asserting a miraculous truth in contradiction to the facts of the natural world but seeking among those facts support for his efforts as a lover, whose language reveals increasing awareness of inevitable change and even death, to control the effects of time:

> What ever dyes, was not mixt equally;
> If our two loves be one, or, thou and I
> Love so alike, that none doe slacken, none can die.

It is by finding such analogies for his feelings in the laws of nature that the lover can argue the possibility for himself and his mistress that if they consciously maintain their love in its present perfection, "none can die." These analogies are not validated by the miraculous power of art but by the accepted truth of the scholastic proposition. This can give authority to the lover's final speculations precisely because it is not a poetic metaphor but a formula for the workings of the natural world. By using analogies from that world to argue for the possibility of the lovers' immortality, the speaker claims that it may be achieved, not in the timeless world of art, but in actual experiences as they are shaped by consciously controlled feeling. From the facts of physical existence in time, like the "pleasures" of the previous night and the beautiful "sights" revealed now by the dawn, this passionate awareness "makes" a relationship so perfectly ordered that the "true plaine hearts" of the lovers can there "rest," meaning "recline," "repose," "remain," without fear of change and loss. In this "rest" they may transcend the limits of mortal experience by most fully experiencing it, in the morning light, in the "little roome," in each other's eyes, not in a poem.

The very choice of "rest," with its added suggestions of arrested motion and of weariness (if not of death, as in the formulas "everlasting rest" and "rest in peace"), reveals the speaker's mounting "feare" of change, however, which even his application of the final, impersonal and authoritative formula cannot allay. For to a lover celebrating the night's "pleasures," and one as aware of sexual innuendo as this speaker, the punning sense of the word "die," meaning "to achieve sexual climax," must be obvious. This meaning creates a conflict, however, for if the lovers reach a state in which "none can die" in the sense of "cease to live," which at the same time means "none can make love," then the meanings cancel each other as desirable possibilities of escape from mutability. For mortal lovers the ideal can be achieved only "now," in the very process of dying.

The lover in "The Sunne Rising," with far less "feare" or uncertainty, claims to control the effects of time from his outrageously impudent opening address:

The Sunne Rising

Busie old foole, unruly Sunne,
        Why dost thou thus,
Through windowes, and through curtaines call on us?
Must to thy motions lovers seasons run?
        Sawcy pedantique wretch, goe chide
        Late school boyes, and sowre prentices,
    Goe tell Court-huntsmen, that the King will ride,
    Call countrey ants to harvest offices;
Love, all alike, no season knowes, nor clyme,
Nor houres, dayes, months, which are the rags of time.

        Thy beames, so reverend, and strong
        Why shouldst thou thinke?
I could eclipse and cloud them with a winke,
But that I would not lose her sight so long:
        If her eyes have not blinded thine,
        Looke, and to morrow late, tell mee,
    Whether both the'India's of spice and Myne
    Be where thou lefst them, or lie here with mee.
Aske for those Kings whom thou saw'st yesterday,
And thou shalt heare, All here in one bed lay.

        She'is all States, and all Princes, I,
        Nothing else is.
Princes doe but play us; compar'd to this,
All honor's mimique; All wealth alchimie.
        Thou sunne art halfe as happy'as wee,
        In that the world's contracted thus;
    Thine age asked ease, and since thy duties bee
    To warme the world, that's done in warming us.
Shine here to us, and thou art every where;
This bed thy center is, these walls, thy spheare.

By personifying the sun in the first stanza as an "old" busybody and a peeping-tom,[19] the speaker cuts him down to a figure which he can then command with lordly contempt, much as the poet-lover in Shakespeare's Sonnet 19 reduces his enemy to an immoral but ineffectual bumbler over whom his own superior skills as an artist might conceivably triumph:[20]

Yet doe thy worst ould Time dispight thy wrong,
My loue shall in my verse euer liue young.

Donne's speaker, by virtue of his own superiority in social position, manner, sophistication, and freedom (for the sun is an "unruly . . . Sawcy pedantique wretch" wearing "rags"), asserts the right to dismiss this shabby intruder. Like Shakespeare's poet-lover, he claims to exist in an unchanging state from which time is excluded (although it is of the utmost importance that he attributes the creation of this ideal to the power of feeling but not of art):

Love, all alike, no season knowes, nor clyme,
Nor houres, dayes, months, which are the rags of time.

He seems here to assert the permanence of his love in contradiction of the facts of temporal experience, immediately impinging on him "Through windowes, and through curtanes." He seems therefore to strive for control over the effects of time by means closer in some ways to those of Shakespeare's eternizing poet-lover than to the efforts of the speaker in "The Good-morrow."

This could be said only of the first stanza, however, for the second opens with the lover acknowledging that his commands have not driven the sun away, that his language, in opposing fact, has not altered it. By implication, then, he admits the limits of the assertion he has just made that "Love, all alike, no season knowes, nor clyme," for not to *know* the effects of time can mean "not to recognize their factual existence in unconscious or willful ignorance" (and indeed the speaker has acknowledged them in his own earlier question, "Must to thy motions lovers seasons run?") The momentary seriousness here in the speaker's tone, even tinged perhaps slightly with sadness, as he describes love's ignorance of passing time, gives a hint, by contrast, of his own awareness of it.

He therefore changes his verbal tactics in the second stanza, no longer relying on bravado to dismiss the facts of his situation but more subtly adjusting his language to interpret them in ways demonstrative of his power to control them:

> Thy beames, so reverend, and strong
> Why shouldst thou thinke?
> I could eclipse and cloud them with a winke,
> But that I would not lose her sight so long.

He admits here that the sun is still shining through his window despite his earlier dismissals, perhaps shining more strongly than before. Yet now he turns that fact to his own advantage by arguments manipulating a selection from other facts of his situation: although he can make the sun disappear by closing his eyes (a quite different power from sending it away from his window by verbally dismissing it), he chooses not to do so because by keeping his eyes open he will not lose "sight" of his mistress for "so long" as a passing instant. His choice of these facts and the construction his words place on them serve his argument that the sun's power to dictate changes in time is not "so reverend, and strong" as its continuing presence, despite his earlier dismissals, or its growing brightness, might prove. His verbal manipulations of these facts also support his argument by locating the sun itself in a mutable world beyond its own control. That is, he describes the physical act of closing his eyes in metaphors—"I could eclipse and cloud them with a winke"—recalling the fact that there are other "unruly" forces in nature which can exert their power over the sun and interrupt the "pedantique" regularity of its appearances. Metaphorically he claims that power for himself, so that by restraining it for his own enjoyment he makes the sun's continuing presence seem to depend on his choice. Its "motions," by the logic of his metaphor, "Must to . . . lovers seasons run."

By the same logic, the fact of the sun's inevitable departure is also made to serve the lover's argument:

> If her eyes have not blinded thine,
> Looke, and to morrow late, tell mee,
> Whether both the'India's of spice and Myne

Be where thou leftst them, or lie here with mee.
Aske for those Kings whom thou saw'st yesterday,
And thou shalt heare, All here in one bed lay.

These lordly commands parallel the imperatives of stanza one,
but with the important difference that they are metaphorical
interpretations of fact rather than contradictions of it. The lover
here "knowes" that "houres, dayes, months" inevitably pass and
makes that knowledge serve him by speaking as if the sun's departures and returns, like those of an ambassador on his
monarch's missions, accord with his wishes and give further
evidence of his command. He "knowes" that "season" and
"clyme" impose limits and divisions (like the "sharpe North" and
"declining West" excluded from the "better hemispheares" of
"The Good-morrow") on the world around which the sun
travels. He talks as if it is the sun on its daily journey which must
be subject to these confinements while he who "knowes" them
remains unchanged. Because he is already familiar with what the
sun must travel to "Looke" for, must "Aske" in order to "heare,"
his knowledge contains "All here" without the restrictions and
divisions of time and space that limit the sun's experience. By
contrast with the fragmented physical world to which the sun is
confined, "here" is a fully achieved ideal world, unchanging and
undivided, like the "better hemispheares" of "The Good-
morrow":

She'is all States, and all Princes, I,
Nothing else is.
Princes doe but play us; compar'd to this,
All honor's mimique; All wealth alchimie.

His phrase, "compar'd to this," acknowledges that he is speaking
metaphorically, since, as we have seen in Shakespeare's sonnets,
the verb "compare" was a formal term for the device of
similitude.[21] Yet because his metaphors derive from an argument
based on physical facts, they have an authority different from
the sheer impudence of his claims to rule the sun in stanza one,
and closer to the kind of validity the lover seeks at the end of

"The Good-morrow" in analogies between his love and the laws of nature. The final grand hyperboles in "The Sunne Rising" are built out of the facts of the sun's "motions," of the distance it must travel around the earth, of its antiquity and its natural heat:

> Thou sunne art halfe as happy'as wee,
> In that the world's contracted thus;
> Thine age askes ease, and since thy duties bee
> To warme the world, that's done in warming us.
> Shine here to us, and thou art every where;
> This bed thy center is, these walls, thy sphaere.

His achievement is to have manipulated language in such a way that he can now generously accept the fact which he first energetically opposed, that the sun has brought day after his night of love. Not only has he accepted it, but the logic of his metaphorical argument has made inevitable the conclusion that he has control over this fact. In the permanent and inclusive state of being—"Nothing else is"—which his language has defined "here," the sun enters by his permission, as in "The Good-morrow" at his invitation:

> Shine here to us, and thou art every where;
> This bed thy center is, these walls, thy sphaere.

By reaching this triumphant conclusion he has demonstrated, with stronger confidence and conviction, the power of consciously controlled feeling described by the speaker in the other aubade, which "makes one little roome, an every where," and he has done so, not as a poet who transforms facts experienced in time into the metaphors of a work of art, but as a lover interpreting his actual experience as it happens. Nor does he step outside his situation as a lover to make a final comment on his argument in a frame provided by the poet, as the lover in Ovid's *Amores* I, xiii (from which "The Sunne Rising" borrows some details), follows his impudent address to the dawn with the ironic reflection:[22]

I had brought my chiding to an end. You might know she

had heard: she blushed—and yet the day arose no later than its wont.

By contrast, Donne does not reflect on his lover's experience by placing it in the past upon which the poet, having recounted the experience in the poem, later comments. (In Ovid's aubade the poet specifically points out the inefficacy of the lover's "chiding" language to alter the sun's course). Instead, Donne underlines the nature of his lover's achievement by making the conclusion of "The Sunne Rising" his final claim, which is built out of his immediate situation in "This bed" surrounded by "these walls," not in "these lines." For although the splendid hyperboles of the third stanza sound more conventionally poetic than the opening, they are spoken by the same voice whose language has grown more elevated with deepening feeling—for the lady whose beauty the sun is gradually revealing but also for his own growing mastery over time—as he talks, not as he has reflected on his emotions in verse. He has created an unchanging "every where" by incorporating into it what he sees and "knowes" as a fully conscious human being of "season" and "clyme" experienced in the "houres, dayes, months" which make up existence in time.

The aubade seems to have provided Donne with the opportunity for a kind of poem in which the lover pits his own power against time by means which claim not to be the distinct gifts of a poet. For it gave him a situation in which it would be comical to imagine the speaker composing verses; a situation which involves an intimate listener while excluding the possibility of a public audience of readers; which includes physical properties—sun, windows, curtains, bed, walls—with defined limits; which exists at a specific moment and so insists on the particularity and mutability of experience; and which, above all, creates a conflict between those facts and the lover's feelings, his desire to preserve unchanged a perfectly realized love.

"The Good-morrow" and "The Sunne Rising," by exploiting these possibilities, though with varying degrees of assurance, represent a kind of anti-conventional eternizing poetry which enacts the struggle of love "in war with Time" while rejecting the figure of the lover who is a poet triumphing over it by the miraculous power of his art. The self-consciousness of Donne's creation of this kind of poetry is shown by his use in "The Good-morrow" of a final couplet which is an eternizing conceit in a new form. For there the lover's promise of immortality is not a transformation of fact into metaphor miraculously expressing a possibility in contradiction of temporal experience, but an analogy with the way things work in nature, not in art. It therefore associates love, and ultimately its celebration in "The Good-morrow," with the physical, temporal world rather than a transcendent world of poetry.

The conventional situation of lovers parting, which attracted Donne more often than the aubade—and, at least in the vale-dictions "of Weeping" and "Forbidding Mourning," with equal effectiveness—offered many of the same possibilities.[23] The lover bidding farewell to his mistress at the moment of separation, like the lover greeting the coming of daylight, struggles to conquer the immediate threat of mutability to feelings he would preserve unchanged. These resemblances between the two great valedictions and the aubades extend beyond the similarities inherent in their situations to uses of language which interpret those situations so that they define a distinct kind of poetry.

The parting, the journey, the beloved's absence, are conventional subjects for Petrarchan lovers, often explored in poems like Shakespeare's Sonnet 51 as representative occasions for the construction of a rhetorical argument — "Thus . . . When . . . Then . . . Therefore . . . Since"—leading inevitably to a conclusion supporting the poet-lover's power "in war with Time." The general and rhetorical uses of language in such a sonnet are themselves instruments for demonstrating that power and for defining it as the special gift of a poet who gives shape to his feelings in literary form:

Thus can my loue excuse the slow offence,
Of my dull bearer, when from thee I speed,
From where thou art, why shoulld I hast me thence,

Till I returne of posting is noe need.
O what excuse will my poore beast then find,
When swift extremity can seeme but slow,
Then should I spurre though mounted on the wind,
In winged speed no motion shall I know,
Then can no horse with my desire keepe pace,
Therefore desire (of perfects loue being made)
Shall naigh noe dull flesh in his fiery race,
But loue, for loue, thus shall excuse my iade,
    Since from thee going, he went wilfull slow,
    Towards thee ile run, and giue him leaue to goe.

Shakespeare's lover demonstrates his control over threatening mutability by generalizing almost as if his parting from his beloved were a theoretical case—"From where thou art, why shoulld I hast me thence"—about which he enjoys leisure to argue "Thus" and freedom to "excuse." His two-line preface to his actual argument, in the present tense, using "when" so that it can mean "whenever," makes it difficult to locate his departure at any particular time, but turns it into an illustration in verse of "perfects loue" victorious in "his fiery race" with time.

In Donne's "A Valediction: of Weeping" the threat of parting is imminent, and the lover's language as he talks of it to the lady shows his painful awareness of the immediacy of his situation and its momentary quality. In this poem, as in the aubades, the lover struggles to establish his control over the flux of experience, again not by preserving it in the "eternall lines" of a poem.

From the opening we might assume that the lover's tears are an expression of his helplessness to protect his love from change and loss:[24]

A Valediction: of Weeping

    Let me powre forth
My teares before thy face, whil'st I stay here,
For thy face coines them, and thy stampe they beare,
And by this Mintage they are something worth,
    For thus they bee
    Pregnant of thee;

Fruits of much griefe they are, emblemes of more,
When a teare falls, that thou falls which it bore,
So thou and I are nothing then, when on a divers shore.

  On a round ball
A workeman that hath copies by, can lay
An Europe, Afrique, and an Asia,
And quickly make that, which was nothing, *All*,
  So doth each teare,
  Which thee doth weare,
A globe, yea world by that impression grow,
Till thy teares mixt with mine doe overflow
This world, by waters sent from thee, my heaven dissolved so.

  O more then Moone,
Draw not up seas to drowne me in thy spheare,
Weepe me not dead, in thine armes, but forbeare
To teach the sea, what it may doe too soone;
  Let not the winde
  Example finde,
To doe me more harme, then it purposeth;
Since thou and I sigh one anothers breath,
Who e'r sighes most, is cruellest, and hasts the others death.

The impression of formless grief is dispelled immediately when the speaker describes his tears as coins which are made precious because they bear the reflected image of his mistress's face, as a disc of metal gains value when it is imprinted with the portrait of the monarch whose mint stamps it. The elaborately wrought detail of this comparison shows his conscious manipulation of language, turning his weeping into a decorous act for which he gravely asks permission: "Let me powre forth / My teares" at this appropriate place and time. His metaphor describes his tears as coins which then become "Fruits," in the sense of "results" but also "organic objects," having solidity, function, and value. He is therefore striving for language which will shape the facts of his experience in such a way as to demonstrate his control over them, as the lovers in "The Good-morrow" and "The Sunne Rising" construe their situations into arguments supporting their efforts to preserve their love unchanged.

Yet mutability is more threatening to the lover here than in the aubades, his situation less adaptable to his advantage in his struggle against inevitable change and loss. His metaphorical interpretations of the facts of his experience are therefore more vulnerable to destruction by them. For though his tears are like coins bearing an image (of a face with regal authority over him), they are unlike because the image is a reflection, ephemeral as flowing drops of water, insubstantial compared to coins or "Fruits," depending even for its momentary impression on the physical presence of the face it mirrors. The conclusion to which these facts point destroys the power of the speaker's metaphor to preserve his love from the destructive effects of change: "So thou and I are nothing then, when on a divers shore."

In the second stanza the speaker begins to describe his tears in a metaphor which would give them form and "worth" and so make them demonstrate his control. By constructing an extended simile, elaborating first the more remote term, his manner suggests detachment or leisured calculation:

> On a round ball
> A workeman that hath copies by, can lay
> An Europe, Afrique, and an Asia,
> And quickly make that, which was nothing, *All*,
>> So doth each teare,
>> Which thee doth weare,
> A globe, yea world by that impression grow.

The hypothetical craftsman who can "quickly make . . . nothing, *All*" is like God creating the world *ex nihilo*, but the meticulous detail of "copies by" prevents his art from seeming miraculous. He is also like the speaker, who has made the "nothing" to which his fallen tears had reduced the lovers at the end of the first stanza "A globe, yea world" bearing an imprint much vaster, more inclusive, more permanent than the sovereign's face on the coin. Because an analogy is drawn between his "globe" and the world created by the "workemen," his mode of creation is implied to be a skillful procedure such as following physical measurements rather than a miraculous art. It therefore derives its authority from seeming conformity to fact rather than transformation of it. The lover seems to have achieved the kind of control that the speaker in "The Good-morrow" attributes to love, which "makes one little roome, an every where," or that the lover more triumphantly asserts at the end of "The Sunne Rising" by declaring "these walls" to be the "spheare" surrounding his contracted "world." Here the speaker has made "each teare" a "globe," and by the logic of that comparison, has made the image which it bears a "world" including every "divers shore" and therefore defying separation and loss.

Then the changing facts of the lover's situation again destroys his metaphorical command over them, because now the lady begins to weep and her tears, mingling with his, blur the image reflected in them:

Till thy teares mixt with mine doe overflow
This world, by waters sent from thee, my heaven dissolved so.

The last stanza, therefore, is the lover's lesson to his mistress on the dangers "of Weeping" without control. For while his grief is decorous, "each teare" bearing its dignified meaning, she weeps in floods which "overflow," which dissolve boundaries, bringing danger and destruction:

O more then Moone,
Draw not up seas to drowne me in thy spheare,
Weepe me not dead, in thine armes, but forbeare
To teach the sea, what it may doe too soone;
    Let not the winde
    Example finde,
To doe me more harme, then it purposeth;
Since thou and I sigh one anothers breath,
Who e'r sighes most, is cruellest, and hasts the others death.

The burden of his lesson is that feeling has power comparable to the vast forces of nature, whose regular cycles, like the tides, can be disrupted by lawless motions. Stormy expressions of emotion can be as destructive as unleashed floods and winds, and can therefore annihilate life itself; the very soul, which is in the breath, may be expended in sighs.[25] The lady must learn to "forebeare" from such wild expressions of grief, by exerting the kind of control that the speaker has used in his struggle to preserve their love by making "that, which was nothing, *All.*" She must practice this skill with her very breathing:

Since thou and I sigh one anothers breath,
Who e'r sighes most, is cruellest, and hasts the others death.

This final couplet makes no promise of immortality for the lovers, however tentative. It does not raise even the possibility left open by the ending of "The Good-morrow" that "If" they achieve a perfect mixture of consciously controlled feelings, "none can die." Yet it does grant to the lovers some power over time and mortality, for sighing "hasts . . . death," and so restrained expression may retard it. This power does not derive, however, from the miraculous "vertue" of art, such as Shakespeare's poet-lover claims for the poetically ordered expression of his love in the conclusion of Sonnet 81:

You still shall liue (such vertue hath my Pen)
Where breath most breaths, euen in the mouths of men.

The power for which Donne's lover argues derives first from the facts of his immediate situation: he and the lady, until the moment when they must actually part, are still physically so close together that their tears mingle and also their breaths. The particular situation he then interprets according to a generally accepted notion about the nature of things: the soul is breathed out in sighs which therefore waste life. From the authority of this proposition, which is not a poet's invention, he derives his argument for the control the lovers may have over time. This power consists in the shape their expressions of feeling can give to the present moment, as they experience it, in one another's "armes," not as it is transformed by the "vertue" of a poet's "Pen."

The beginning of "A Valediction: Forbidding Mourning" sounds at first more as if it were the consideration of a poet than does the direct opening plea of "A Valediction: of Weeping" or the impudent tones heard at the beginning of "The Good-morrow" or "The Sunne Rising":

A Valediction: Forbidding Mourning

As virtuous men passe mildly'away,
 And whisper to their soules, to goe,
Whilst some of their sad friends doe say,
 The breath goes now, and some say, no:

So let us melt, and make no noise,
 No teare-floods, nor sigh-tempests move,
'Twere prophanation of our joyes
 To tell the layetie our love.

Moving of th'earth brings harmes and feares,
 Men reckon what it did and meant,
But trepidation of the spheares,
 Through greater farre, is innocent.

Dull sublunary lovers love
 (Whose soule is sense) cannot admit
Absence, because it doth remove
 Those things which elemented it.

But we by'a love, so much refin'd,
 That our selves know not what it is,
Inter-assured of the mind,
 Care lesse, eyes, lips, and hands to misse.

Our two soules therefore, which are one,
 Though I must goe, endure not yet
A breach, but an expansion,
 Like gold to ayery thinnesse beate.

If they be two, they are two so
 As stiffe twin compasses are two,
Thy soule the fixt foot, makes no show
 To move, but doth, if the'other doe.

And though it in the center sit,
 Yet when the other far doth rome,
It leanes, and hearkens after it,
 And growes erect, as it comes home.

Such wilt thou be to mee, who must
   Like th'other foot, obliquely runne;
Thy firmnes makes my circle just,
   And makes me end, where I begunne.

The impression that the speaker is using a poet's language for his "Valediction" here is created first by the opening simile (and it is significant that this is the only one of Donne's *Songs and Sonets* beginning with such a device). Because it is an extended comparison, with an entire stanza devoted to each term, and because he begins by explicating the more remote term to which he will then liken his own experience, the simile gives an impression of detachment and leisurely preparation even stronger than that made by the comparison of the globe-maker in the middle stanza of "A Valediction: of Weeping." This opening simile is also more conventionally poetic because it points to its structure by the prominence of the formal terms for comparing, "As . . . So"; because it draws on such traditional materials as a holy death-bed scene and a pair of lovers sanctified by the sublimity of their feelings; because it uses religious diction like "soules" and "prophanation"; because its tone is hushed and reverent; even because its unusually simple stanza form (only five other *Songs and Sonets* use a four-line stanza)[26] with relatively regular meter and closely proximate rhymes sounds more like song than the complex stanzas of "A Valediction: of Weeping."

The speaker continues to use elevated, literary language resembling Petrarchan love poetry through the first five stanzas. They contain formal and conventional comparisons, elevating because drawn from astronomical "spheares" and "refin'd" feelings, detached and general because free of any direct mention of the lovers' immediate situation or the imminent threat of their parting. For the comparative "So let us melt" is sufficiently undefined and the mention of "Absence" (by contrast with "thou and I . . . on a divers shore") so general, even hypothetical, that they could refer to the sort of representative condition evoked to illustrate the poet-lover's feelings in Shakespeare's Sonnet 98, "From you haue I beene absent in the spring." Even the last line of stanza five, "Care lesse, eyes, lips, and hands to misse," although it refers to the speaker and his mistress, sounds like part of a generalized definition of a category of feeling because it completes the contrast of "refin'd" with "Dull sublunary" love.

These first five stanzas, in marked contrast to the aubades and "A Valediction: of Weeping," sound very like a poet-lover's contemplation upon the conventional subject of absence from his beloved, in which he claims for their feelings a purity so far transcending "sublunary" experience "That our selves know not what it is." A seemingly predictable conclusion—"therefore"—to such a poetic argument comes in stanza six:

> Our two soules therefore, which are one,
> Though I must goe, endure not yet
> A breach, but an expansion,
> Like gold to ayery thinnesse beate.

Almost without alteration this stanza could conclude a conventional love poem. The metaphor of "two soules . . . which are one" is a Petrarchan commonplace, characteristically a paradox which asserts a metaphysical or psychological truth in contradiction of physical fact[27] (and therefore altogether different in kind from such metaphors as the "better hemispheares" or the "globe, yea world" derived by the lovers in "The Good-morrow" or "A Valediction: of Weeping" from the facts of their immediate situations). The metaphor of "two soules . . . which are one" transforms what is divided into a new creation transcending mundane limits as the perfection of feeling "so much refin'd" seems to the lover to escape the threat of physical separation, change, and loss. The speaker's language therefore claims for such love a power, like the eternizing poet's miraculous art of metaphor, to alter the facts of the temporal world, a power hinted in the beautiful conceit of "gold to ayery thinnesse beate," which suggests the metamorphosis of "sublunary" matter into an ethereal state.[28]

Yet "gold to ayery thinnesse beate" is not quite transmuted into *air*, and a union of "soules" which "endure not yet" a separation is not *eternally* free from mutability.[29] The unarguable fact, "Though I must goe," points to the limits of the speaker's metaphorical claims. His lofty generalizing about "Absence" has not altered the fact, which therefore calls in question the authority of his elevated poetic language to rescue his love from temporal existence. For like "gold to ayery thinnesse beate," human feeling, however "much refin'd," cannot altogether free itself from its "elemented" nature,[30] can only "care *lesse*, eyes, lips, and hands to misse," and therefore does not have the miraculous power to transcend "sublunary" experience which inevitably involves change.

The speaker, whose awareness of the facts of his immediate situation has here for the first time directly impinged on his argument, cannot therefore gain control over them by metaphorical claims to contradict or alter them. He must now seek another kind of authority in an apparently new language, which announces itself by first dismantling the conceit of "two soules . . . which are one" (somewhat the way the lover in the final couplet of "The Good-morrow" proposes an alternative "or" to "If our two loves by one"), and replacing it with an altogether different sort of metaphor.[31]

If they be two, they are two so
  As stiffe twin compasses are two,
Thy soule the fixt foot, makes no show
  To move, but doth, if the'other doe.

And though it in the center sit,
  Yet when the other far doth rome,
It leanes, and hearkens after it,
  And growes erect, as it comes home.

Such wilt thou be to mee, who must
  Like th'other foot, obliquely runne;
Thy firmnes makes my circle just,
  And makes me end, where I begunne.

This is even more extended than the simile in stanzas one and two, showing by its elaboration the speaker's conscious effort to master his situation, but in every other way it seems designed not to sound like Petrarchan love poetry. The comparison is not drawn from the "stocks intire" of the conventional poet-lover but from the speaker's apparent familiarity with practical life, specifically the tools and techniques used by a skilled craftsman to shape his materials (like the "workeman" making a globe in "A Valediction: of Weeping").[32] It is not formally introduced by the conventional terms of literary comparison, "As . . . So," but by the cautious, speculative and somewhat awkward phrasing, "If they be two, they are two so / As." It does not include religious diction or evoke associations with either grand or precious aspects of nature, but confines itself to a plain vocabulary full of relatively unevocative descriptive terms like "stiffe," "fixt," "erect," "obliquely." Its tone is less hushed and reverent than careful, patiently explanatory and exact rather than suggestive of mystery. Instead of implying a state of feeling "so much refin'd" in the moral or metaphysical sense of "refin'd" that it transcends human limitations and therefore human comprehension, the comparison with compasses seems to insist that this love can be described in terms of physical operations. Its "much refin'd" state is therefore like the condition of metal from which impurities have been distilled, increasing its value (like metal which has gained "worth" by being minted into coins) and also its "firmnes" and durability.[33] The motions of the lovers' feelings are comparable to the movement of a pair of compasses, which "must" inevitably follow the pattern determined by its nature. The lovers' means of defeating mutability are therefore not like the paradoxical workings of miracle, but like the operations of natural, physical laws. These are detailed in the comparison, which is offered as an explanation rather than a transformation of fact.

The speaker's argument here derives its authority from its acknowledgment, rather than its contradiction, of the facts of his situation and from his exactitude in finding analogies—not derived from literary tradition—for the lovers' feelings in recognized workings of natural objects. He establishes his control over the flux of experience, not finally by the kind of poetic power associated with elevated diction and hyperbolic metaphor, but by careful explication of the terms of his comparison in objective, relatively impersonal although carefully wrought language:

> Thy soule the fixt foot, makes no show
> To move, but doth, if the'other doe.

> And though it in the center sit,
> Yet when the other far doth rome,
> It leanes, and hearkens after it,
> And growes erect, as it comes home.

By using "it", and "the'other" repeatedly, the speaker makes the simile seem as much a literal description of a physical object as a personification of it, and even in the last stanza, where personal pronouns replace "it," the language is noticeably matter-of-fact, unevocative, unelevated by hyperboles:

> Such wilt thou be to mee, who must
> Like th'other foot, obliquely runne;
> Thy firmnes makes my circle just,
> And makes me end, where I begunne.

The final metaphor triumphantly concludes the speaker's struggle to demonstrate his power over changing experience by scarcely appearing to be a metaphor, although it is a carefully elaborated verbal construct (as is also true of the figurative language in the last lines of "The Good-morrow"). It is presented almost as if it were a literal description of how love moves—like compasses—by simple, physical operations, so that it "makes me end, where I begunne," defying the divisions of space and limits of time and so defeating mutability.

Using this simile to show his command over the flux of experience, the speaker does not reject his earlier, seemingly more literary comparisons (as the poet-lover in Shakespeare's Sonnet 64 is forced by the fact "That Time will come and take my loue away" to reject his grand generalizing) but charges them for the reader with a new kind of significance. That is, we have seen the way the phrase "a love, so much refin'd" which first seems to claim for the lovers a moral or metaphysical state of elevation and purity, becomes a definition of love that has undergone a process like the distillation of imperfections from metal. In the same way, "So let us melt," which seems on first reading to be a vaguely metaphorical reference to parting, is a comparison to a physical change in substances which unexplosively dissolves their boundaries and allows them to expand beyond their original limits, "Like gold to ayery thinnesse beate," another phrase in which poetic qualities at first distract from its exactness as a description of a physical operation. For "gold" one first assumes to be chosen because of its literary and mythological associations in poems like Shakespeare's Sonnets 3 and 18, associations of radiance, preciousness, and unfallen purity, but actually the logic of the simile depends on the physical fact that gold is a particularly ductile metal, more easily malleable into an expanded shape than silver, brass or iron.[34] Similarly, the comparison of the lovers' motions to the "trepidation of the spheares" can be seen to have precise meanings in addition to the lofty effects of that phrase, or the moral and religious connotations of "Though greater farre, is innocent." For "spheares" are astronomical bodies whose movements are "innocent" in the sense that they do not have the harmful effects of earthquakes and that they are free of intention,[35] simply operating according to the laws of their nature, with a geometric regularity that makes their spherical patterns like the motions of the compass.

The final simile, therefore, in retrospect makes the reader aware of some of its own qualities in earlier comparisons of the lovers' feelings with the workings of natural objects. Their more conventionally literary effects do not prevent them from sharing the kind of factual basis that gives the analogy of the lovers to compasses its seeming exactitude and therefore its particular kind of authority. These resemblances point then to others: the comparisons liken the lovers' feelings to natural processes which are so regular and controlled as to be imperceptible. The "trepidation of the spheares" is "innocent" because unseen, like the perfectly restrained passing from life to death of the "soules" of "virtuous men." Both are therefore like the "fixt foot" of the compass which "makes no show / To move, but doth," by the necessity of its physical nature (which joins it to the other), drawing a "circle just," figure of perfect regularity and control.[36]

The speaker's argument "Forbidding Mourning" endows consciously controlled feeling with power over the facts of experience because it "makes me end, where I begunne," overcoming the divisions of space and time that threaten the lovers' feelings. This "love, so much refin'd" has power like that attributed to the elements "mixt equally" at the end of "The Good-morrow": the lovers' feelings are so perfectly matched in "firmnes," like the legs of a compass, that by analogy with the argument in the aubade, if "none doe slacken, none can die."

As in "A Valediction: of Weeping," the lover here contrasts the shaping power of decorously restrained feeling with uncontrolled expression, having the destructiveness of unruly forces in nature, floods and storms:

> So let us melt, and make no noise,
> No teare-floods, nor sigh-tempests move,
> 'Twere prophanation of our joyes
> To tell the layetie our love.

Again he is educating the lady in this distinction, but here the wild tears and sighs are not hers, to be contrasted with his own controlled expression. He and she are "one" in their feelings, not separated into "Thy" and "mee" until the final comparison (although as two legs of a compass they are physically joined and so ultimately inseparable).[37] The "teare-floods" and "sigh-tempests" are the unruly motions of hypothetical lovers, contrasted by the speaker with "us," who "make no noise" and so guard the sacred mysteries of love, as "virtuous men" keep secret the chosen moment of the soul's departure.

The speaker's opening simile implies such a contrast between "us" and others, presumably the "Dull sublunary lovers" of stanza four, who indulge in ostentatious shows of feeling and so publicize their passion. Although no explicit mention is made of poetry as their mode of display, the "teare-floods" and "sigh-tempests" of these others are the conventional expressions of Petrarchan lovers, unmistakable to readers of love poetry, including Donne's *Songs and Sonets*, where the formula of tears and sighs appears in many combinations and contexts.[38]

The speaker in "Loves Infiniteness" lists as his "stocks intire" for purchasing the lady "Sighs, teares, and oathes, and letters." In similarly playful mockery, "one sigh a day" and one briney "teare" are allowed as sustenance for "Loves Diet." The lover in "The Will," about to "sigh my last gaspe," bequeathes "To women or the sea, my teares"; in "Loves Exchange" the speaker begs no "dispensation now / To falsifie a teare, or sigh, or vow"; in "The Computation" absence from the beloved is measured in seeming years as "Teares drown'd one hundred, and sighes blew out two"; while in "The Prohibition" it is the lady's "sighes, and teares" which are lightly mocked. The "materialls" composing the lover in "The Dissolution" include "sighes of ayre, / Water of teares" and the speaker of "Twicknam Garden" complains stylishly of his condition, "Blasted with sighs, and surrounded with teares."[39]

Contrasting himself and his mistress to Petrarchan lovers, the speaker by "Forbidding Mourning" points to differences in modes of expression which in turn distinguish his "Valediction" from the poems in which conventional poet-lovers "tell" their feelings (and it is significant that Donne uses for his titles in the valedictions and "The Good-morrow" terms for forms of address, calling attention to his speaker's *way of saying farewell* or his *way of greeting the day*).

His "Valediction," we have seen, only sounds at first like a conventional poet-lover's metaphorical transformation of "sublunary" experience into a generalized ideal transcending mortal "harmes and feares" and presenting an image, like the "goulden time" of Shakespeare's Sonnet 3, eternally present to readers of poetry. The addition of the final comparison between the lovers and the pair of compasses insists that this analogy and all others in the poem—however seemingly generalized, hyperbolic, figurative—derive from the way things work in the natural world rather than from miraculous contradictions of fact. The presence of this simile therefore has the effect of making "A Valediction: Forbidding Mourning" a kind of criticism of the poetry it first seems to resemble. By insistence that the speaker is not a poet expressing his feelings in the timeless form of a work of art, but a lover struggling to give shape to his experience at the very moment of its occurrence, he denies the distinction implied by the kind of eternizing poem this first seems to imitate, between immediate situations and their transformation into general, idealized images.

His "Valediction" is an interpretation of such an experience, which draws it into a meaningful shape and so "makes" the facts of the situation support the speaker's argument, proving his mastery over time and change, as he experiences them, not as he reflects upon them in verse. His ability to find analogies for his feelings in the workings of natural objects makes possible his claims for the immutability of those feelings, while his patiently exact explication of similitudes shows his present freedom from "harmes and feares." He is talking this way to his mistress now, not in a poem but at the very moment of parting, which is like a death; he is therefore in control of his mortal condition in the manner of "virtuous men" who "whisper to their soules, to goe,"[40] not of poets who vow to defeat death with the living record of their poetry.

"A Valediction: Forbidding Mourning" defines itself as an anti-conventional eternizing poem, and it does so by devices of language as self-conscious and explicit as the version of the eternizing conceit at the end of "The Good-morrow" or the simile of the "workeman" who can "quickly make that, which was nothing, *All*" in the middle stanza of "A Valediction: of Weeping." These three poems, in addition to sharing many such verbal devices, have in common a preoccupation with the threat of death, which is certainly not inherent in the situation of the aubade or even of the valediction, that further defines them in relation to the conventions of a poetry pledging the eternizing power of art against the fact of mortality. In these poems, and most radiantly in "The Sunne Rising" (where awareness of mortality is only hinted in the reference to love's ignorance of time's passage and in the final admission that even lovers need "warming" by the sun), Donne's lovers seem to proclaim that their defeat of mutability and death is wrought out of the materials of this timebound world. Their power over ever-changing experience is not miraculous, although when "love . . . controules" such experience it "makes" from its limits and divisions, its fragments, "which are the rags of time," an "every where" including and therefore transcending them "*All.*"

In "The Anniversarie" the speaker promises his mistress "To write" in celebration of the "everlasting day" of their love. In "The Relique" the lover pledges "by this paper" to teach readers yet unborn "What miracles wee harmlesse lovers wrought." The speaker in "The Canonization" vows to "build in sonnets pretty roomes" by which, after he and his beloved are dead, "all shall approve / Us *Canoniz'd* for Love." These poems therefore establish connections with eternizing verse in ways seeming to distinguish them from the aubades and valedictions previously discussed. For they adopt the convention avoided with pointed significance in those four poems and most of the other *Songs and Sonets*, the figure of a speaker promising to give permanence to his ideal love in a verbal record which will escape the subjection to time of "All other things."

In the first stanza of "The Anniversarie" the speaker claims his love to be exempt from mutability in sweeping hyperboles which oppose the facts he himself has acknowledged, that the world is "elder by a yeare, now, then it was," and so "things, to their destruction draw." The language of the first stanza alone does not violate the conventions of eternizing verse, for although it begins by evoking a courtly society of "honors, beauties, wits," it then seems to transcend that world by adopting a language closer to Shakespeare's in his contemplations of temporal "decay";[41]

> All Kings, and all their favorites,
> All glory'of honors, beauties, wits,
> The Sun it selfe, which makes times, as they passe,
> Is elder by a yeare, now, then it was
> When thou and I first one another saw:
> All other things, to their destruction draw,
>   Only our love hath no decay;
> This, no tomorrow hath, nor yesterday,
> Running it never runs from us away,
> But truly keepes his first, last, everlasting day.

From his assertion that "Only our love hath no decay" the speaker derives the metaphorical identification of "This" love with the "Sun it selfe" which, though "Running" unceasingly, "never runs" from its own source of light, and therefore "keepes" a perpetual "day." By the force of this hyperbolic, figurative, elevated language he claims a transcendance for his love, metaphorically transformed into a sun, because paradoxically it exists in "times, as they passe" and yet is "everlasting." This paradox is endowed with miraculous qualities by the speaker's language which, in the last line, adopts the diction and cadences of prayer, particularly the formulaic pattern of endings for many liturgical supplications familiar to Anglican readers.[42]

This stanza sounds actually like the triumphant conclusion to a poem celebrating an ideal love. Specifically it resembles in certain respects the last stanza of "The Sunne Rising," by the radiant confidence, the inclusive grandeur, the finality in the lover's voice, as well as by similarities in metaphorical language about the world and the sun. Yet there are all-important differences. For here the argument is not derived from the lover's manipulation of the actualities of his immediate situation, but is asserted in opposition to fact, and in language which derives its authority from its nature as a literary invention, using elevation and generality to illustrate the poet's argument. Most significantly, this is not a conclusion but the opening of a poem, and one ultimately very different in kind from the poem seemingly predicted by the language of the opening stanza itself, from which we would expect the poet to dedicate his verse to creating a timeless world matching the ideal love described at the beginning:

The Anniversarie

   All Kings, and all their favorites,
    All glory'of honors, beauties, wits,
The Sun it selfe, which makes times, as they passe,
Is elder by a yeare, now, then it was
When thou and I first one another saw:
All other things, to their destruction draw,
    Only our love hath no decay;
This, no tomorrow hath, nor yesterday,
Running it never runs from us away,
But truly keepes his first, last, everlasting day.

    Two graves must hide thine and my coarse,
    If one might, death were no divorce.
Alas, as well as other Princes, wee,
(Who Prince enough in one another bee,)
Must leave at last in death, these eyes, and eares,
Oft fed with true oathes, and with sweet salt teares;
    But soules where nothing dwells but love
(All other thoughts being inmates) then shall prove
This, or a love increased there above,
When bodies to their graves, soules from their graves remove.

    And then wee shall be throughly blest,
    But wee no more, then all the rest.
Here upon earth, we'are Kings, and none but wee
Can be such Kings, nor of such subjects bee;
Who is so safe as wee? where none can doe

Donne   103

Treason to us, except one of us two.
    True and false feares let us refraine,
  Let us love nobly'and live, and adde againe
  Yeares and yeares unto yeares, till we attaine
To write threescore: this is the second of our raigne.

The argument of the second stanza might be predicted from the first, for it expands the conventional claim (similar to that first seemingly made for "a love, so much refin'd" in "A Valediction: Forbidding Mourning") that the lovers can escape the limits of mortality because their purified "soules where nothing dwells but love" can transcend the separation imposed by death to flourish "above" the "sublunary" world where less perfect lovers are confined. The effects of this argument in stanza two are disturbed, however, by details of language not in harmony with its claims.

Most indecorous are the first two lines, which come between the lofty religious hyperboles at the end of the first stanza and a similar style in the later lines of the second with a very different kind of language:

Two graves must hide thine and my coarse,
If one might, death were no divorce.

There is a conversational directness about these lines to distinguish them, a worldliness belonging to the society briefly evoked in the first stanza, for instance in the identification of the grave and a marriage bed. This makes the regretful exclamation "Alas," that the lovers "Must leave at last in death, these eyes, and eares" a partly joking suggestion that their intense interest in each other's bodies will "last" until death parts them, and even after.

These indecorous hints, casting doubt on the solemnity of the speaker's religious language in lines 17 to 20, prepare for his rejection in the last stanza of spiritual bliss "above" the world and outside the body:

And then wee shall be throughly blest,
But wee no more, then all the rest.

Here upon earth, we'are Kings, and none but wee
Can be such Kings, nor of such subjects bee;
Who is so safe as wee? where none can doe
Treason to us, except one of us two.

They belong to the category of "All Kings" who, with "All glory" must "passe" according to the motions of the sun,[43] but these lovers are unique among "Kings" because perfectly matched in ruling and subjection, like "All States, and all Princes" in "The Sunne Rising." They alone are therefore "safe" in maintaining their power, resembling the lovers in "The Good-morrow" who "watch not one another out of feare." To maintain this control over the threat of change, the speaker prescribes a kind of restraint, recalling also the two valedictions, when he urges: "True and false feares let us refraine." What the lovers might fear is no more clearly specified here than in "The Good-morrow," so that again such "feares," some defined and some unlocated, are implied to be an inevitable part of all human feeling. The context, however, makes the reader identify "false feares" with the suspicions of betrayal that haunt lesser lovers, "true . . . feares" with awareness of change and therefore of inevitable death, which here again casts its shadow over the speaker's thought although nothing inherent in the occasion of the poem, the first anniversary of their meeting, would suggest that the actual death of either lover is imminent. His urgings, with his repetitions of "Let us" (like the imperatives of "The Good-morrow"), insist on the power which the lovers can exert if they consciously "refraine" from such "feares":

Let us love nobly,'and live, and adde againe
Yeares and yeares unto yeares, till we attaine
To write threescore: this is the second of our raigne.

To control the feelings that threaten less pure "soules" with change is to "love nobly," and that accomplishment is equated with the decision to "live," to "adde yeares unto yeares," giving the kingly lovers power like that of "The Sun it selfe, which makes times, as they passe." For it is they who willingly "adde

. . . yeares" by joyfully accumulating them and also by triumphantly recording their chosen number. By the style in
which they "live," they dictate the passing of time and "write"
the history of their love as a monarch with their power might
chronicle his own "raigne" and so shape it to match his ideal,
excluding from it the threat of mutability which causes "feares"
in more vulnerable men.

"To write threescore" is to triumph over temporal experience
by fully experiencing it through "yeares and yeares," not to
transform it into the "eternall Sommer" of a poem. The lover,
like the speakers in the aubades and valedictions discussed
earlier, has claimed the possibility of controlling the facts of his
experience in accepting, rather than dismissing, opposing, or
altering them by the miraculous power of his art. His promise
"To write" is the vow of a lover who does not wish his ideal to be
eternized in verse but to be perpetually enjoyed in the "everlasting day" composing the "yeares" in which the lovers "live"
unchanged in their feelings, growing together to a flourishing
age, "fed" with the "sweet" messages by which the body communicates love to the soul. The verbal record of his ideal with
which he concludes his argument—"this is the second of our
raigne"—is the lover's triumphant rejection of conventional
eternizing verse, such as the first stanza seems to predict that he
will write, in favor of the kind of poem represented by "The
Anniversarie" (and by the aubades and valedictions which it
ultimately resembles), a celebration of human love in the body,
"Here upon earth."

The speaker in "The Relique" assumes at the end of the second
stanza the conventional posture of the lover who is a poet recording for posterity "What miracles wee harmlesse lovers
wrought." Alone among speakers in Donne's *Songs and Sonets*
he refers to his celebration of his ideal as "this paper,"[44] by which
a future age will be "taught" after he and his beloved are dead.
Yet that reference to his verse, itself phrased in rather dryly unelevated terms compared to "eternall lines" or "immortall

Song,"[45] is preceded by two stanzas spoken to the lady, not apparently composed for posterity, and in a language altogether unlike, and unsuited to, conventional eternizing poetry. This introduction, of course, directs the reader's response to the speaker's "paper," which is stanza three:

The Relique

When my grave is broke up againe
Some second ghest to entertaine,
(For graves have learn'd that woman-head
To be to more then one a Bed)
And he that digs it, spies
A bracelet of bright haire about the bone,
Will he not let'us alone,
And thinke that there a loving couple lies,
Who thought that this device might be some way
To make their soules, at the last busie day,
Meet at this grave, and make a little stay?

If this fall in a time, or land,
Where mis-devotion doth command,
Then, he that digges us up, will bring
Us, to the Bishop, and the King,
To make us Reliques; then
Thou shalt be'a Mary Magdalen, and I
A something else thereby;
All women shall adore us, and some men;
And since at such times, miracles are sought,
I would that age were by this paper taught
What miracles wee harmlesse lovers wrought.

First, we lov'd well and faithfully,
Yet knew not what wee lov'd, nor why,
Difference of sex no more wee knew,
Then our Guardian Angells doe;
Comming and going, wee
Perchance might kisse, but not between those meales;
Our hands ne'r toucht the seales,
Which nature, injur'd by late law, sets free:
These miracles wee did; but now alas,
All measure, and all language, I should passe,
Should I tell what a miracle shee was.

The speaker's playfulness (rather like the opening of stanza two in "The Anniversarie"), even as he concretely imagines his skeleton in the grave—here a physical place rather than a metaphorical tomb or eternizing poem—shows his ease and comfort while talking to the lady. He jokes with assurance that she will understand and be amused, not offended by ribaldry or irreverence. The freedom and variety of his witticisms imply common language and values, a shared worldliness and social flexibility, an intimacy which sets them apart—from the intruding grave-digger, and from the false believers of the "time, or land, / Where mis-devotion doth command." These blundering figures, by contrast with the speaker and the lady, have in common a kind of naïve literal-mindedness which makes them misread what the two know themselves to represent. The grave-digger, seeing the braceleted skeleton, will "thinke that there a loving couple lies," which is true only in a symbolic sense that he does not understand. For the reader learns in stanza three that the emblem of her affection is not only all of the lady that will be in the grave, but all of her body that she has given to the speaker. From his mistaken notion that they are lovers in a physical sense, the grave-digger derives a comically literal explanation of the bracelet's function to provide an excuse for a rendezvous between their "soules, at the last busie day." With similar naïvete, the false-believers will take the contents of the grave for saints' relics, and will expect them to perform the kind of demonstrable "miracles" that pharasaical minds seek as outward and visible proofs of their faith, utterly different from the "miracles" which the lover later claims to have "wrought."[46]

The speaker's tolerantly amused ways of imagining these intruders upon himself and the lady intensifies the sense of their privacy and intimacy. Because their mutual understanding is perfect, they can be entertained by the misinterpretations of others, as the speaker obviously enjoys and expects the lady also to appreciate the grave-digger's fantasy that they are lovers who have arranged a rendezvous during the "busie" moving day which is the Last Judgment; or the adoration by "All women . . . and some men" of the token from the lady's "bright haire" as a lock from the famous golden tresses of Mary Magdalen, a reformed prostitute.[47] The mutual understanding of the two is emphasized by the speaker's use of innuendo and shorthand, which the lady must be able to interpret if his fantasy is to be appreciated:

> Thou shalt be'a Mary Magdalen, and I
> A something else thereby.

The hidden meaning of "something else," most probably a substitution for "Jesus Christ,"[48] is a private joke between them which anyone overhearing their conversation, and certainly the imagined false-believers, could easily misinterpret or reject as offensive, blasphemous.

The speaker's ways of talking to the lady in these first two stanzas create a sense of understanding so full that even intruders who curiously try to interpret it cannot violate its privacy. This exclusiveness casts suspicion on the speaker's vow to publicize the nature of his intimacy with the lady:

> I would that age were by this paper taught
> What miracles wee harmlesse lovers wrought.

This pledge to perpetuate his ideal beyond the mortal span of the "lovers" is not made to a generalized "age vnbred" or to "times in hope" or to the "eyes of all posterity," but pointedly to "that age" of "mis-devotion," itself an invention of the speaker's imagination like the grave-digger, which the speaker has teased for seeking "miracles,"[49] literal evidence of the supernatural such as idolaters believed to be performed by the relics of saints. The likelihood of "that age" learning to understand whatever the speaker calls "miracles" has been cast in doubt by his sophisticated condescension toward it, and by his exclusiveness, but still he begins his promised lesson, with the mock-pomposity of "First."

What follows in stanza three is a description of those "miracles wee harmlesse lovers wrought" in a language as various, witty, social, confident of an understanding response, as the first two stanzas. The sexual innuendo in the plays on the biblical use of "knew" to mean "physical familiarity," the smiling comparison with sociable "Guardian Angells," the Ovidian joke in defense of "nature, injur'd by late law,"[50] imply the same sympathetic listener. It is the lady who can enjoy this equation of chastity with "miracles," and therefore of their sexual restraint as evidence of their supernatural power, who can appreciate the sophisticated mingling of ribaldry and reverence, worldliness, and wonder in the speaker's description of their ideal love.[51] So it is she to whom "this paper" must be written, for urbane entertainment and compliment, not the false-believers—themselves imaginary—to whom it is supposedly addressed. Such mock-publicity no more violates the shared privacy of this miraculous love than does the imaginary grave-digger who "spies" on the braceleted skeleton.

The sense of shared secrecy remains even in the last lines, where the speaker for the first time refers to the lady in the third person, as if she were no longer present to listen. This is also implied by the change from the past tense in which they performed their "miracles" to "now" when the lovers are imagined to be dead and "this paper" lives on to eternize them:

These miracles wee did; but now alas,
All measure, and all language, I should passe,
Should I tell what a miracle shee was.

This conclusion is made to sound like a conventional apology by a poet to a public audience of readers for the inadequacy of his verse to celebrate the supernatural worth of the lady. A pure example is Spenser's *Amoretti* 3:

The souerayne beauty which I doo admyre,
    witnesse the world how worthy to be prayzed:
the light wherof hath kindled heauenly fyre,
    in my fraile spirit by her from basenesse raysed.
That being now with her huge brightnesse dazed,

base thing I can no more endure to view:
but looking still on her I stand amazed,
at wondrous sight of so celestiall hew.
So when my toung would speak her praises dew,
it stopped is with thoughts astonishment:
and when my pen would write her titles true,
it rauisht is with fancies wonderment:
Yet in my hart I then both speak and write
the wonder that my wit cannot endite.

The likeness of Donne's conclusion to such a poem chiefly defines their dissimilarities, however, for the conventional posture of the "base" worshipper apologizing to his "world" of readers for being struck mute with awe as he gazes up in wonder at his "celestiall" mistress is utterly incongruous with the tone of Donne's speaker, whose claims for "What miracles wee harmlesse lovers wrought" depend on their private understanding and also on their equality. When he uses the same word "miracle" to refer separately to what "shee was," he does not elevate her to "heauenly" heights in a poetic firmament above himself, but makes a compliment which is playfully phrased in terms so obviously conventional that they will at once praise and amuse the lady.[52] Far from worshipping her in silence as a mysterious being remote from himself, he talks easily of "wee" and "our." He too is familiar with the supernatural, himself a daily maker of true "miracles," an initiate in love's mysteries. His secret knowledge, shared only with the lady, therefore surpasses "All measure"—moderation, limit, calculation, metrics—and "all language," and in the end he withholds it from his imagined future audience. He chooses not to "tell" those unworthy listeners the truth which only the miraculous lovers know of the lady and his feelings for her, and so playfully denies his intention to eternize his ideal in poetry, pretending that he is not actually accomplishing that "miracle."[53]

The speaker in "The Relique," then, in a sense only pretends to adopt the conventional role of the poet-lover promising that his ideal will live "So long as men can breath or eyes can see" his verse. The imagined audience of stanza three is actually not the public of future readers assumed as the ultimate audience in conventional eternizing verse, which obviously depends on that assumption (even in poems where an immediate listener is also addressed), as a means of validating its claim to escape destruction by time. Here "that age" is, like the spying grave-digger, a device for amusement and compliment in his conversation with the lady. The third stanza, then, is the speaker's parody of poetic addresses to posterity, designed for the immediate entertainment of the lady, who shares his familiarity with the fashions of love poetry (in which miraculous ladies strike poets dumb) and his freedom to play games with them. The function of "that age" in "The Relique" is more nearly comparable to the personified sun imagined as audience in "The Sunne Rising" than to the future readers intended to hear the poet's vows in Shakespeare's eternizing sonnets. The ultimate effect of this use of a mock-audience is to insure that "The Relique," like the aubade, remains throughout an intimate conversation with the lady, whose response to the lover's pretended address to "that age" is what the device is supposedly invented to evoke.

The reader is initially in the position of someone overhearing a private conversation, as in the aubades and the valedictions, where Donne's exploitation of the lovers' immediate situations pointedly excludes an audience of readers. In those poems, however, our eavesdropping is boldly ignored throughout, whereas in "The Relique" it is ultimately made the butt of a joke, although one with which we are in complicity since its effect must depend on our capacity to appreciate it. For our position at the end of the poem is equated with that of the false-believers hearing a mock-lecture in a language they are too unsophisticated to understand, and like them we are finally excluded from the secret knowledge which the speaker refuses to "tell."

The implications of this kind of game with the reader, as an expression of what may be called Donne's anti-conventional eternizing attitudes, can be explored if "The Relique" is set beside

All in War with Time

"The Canonization," which it resembles in some obvious and some indirect ways. Initially, the comparison is suggested by the presence, so unusual in Donne's *Songs and Sonets,* of another speaker who appears to identify himself in the second-to-last stanza as a poet in love, promising to celebrate his ideal in "verse" which will survive after the death of himself and his mistress to teach "all" future readers a "patterne" of perfect love:

> Wee can dye by it, if not live by love,
>   And if unfit for tombes or hearse
> Our legend bee, it will be fit for verse;
> And if no peece of Chronicle wee prove,
>   We'll build in sonnets pretty roomes;
>   As well a well wrought urne becomes
> The greatest ashes, as halfe-acre tombes,
>   And by these hymnes, all shall approve
>   Us *Canoniz'd* for Love.

It is in part a familiarity with the rest of Donne's love poetry which causes uncertainties about the appropriate response to this fourth stanza of "The Canonization": recognition that the conventional figure of the poet-lover and his promise to eternize his ideal are elsewhere pointedly avoided; that only in one other love poem does the speaker refer to his "Sonnets," and there satirically;[54] that "pretty" is an unlikely adjective of praise for Donne, usually associated in the verse of the period with the diminutive innocence of children and lambs, and not one that any reader, or presumably Donne himself, would choose to praise his own poems;[55] that by comparison with claims in other poems for love's power to escape the threat of mutability, the promise to "build in sonnets pretty roomes" seems diminished if not actually belittling. For the phrasing of the vow insists on smallness and limits whereas the lovers in "The Good-morrow" or "The Sunne Rising" make "one little roome" or "these walls" include "every where" or the "world," while the speaker in "A Valediction: of Weeping" can make out of "nothing, *All.*" Even the less diminutive comparison of the speaker's eternizing verse to a "well wrought urne" containing the "greatest ashes" seems built on a smaller scale than the heroic claims of Donne's other lovers to embody "All States, and all Princes," or to "raigne" supremely powerful among all the "Kings" that rule "Here upon earth." The prediction that the poet and his mistress will become lifeless "ashes," however artistically enshrined, makes them static and finite compared to the lovers in other poems, who seem to go on passionately existing and feeling, as souls in animate bodies, even after they are buried. [56]

These are some of the questions raised by the speaker's claims in the fourth stanza of "The Canonization" read in the light of others of Donne's *Songs and Sonets*, and the poems previously discussed are precisely the ones with which it is most often grouped. [57] These questions are not easily answered, but actually become further complicated when the stanza is considered in the context of the poem as a whole. For there seem to be puzzling contradictions between the lover's claims here and the attitudes he expresses in the three preceding stanzas, while the language of his fantasy in the concluding stanza raises still more difficulties of interpretation: [58]

The Canonization

For Godsake hold your tongue, and let me love,
   Or chide my palsie, or my gout,
My five gray haires, or ruin'd fortune flout,
With wealth your state, your minde with Arts improve,
    Take you a course, get you a place,
    Observe his honour, or his grace,
And the Kings reall, or his stamped face
    Contemplate; what you will, approve,
     So you will let me love.

Alas, alas, who's injur'd by my love?
   What merchants ships have my sighs drown'd?
Who saies my teares have overflow'd his ground?
When did my colds a forward spring remove?
    When did the heats which my veines fill
    Adde one man to the plaguie Bill?
Soldiers finde warres, and Lawyers finde out still

Litigious men, which quarrels move,
  Though she and I do love.

Call us what you will, wee'are made such by love;
  Call her one, mee another flye,
We'are Tapers too, and at our owne cost die,
And wee in us finde the'Eagle and the Dove;
  The Phœnix ridle hath more wit
  By us, we two being one, are it,
So, to one neutrall thing both sexes fit.
  Wee dye and rise the same, and prove
  Mysterious by this love.

Wee can dye by it, if not live by love,
  And if unfit for tombes or hearse
Our legend bee, it will be fit for verse;
And if no peece of Chronicle wee prove,
  We'll build in sonnets pretty roomes;
  As well a well wrought urne becomes
The greatest ashes, as halfe-acre tombes,
  And by these hymnes, all shall approve
  Us *Canoniz'd* for Love.

And thus invoke us; You whom reverend love
  Made one anothers hermitage;
You, to whom love was peace, that now is rage;
Who did the whole worlds soule extract, and drove
  Into the glasses of your eyes,
  So made such mirrors, and such spies,
That they did all to you epitomize,
  Countries, Townes, Courts: Beg from above
  A patterne of your love!

Like the lover in "The Sunne Rising," the speaker begins by immediately dismissing an intruder hostile to his feelings, in impudent tones and with playfully theatrical exaggerations reminiscent of Ovid's *Amores*, which contributed some details to both poems.[59] Also like the speakers in the aubades—though here with even more sweeping contempt and a touch of comic self-pity—he dismisses the busy world that preoccupies other men, including the listener, in place of love. In the second stanza the speaker, here as in "The Relique," claims that his love is harmless; like that of the "refin'd" lovers in "A Valediction: Forbidding Mourning," it causes no destruction to the larger world, no storms or other disruptions of nature—the "teare-floods" and "sigh-tempests" associated with the uncontrolled feelings of noisier and more publicly demonstrative lovers.

In these first two stanzas the speaker has lectured his obviously unsympathetic listener on the complete independence of his love from the scrambling and quarrelsome world of kings and their would-be favorites, of courtiers, scholars, merchants, soldiers, and lawyers, the world which is traditionally the target of the satirist's railings.[60] Having dismissed it with loud contempt, he shows his indifference to it in the third stanza by inviting the listener, representative of that alien world, whom he first told to be silent, now to "call" the lovers whatever he pleases.[61] Like the speaker and the lady in "The Relique," these share an enjoyment of each other which cannot be threatened by misinterpretation and which to the observer, however pryingly inquisitive, will remain "Mysterious."

The speaker's almost flippant tone in this third stanza, the gaiety with which he multiplies names for the listener to "Call us," in the sense of "identify or define us" but also "insult us," the bawdiness and irreverence of his jokes about his love resemble the lover's way of talking in "The Relique." Here, however, the jokes as well as the love-affair are much more frankly, even coarsely physical and sexual. This Ovidian manner characterizes not only the comparisons to the fly, the taper, the eagle and the dove, but also, and with at least matching bluntness, to the Phœnix, a mythological bird which could be used with serious religious significance as an emblem of Christ but also for bawdy joking and compliment, as Donne uses the figure in the second stanza of "An Epithalamion, Or Mariage Song on the Lady Elizabeth, and Count Palatine Being Married on St. Valentines Day":

Till now, Thou warm'dst with multiplying loves
　　Two larkes, two sparrowes, or two Doves,
　　　　All that is nothing unto this,
For thou this day couplest two Phœnixes;
　　　　Thou mak'st a Taper see
What the sunne never saw, and what the Arke
(Which was of soules, and beasts, the cage, and park,)
Did not containe, one bed containes, through Thee,
　　　　Two Phœnixes, whose joyned breasts
　　Are unto one another mutuall nests,
Where motion kindles such fires, as shall give
Yong Phœnixes, and yet the old shall live.
Whose love and courage never shall decline,
But make the whole year through, thy day, O Valentine.

In the third stanza of "The Canonization" the comparison with the Phœnix is a "ridle," a verbal puzzle or game intended to perplex, which the speaker seems to explicate almost casually, with a literary cliché, "we two being one, are it." This figure provides the cryptic but far from elevated image of the "neutrall thing" created when male and female "fit" together, literally in the posture of love-making,[62] from which these lovers "dye and rise the same." Of course this phrase is recognizable as religious language, but here, rather than implying a seriously explored analogy between sexual and sacred patterns of experience, it makes the outrageous suggestion that these lovers are more than human, supernatural, as if already resurrected into eternal life, because they "dye" over and over in the common punning sense of the verb for achieving sexual consummation, and yet their flesh can still "rise the same," not satiated or diminished in virility by continuous love-making,[63] and with perhaps less bawdy meaning, not bored or disappointed with each other. The use of religious language—"Wee dye and rise the same"—combined with the conventional paradox of Petrarchan poetry—"we two being one"—does not here have the gravely elevating force of seemingly similar diction in a poem like "A Valediction: Forbidding Mourning," but the wittily parodic effect of such language in "Loves Infiniteness":

> Thou canst not every day give me thy heart,
>> If thou canst give it, then thou never gav'st it:
> Loves riddles are, that though thy heart depart,
>> It stayes at home, and thou with losing sav'st it:
> But wee will have a way more liberall,
> Then changing hearts, to joyne them, so wee shall
>> Be one, and one anothers All.

When the speaker in "The Canonization" claims that because they "dye and rise the same," the lovers will "prove / Mysterious" to those who "Call" them names, he may be drawing on the religious associations of "Mysterious" as a joking assertion of the lovers' initiation into the sacred mysteries—of their kind of dying. He is also boasting that they are "Mysterious" in the sense of "inscrutable" or "enigmatic." The "ridle" they pose to the intruding world has not, for all his mock-explication in this stanza, been answered.

In stanza four the speaker then promises a future publication of love's mysteries in "sonnets" or "hymnes" by which "all" who have formerly criticized or misinterpreted the lovers will learn to "approve / Us Canoniz'd for Love." The category "all" is sufficiently general (by contrast with "that age" in "The Relique") to stand for posterity. It may also refer to "all" who read "sonnets," and therefore make an absurd equation between devotees of love poetry and "all" posterity, as well as a satirical comment on the arrogance of conventional eternizing poets who assume that "all" will read them.

This assertion of future acclaim is said as if in self-vindication, to silence attacks and name-calling, to justify the renunciation of the world for love by claiming ultimate approval of the lovers' values by that world. Such a reading cannot be accepted uncritically, however, because it raises many disturbing questions in relation to preceding stanzas. For the speaker has satirized the world in terms which have already dismissed it so wholeheartedly that he is then free to enjoy its misjudgments, even to encourage its attacks by teasing it with enigmatic metaphors for the lovers' private experience. Those descriptions, although in a sense cryptic or gnomic, unquestionably convey the lovers' enjoyment of triumphant sexuality, with a robustness, a humorous vigor of language, that could scarcely be made "fit" for the "pretty roomes" of "sonnets" or for "hymnes," the term for elevated or sacred verse such as the "Larke" sings "at Heauens gate" in Shakespeare's Sonnet 29. The promise to explicate the "ridle" of their "Mysterious" love in such "verse" seems purposely indecorous, and therefore suspect. Finally, the desire to explain his love to the world, to publicize it in order to win approval of "all," is seriously questioned by reminders of the lover's contemptuous exclusiveness—"what you will, approve / So you will let me love"—in the preceding stanzas, specifically by his extravagant mockery of Petrarchan lovers, who display their feelings with loud ostentation, as if their publicized "sighs" and "teares" influenced the course of nature, as if the "colds" and "heats" of their blood created national disasters.

These questions raised by apparent conflicts between the lover's vows in stanza four and his attitudes earlier in the poem point to two alternative conclusions. One is simply that the poem is self-contradictory, that it is ultimately unsatisfactory because the lover's feelings are not sufficiently in control, his ambiguities of tone never adequately resolved, to prevent their range and complexity from disintegration.[64] Another possible conclusion, to be explored in this discussion, is that the speaker's promise here to eternize his love for the edification of future readers is a joke similar in some respects to the device of "this paper" in "The Relique," which the speaker only pretends to compose to educate the future "age" of "mis-devotion" in the true "miracles" of love.

If the speaker is continuing to tease in stanza four, with further pretenses of accommodatingly explaining his love to his critic, then the absurdity of promising to explicate his "Mysterious" sexual experience in "pretty" little poems or in conventional "hymnes," is part of his riddling game.[65] The triumphant assertiveness of the last two lines of stanza four is then less self-vindicating than jokingly derisive:

And by these hymnes, all shall approve
Us *Canoniz'd* for Love.

The speaker's secret amusement derives from his sense of how scandalized the world would be if it could interpret the "ridle" of his love; how little it would be suited as a subject for celebration in the "pretty" or sublime forms of poetry in which the world is accustomed to reading about what it calls "Love"; how easily "all" may be duped into approval by the flattering deference to a public audience in the kind of conventional eternizing poetry he is parodying.

In the final stanza he imagines the form in which the world, edified by such "hymnes," would express its approval. The reader who interprets this stanza as a fundamentally serious philosophic statement about the nature of love, comparable to the claims for its power by the speakers in the aubades and valedictions previously discussed, must initially be able to accept the necessary corrolaries that the lover has willingly and successfully explained his "Mysterious" experience in "sonnets" and "hymnes" and that the world, previously rejected by him as contemptibly vicious and vulgar, has somehow proved capable of conversion to his vision, his values, which it then celebrates with true understanding in the last stanza.

An alternative possibility is that the lover's "sonnets" or "hymnes" have duped "all" who inquire into the mysteries of love to find in this "verse" confirmation of their own false values, which are expressed then in their invocation of the "Canoniz'd" lovers. The very fact that they pray for the intercession of saints might suggest a resemblance between "all" here and "that age" of "mis-devotion" in "The Relique," which mistakes the lovers' remains for those of figures representing altogether different kinds of love and sanctity. The practice of such invocations, as well as the worship of relics, was rejected by the Anglican Church, and Donne in one letter makes a joke about "praying to Saints, to whom God must tell first, that such a man prays to them to pray to him."[66] If "all" are indeed such false-believers, then they are incapable of rightly understanding love's mysteries and therefore interpret the speaker's enigmatic language in the light of their own vulgar values.

If such a reading is supported by the language of the invocation, it would make "The Canonization" a poem different in kind from the aubades and valedictions discussed earlier, but much closer in its effects to the satirical "A Valediction: of the Booke." There the lover sarcastically encourages his mistress to "vent thy thoughts" by writing the "Annals" of their love in which representatives of the world—scholars, lovers, lawyers, statesmen "or of them, they which can reade"—will each "their nothing see, / As in the Bible some can finde out Alchimy." The suggestive parallels between this parody of conventional eternizing verse and "The Canonization" justify quoting at least the first four of its seven stanzas:

> I'll tell thee now (deare Love) what thou shalt doe
>   To anger destiny, as she doth us,
>   How I shall stay, though she esloygne me thus,
> And how posterity shall know it too;
>   How thine may out-endure
>   Sybills glory, and obscure
>   Her who from *Pindar* could allure,
> And her, through whose helpe *Lucan* is not lame,
> And her, whose booke (they say) *Homer* did finde, and name.
>
> Study our manuscripts, those Myriades
>   Of letters, which have past twixt thee and mee,
>   Thence write our Annals, and in them will bee,
> To all whom loves subliming fire invades,
>   Rule and example found;
>   There, the faith of any ground
>   No schismatique will dare to wound,
> That sees, how Love this grace to us affords,
> To make, to keep, to use, to be these his Records.
>
> This Booke, as long-liv'd as the elements,

Or as the worlds forme, this all-graved tome,
In cypher write, or new made Idiome;
Wee for loves clergie only'are instruments.
When this booke is made thus,
Should againe the ravenous
Vandals and Goths inundate us,
Learning were safe; in this our Universe
Schooles might learne Sciences, Spheares Musick, Angels Verse.

Here Loves Divines, (since all Divinity
Is love or wonder) may finde all they seeke,
Whether abstract spirituall love they like,
Their Soules exhal'd with what they do not see,
Or, loth so to amuze
Faiths infirmitie, they chuse
Something which they may see and use;
For, though minde be the heaven, where love doth sit,
Beauty'a convenient type may be to figure it.

If "all" who have studied the speaker's "hymnes" at the end of
"The Canonization" are meant to be types comparable to "Loves
Divines" here, searching its mysteries "In cypher . . . or new
made Idiome" to "finde all they seeke" in confirmation of their
own values, the evidence that Donne so intended them must be
in the actual language of the invocation which his speaker invents for them:

You whom reverend love
Made one anothers hermitage;
You, to whom love was peace, that now is rage;
Who did the whole worlds soule extract, and drove
Into the glasses of your eyes,
So made such mirrors, and such spies,
That they did all to you epitomize,
Countries, Townes, Courts: Beg from above
A patterne of your love!

This is certainly serious, even solemn, and philosophical language, but it does not sound like the speaker of the previous
stanzas growing more grave or intense as he enlarges genuinely
felt claims for the power of his love. The praises of the represent-

atives of "reverend love" (a phrase suggesting an elderly and respectable figure such as the lover in "The Sunne Rising" mocks the sun for thinking himself) as "one anothers hermitage" whose "love was peace" encompassing, distilling, epitomizing the "whole worlds soule,"[67] lack the sexual energy of the speaker's own earlier claims. They make this love sound almost ascetic, disembodied like the "abstract spirituall love" that some "Divines" find in "A Valediction: of the Booke," rather than passionate and robust like the lover's parodic religious language in stanza three or his bawdy posturing as a martyr to sexual pleasure, "Wee can dye by it, if not live by love."[68]

Nor do the final claims for the lovers by their worshippers sound like the impassioned assertions of love's power made by the speakers in the aubades or in the valedictions "of Weeping" or "Forbidding Mourning," despite the recurrence of the metaphor of the lovers' eyes reflecting the "world" for each other. In fact the differences in the way that metaphor is used here are particularly telling evidence that "all" are worshipping a false image of "Canoniz'd" love. Their language of highest praise is that the "eyes" of the saints—"glasses," "mirrors," "spies"—"did all to you epitomize." This "all," which presumably each lover's "eyes" could reflect and therefore "mirror" in contracted form for the other to share, is then defined by the formula, "Countries, Townes, Courts." This is unmistakably the world contemptuously dismissed by the speaker in the first stanza, which has for him none of the excitement and diversity of the newly discovered "worlds" that the lovers in "The Good-morrow" embrace in their "every where," nor the glamorous sensuality, even sexuality, of "the'India's of spice and Myne"[69] or the opulent grandeur of superfluous "Kings" contained in "This bed" of "The Sunne Rising." The world reflected in the eyes of the lovers invoked as saints is the vulgar and venal society defined by a formulaic phrase conventional to satire, one which Donne himself uses satirically elsewhere,[70] in a verse epistle "To Sr Henry Wotton":

Life is a voyage, and in our lifes wayes
Countries, Courts, Towns are Rockes, or Remoraes;
They breake or stop all ships, yet our state's such,
That though then pitch they staine worse, wee must touch.

He uses it also in "Loves Usury":

From country grasse, to comfitures of Court,
Or cities quelque choses, let report
My minde transport.

In defining the world epitomized to the lovers by this formula, the worshippers reveal their own undiminished attachment to that world, its viciousness betrayed by the equation of "eyes" with "spies," a word used with great frequency by Donne, and almost always for the kind of prying intruder that the lover contemptuously dismissed in the first stanza, and that "all" his readers are here made to show themselves.[71] The "patterne" they seek is not that truly embodied in the lovers they invoke, who represent themselves in the "Phœnix ridle," but their vulgar misinterpretation of a love which to them and the world will remain forever "Mysterious."

By this reading "The Canonization," like "The Relique," begins as if it were part of a private conversation during which the speaker devises for his immediate listener a parody of conventional eternizing verse where he pretends to address future readers. In both poems the actual reader is initially in the position of an eavesdropper whose presence is ignored, as in the aubades, the valedictions "of Weeping" and "Forbidding Mourning," and "The Anniversarie." But in "The Canonization," as in "The Relique," our presence is ultimately acknowledged by becoming part of an elaborate joke, since as readers of a future time we are in the position of "all" who will study and misunderstand the speaker's "verse," who will be deluded by its flattering promises to seek our approval, but for whom he refuses to explicate the "ridle" of his "Mysterious" love.

This device of making the speaker deliver a parody of poetry addressed to future readers has a somewhat different effect in the two poems, however, because even at the end of "The Relique," when the reader becomes part of its imaginary audience, the sense of the lady's intimate presence as listener is never really lost, and the poem retains its private and dramatic character. In "The Canonization," however, the critical listener, whose presence is passionately felt in the opening, which has the explosive immediacy of "The Sunne Rising," gradually disappears from the poem. By the last stanza that listener is virtually forgotten, or absorbed into the larger audience of "all," as the lady, for whom the wit and compliment of "The Relique" are designed, is never submerged.

The effect is to turn "The Canonization" into a poem which ceases to be private or dramatic, which is actually closer in kind to "A Valediction: of the Booke." In stanzas two through six of that "Valediction" the lady's presence as listener is scarcely felt; mentions of her in the first and last stanzas seem to be the invention of Donne to provide opportunity for the parody of eternizing verse whose satiric thrust is not directed toward her. With something like the same effect, the listener whose presence is strongly felt in the first stanza of "The Canonization," in the end is so nearly obliterated as to seem like a device invented by Donne to open an argument that could include the riddling games of the last three stanzas.[72] It is perhaps for this reason that some readers find it a "faintly unsatisfactory" poem.[73]

Whether or not it is fully successful, "The Canonization" is ultimately different in kind from the *Songs and Sonets* with which it is usually grouped, and yet, like them, it defines itself in relation to conventional eternizing poetry, which seems to have embodied for Donne attitudes toward which his imagination was deeply hostile. By satirizing its conventions here, Donne rejects them, as he does in the *Songs and Sonets* previously discussed, in favor of a kind of poem that does not "Beg from above / A patterne" of the ideal, but finds it in the "Mysterious" and mutable experience of mortal lovers.

3

Jonson

In the dedicatory letter to his volume of *Epigrammes* Jonson proudly introduces himself as a poet whose *"verses"* present *"good, and great names . . . to their remembrance with posteritie,"*[1] and in the poems themselves the speaker is characteristically identified as a writer, and often one who, like Petrarchan poet-lovers but also classical authors,[2] sings praises which "shall out-last common deeds," which celebrate worth "Whose rellish to eternitie shall last," which confer immortality by their power to "publish" to all ages the ideal they crown with fame:[3]

> Weare this renowne. 'Tis iust, that who did giue
> So many *Poets* life, by one should liue.

The speakers in these poems of praise present themselves in the act of composing verses complimenting a particular listener named in the title, as in *Epigrammes* CIIII addressed "To Svsan Covntesse of Montgomery," while also publishing the subject's worth to the "world," an audience universalized by "comparison" with the past, by references to "our times" and predictions about "posteritie."

Within such poems the speaker, the individual listener, and the public audience of readers share a timeless present created by the language of the poem. For the poet is represented in traditional figures: the painter of "A picture, which the world for yours must know"; the builder of "An obeliske, or columne to thy name" immortalized in verse rather than "in brasse or marble writ"; like a "trumpet . . . whose euery breath was fame"; even as a metaphor for poetic inspiration:[4]

> Who now calls on thee, Nevil, is a *Muse*,
>   That serues nor fame, nor titles; but doth chuse
> What vertue makes them both, and that's in thee.

These conventional metaphors make the poet a figure to be identified with authors of other countries and different ages, and therefore, like the many other classical and biblical allusions, contribute to the effect of lifting both poet and subject out of specific time and place.

In poems of praise which hint at actual, contemporary incidents, these are characteristically generalized, even mythologized, so that they become representative illustrations of the poet's ideal, like the virtues of the figure praised in a Petrarchan love-sonnet. For example, Lady Wroth, whose participation in masques and other courtly entertainments is the source of Jonson's compliments in *Epigrammes* CV, is transformed into "Natures Index" of a lost golden "age," much like the friend celebrated in Shakespeare's Sonnet 68, whose "holy antique" beauty "for a map doth Nature store." As the friend is praised for loveliness which has power to correct "faulse Art," Lady Wroth is also made the source of inspiration for poets "Who could not but create" from her image "all antiquitie" and "All historie." Jonson's adaptations of such conventions are themselves a means of generalizing his compliments and also enhancing them since they cast him as if in the traditional position of the poet in love with the lady he praises, although his language is not intended to express intimate or passionate feelings.

Without the cold formality of some of Jonson's verse compliments to aristocratic ladies, yet with equal self-consciousness, his speaker assumes the role of a poet-lover praising "my Lady" in part four of "A Celebration of Charis in Ten Lyrick Peeces":[5]

Her Triumph

> See the Chariot at hand here of Love,
>   Wherein my Lady rideth!
> Each that drawes, is a Swan, or a Dove,
>   And well the Carre Love guideth.

As she goes, all hearts doe duty
            Unto her beauty;
And enamour'd, doe wish, so they might
            But enjoy such a sight,
That they still were to run by her side,
Th(o)rough Swords, th(o)rough Seas, whether she would ride.

Doe but looke on her eyes, they doe light
    All that Loves world compriseth!
Doe but looke on her Haire, it is bright
    As Loves starre when it riseth!
Doe but marke, her forehead's smoother
            Then words that sooth her!
And from her arched browes, such a grace
            Sheds it selfe through the face,
    As alone there triumphs to the life
All the Gaine, all the Good, of the Elements strife.

Have you seene but a bright Lillie grow,
    Before rude hands have touch'd it?
Have you mark'd but the fall o'the Snow
    Before the soyle hath smutch'd it?
Have you felt the wooll o' the Bever?
            Or Swans Downe ever?
Or have smelt o'the bud o'the Brier?
            Or the Nard i' the fire?
    Or have tasted the bag o'the Bee?
O so white! O so soft! O so sweet is she!

Although the speaker refers to "my Lady," he never addresses
her but pointedly directs all his praise of her to another audience,
the witnesses whom he urges to "See" her ride in triumph, as in a
royal procession or spectacle designed for public display. He directs us to "See" what is apparently visible near "at hand here,"
and yet there is a sense in which he is also creating the picture,
since until he names its details—"Each that drawes, is a Swan, or
a Dove"—we cannot visualize them, nor do we know until he
tells us what "all hearts" feel at "such a sight." His praise of the
lady in the first stanza is therefore that of an artist who portrays
and interprets a figure, generalized and even mythologized by
his language, embodying moral and aesthetic values to which

"all hearts doe duty." The political or military imagery of the triumphal chariot-ride relates the lady to the conventional figure of the sovereign mistress for whom the poet-lover composes "words that sooth her." Yet the tone in which the speaker offers to "enjoy" her beauty with all "hearts" distinguishes him from the suffering servant of such a powerful lady.[6] For his tone is proud and gaily appreciative, his delight unmixed with pain or humble pleading, and his intention throughout seems more to enlighten his audience than to supplicate the lady.

The delighted imperatives of the second stanza—"Doe but looke . . . Doe but looke . . . Doe but looke . . . Doe but marke"— increase the impression that she is a "sight" intended for public view and admiration. Although she is brought nearer so that we may observe her features, these are generalized by the poet's hyperbolic comparisons. He controls this "sight," meaning both her appearance and our view of it, by his metaphorical language which, in the third stanza, creates a poetic world seeming, until the last line, to exist independently of the lady:

> Have you seene but a bright Lillie grow,
>   Before rude hands have touch'd it?
> Have you mark'd but the fall o'the Snow
>   Before the soyle hath smutch'd it?
> Have you felt the wooll o' the Bever?
>   Or Swans Downe ever?
> Or have smelt o'the bud o'the Brier?
>   Or the Nard i' the fire?
> Or have tasted the bag o'the Bee?
> O so white! O so soft! O so sweet is she!

These rhetorical questions to the reader evoke a pastoral world combining innocence and elegance in some ways resembling the world of Marlowe's "The Passionate Shepherd to His Love," but here it is the reader rather than the lady who is invited to "enjoy" it with the poet as an imaginative ideal. His images, resonant with associations from nature or poetry, create a landscape pure and precious and permanently preserved in that state by his language. They have a clarity and delicately loving exactitude which enhance his authority to teach us just appreciation of the beauty celebrated in his poem.

Its last line tells us that this pastoral scenery is itself an extended comparison to the lady—"O so white! O so soft! O so sweet is she!"—which is at once hyperbolic and precise, for "so" means both "so very" and "just exactly as." By the workings of these similitudes, therefore, the lady, with the lily or the swan, becomes a figure in the landscape of the speaker's poem, like the friend in Shakespeare's Sonnet 15, whose youthful beauty is set before the poet-lover's "sight" as a "conceit" in his poem.

Yet here a public audience is insistently addressed, but never the "Lady," who is called only by that title, not by name, not "my love," or any other endearment. Because the speaker's appreciation of this universally admired figure is so eagerly shared throughout with his audience, and is so untroubled by any such conflicting feelings as pain or fear or grief or desire, his identity as a poet celebrating an embodiment of ideal beauty emerges far more strongly than as an intimate or impassioned lover. His use of "my" to describe the "Lady" therefore seems decorous to the convention in which he is writing, or perhaps even an author's proprietary feeling for his subject, more than a term intended to convey intimacy or private feeling, such as we hear in Shakespeare's Sonnet 15 when the poet-lover turns from large generalizing to speak directly to his friend:

Then the conceit of this inconstant stay,
Sets you most rich in youth before my sight.

Jonson's speaker is preeminently a poet who adopts the role of lover for literary effects which his readers, assumed to share his poetic inheritance as they share his "duty" to appreciate "such a sight," are expected to recognize.

Even in poems which seem not to be published to the "world" or elaborated as if to inspire an "age" of poetry, but appear to be addressed only to the admired lady herself, Jonson's speaker assumes a verse-writing posture conventional to the figure of the poet-lover, unlike one of Donne's speakers talking directly and privately to his mistress on an occasion or in a situation made immediate by his ways of speaking. This role may be chosen for a variety of literary effects, as in *Epigrammes* CXXVI:

To His Lady, Then Mrs. Cary

Retyr'd, with purpose your faire worth to praise,
    'Mongst *Hampton* shades, and Phoebus groue of bayes,
I pluck'd a branch; the iealous god did frowne,
    And bad me lay th'vsurped laurell downe:
Said I wrong'd him, and (which was more) his loue.
    I answer'd, Daphne now no paine can proue.
Phoebus replyed. Bold head, it is not shee:
    Cary my loue is, Daphne but my tree.

The poet "Retyr'd" to a pastoral landscape for the purpose of receiving inspiration from the god of poetry to praise the lady's "faire worth" is mythologized with the narrated episode, and the lady it is designed to compliment, in something like the same way as the figure of the poet-lover is mythologized in a sonnet like Sidney's *Astrophil and Stella* 17:

His mother deare *Cupid* offended late,
    Because that *Mars*, growne slacker in her love,
    With pricking shot he did not throughly move,
To keepe the pace of their first loving state.
The boy refusde for feare of *Marse's* hate,
    Who threatned stripes, if he his wrath did prove:
    But she in chafe him from her lap did shove,
Brake bow, brake shafts, while *Cupid* weeping sate:
    Till that his grandame *Nature* pittying it,
Of *Stella's* browes made him two better bowes,
And in her eyes of arrowes infinit.
O how for joy he leapes, ô how he crowes,
    And straight therewith, like wags new got to play,
    Fals to shrewd turnes, and I was in his way.

Both Jonson's poem and Sidney's seem to place the lady and the poet in a timeless literary world, transforming them into mythological figures different in kind from the lovers in Donne's

Songs and Sonets previously discussed. Both poets might therefore imply a shared definition of their art fundamentally unlike Donne's in those poems using situations which avoid the possibility of a lover expressing his feelings in verse, and which define their nature partly by that exclusion. Yet it is finally significant for an understanding of Jonson's most distinctive, most impressive poetry that here in the mythologized tale which his poet narrates, his pastoral "shades, and Phoebus groue" are actually located at the royal court of "Hampton" and his lady is identified in the poem itself, as well as in its playful title, by the family surname of Cary rather than by a literary or metaphorical name—Stella, Delia, Parthenope, Zepheria, Coelia, Chloris, Fidessa, Diana, Cynthia, Idea—such as abound in English sonnets in imitation of classical, Italian, and French love poetry.

Jonson's amusement with this fanciful practice of naming, and with his own participation in it in his poems to Celia, is shown in *The Vnder-wood XXVII:*

An Ode

Helen, did *Homer* never see
Thy beauties, yet could write of thee?
Did *Sappho* on her seven-tongu'd Lute,
So speake (as yet it is not mute)
Of *Phao[n]s* forme? or doth the Boy
In whom *Anacreon* once did joy,
Lie drawne to life, in his soft Verse,
As he whom *Maro* did rehearse?
Was *Lesbia* sung by learn'd *Catullus?*
Or *Delia's* Graces, by *Tibullus?*
Doth *Cynthia,* in *Propertius* song
Shine more, then she, the Stars among?
Is *Horace* his each love so high
Rap't from the Earth, as not to die?
With bright *Lycoris, Gallus* choice,
Whose fame hath an eternall voice?
Or hath *Corynna,* by the name
Her *Ovid* gave her, dimn'd the fame
Of *Caesars* Daughter, and the line
Which all the world then styl'd divine?

Hath *Petrarch* since his *Laura* rais'd
Equall with her? or *Ronsart* prais'd
His new *Cassandra*, 'bove the old;
Which all the Fate of *Troy* foretold?
Hath our great *Sydney*, *Stella* set,
Where never Star shone brighter yet?
Or *Constables* Ambrosiack Muse
Made *Dian*, not his notes refuse?
Have all these done (and yet I misse
The Swan [that] so relish'd *Pancharis*)
And shall not I my *Celia* bring,
Where men may see whom I doe sing?
Though I, in working of my song,
Come short of all this learned throng,
Yet sure my tunes will be the best,
So much my Subject drownes the rest.

The mere accumulation here of so many long and elaborate
names, both those of "all this learned throng" of poets and of the
ladies for whom they chose the "name" which gave them "fame,"
has in itself a parodic effect, especially in a series of tetrameter
couplets whose "tunes" are so loud. The broadest stroke, however, is saved for the inclusion, as the climax of the list, of the
parenthesis:

Have all these done (and yet I misse
The Swan [that] so relish'd *Pancharis*).

This reference to a poem by Hugh Holland, to which Jonson
wrote a prefatory ode, is obviously chosen, not for the distinction of the original, scarcely belonging in such noble company,
but for the absurdity of the lady's name as well as the poet's
mythological transformation of himself into a swan, a form assumed by Jove when he became a lover. This allusion allows for
the bawdy suggestions of "so relish'd," since Jove as swan raped
Leda and since the swan in legend was thought to sing before
"dying."[7]

By comparison to Holland's, the speaker's own song will
scarcely "Come short," yet he ends with the conventional claim
to surpass the achievements of the other poets only because his

"Subject drownes the rest." This concluding line directs the parody to include his own choice of the name "Celia," deriving from the Latin *caelum* and therefore elevating her to heaven, from which height she will surpass all other mythologized ladies, particularly by her capacity to overflow with bad weather that "drownes the rest."

In the poem "To His Lady, Then Mrs. Cary," the substitution of "Cary" for "Daphne" alludes playfully to this fashion for choosing literary names, but it also has another, more important function. For within the language of the poem, the mythological world of the poet's narrative is placed in relation to the actual geographical and social world evoked by "Hampton" and "Cary," but excluded from Sidney's sonnet, in which all details, including Stella's eyebrows, are wholly mythologized.[8]

Jonson's inclusion of such historical names in this epigram as a device to define his poetic intentions, as well as for literary parody and social compliment, is emphasized by the close connection between his poem to Mrs. Cary and the fifth sonnet of Petrarch's *Canzoniere*, itself a play on the resemblance between the name Laura and the Italian word for praising, *laudando*. This sonnet was a favorite source for motifs often used by English sonneteers, and was therefore a poem which Jonson could expect his readers to know.[9] The nature of his borrowing makes clear that he designed the comparison as a means of pointing to his own literary intentions in the epigram to Mrs. Cary, by contrast with Petrarch's sonnet:

> When I summon my sighs to call you near
> With the name that Love wrote within my heart,
> "LAUdable," one seems suddenly to hear
> The sound of its first sweet melodies start.
>
> Your REgal state that I wish to define
> Doubles my valour to the enterprise;
> "TAcitly," for her honour, the end cries,
> Is load for other shoulders than are thine.
>
> Thus to LAUd and REvere teaches and vows

The voice itself, if someone tries to call,
O worthy of all praise and reverence;

Unless perhaps Apollo take offence
That mortal tongue his ever-verdant boughs
Presumptuously endeavour to extol.

Jonson's elaboration of Petrarch's suggestion that the god of poetry might be offended if a mere "mortal tongue" were to utter the sacred name of his love, now immortalized in the laurel with "ever-verdant boughs," wittily calls attention to his substitution of the name "Cary," the real human being, for that of the mythologically transformed "Daphne." The actual, flesh-and-blood woman, not the symbolic tree, is the proper object of "loue," both Apollo's and the speaker's, and therefore it is her name which poetry must celebrate. His role as poet is to "praise" such physical embodiments of worth, "Then Mrs. Cary," in another poem some other living lady. His posture as poet-lover, in imitation of Petrarch, is understood to be assumed for the occasion of this particular retirement to "Hampton" to write *Epigrammes* CXXVI.

The significance of such differences between Jonson's poem and its Petrarchan model can be shown most clearly in other poems where Jonson arouses the expectations which the presence of a poet-lover evokes in a reader familiar with English love poetry, seemingly in order to defy those expectations. These poems, like the *Songs and Sonets* explored in Chapter 2, define their own character through alterations or violations of the conventions of love poetry. They also show parallels between Jonson's poems and Donne's which point to some similarities of interest amid their apparent differences. [10]

Epigrammes CIII to Lady Wroth, one of Jonson's rare sonnets, begins with the hyperboles of a Petrarchan poet, addressed at once to the "faire" lady it praises, and to an imagined audience of readers. The fact that in his love poetry Jonson, like Donne, largely avoided the sonnet form, is itself a long recognized mark of divergence from the interests of other English poets writing in the 1590s.[11] His pointed use of the form here is part of his compliment to Lady Wroth, niece of Sir Philip Sidney and herself a sonneteer, according to another of Jonson's rare sonnets.[12] The choice of form is also a means for defining his own concerns by inviting comparison with the kind of sonnet it resembles:

To Mary Lady Wroth

How well, faire crowne of your faire sexe, might hee,
  That but the twi-light of your sprite did see,
And noted for what flesh such soules were fram'd,
  Know you to be a Sydney, though vn-nam'd?
And, being nam'd, how little doth that name
  Need any *Muses* praise to giue it fame?
Which is, it selfe, the *imprese* of the great,
  And glorie of them all, but to repeate!
Forgiue me then, if mine but say you are
  A Sydney: but in that extend as farre
As lowdest praisers, who perhaps would find
  For euery part a character assign'd.
My praise is plaine, and where so ere profest,
  Becomes none more then you, who need it least.

The sonnet form itself, the metaphor of the lady—"faire crowne"—as a sovereign creature whose virtue is by "faire" defined as both inward and outward beauty, the use of religious terms—"sprite" and "soules"—to elevate her worth, the reverent yet confident tone of the poet's rhetorical questions, all establish connections between this "praise" and Petrarchan love poetry. Even the rejection of the elaborate literary language of "lowdest praisers," whose poetry he contrasts with what he calls his own "plaine" verse, is itself conventional to poems like Shakespeare's Sonnets 21 and 130 or Sidney's *Astrophil and Stella* 28.[13] Sidney's sonnet, imitating Petrarch's celebration of the lady's name as a kind of prayer, argues that it may be repeated by her admirer "in pure simplicitie" without need of poetic ornament:

You that with allegorie's curious frame,
  Of other's children changelings use to make,
  With me those paines for God's sake do not take:

> I list not dig so deepe for brasen fame.
> When I say '*Stella*', I do mean the same
>> Princesse of Beautie, for whose only sake
>> The raines of *Love* I love, though never slake,
> And joy therein, though Nations count it shame.
>> I beg no subject to use eloquence,
> Nor in hid wayes to guide Philosophie:
> Looke at my hands for no such quintessence;
> But know that I in pure simplicitie,
>> Breathe out the flames which burne within my heart,
>> *Love* onely reading unto me this art.

Jonson is therefore following a convention when his speaker attributes the entire burden of his "praise" to the unornamented name "Sydney" itself, as Astrophil claims "When I say '*Stella*'" to have uttered the full message that "Love" has read to his "heart." This resemblance, then, points to the most prominent difference in detail between the two sonnets, which is again the character of the name invoked by the poet, a distinction emphasized here by the sequence of "vn-nam'd," "nam'd," "name," and the repetition of "a Sydney." The name of "Stella" is a metaphorical title like Petrarch's "Laura," which transforms the lady into the most brightly shining "Star," according to Jonson's parodic ode, "set" above the worshipful Astrophil, himself mythologized by his name as a star-lover inspired and guided by this remote celestial light.[14] "Sydney," by contrast, is a name different in kind and therefore capable of carrying different sorts of meanings.

To praise the lady as "a Sydney" is to place her in a family, a social class, a country and period, and therefore to set the poet, who can "Know" by looking at her that she is "a Sydney," in the same historical world. This world may have the glamor and grandeur of the heroic tradition associated with it, "the *imprese* of the great, / And glorie of them all." It may have the imaginative force of poetic associations since the name Sydney meant not only aristocratic position and wealth but literary inheritance from the author of *Astrophil and Stella*, at whose "great birth

. . . all the Muses met."[15] Yet for all its wealth of associations, which allow the name of Sydney metaphorical meanings in the poem, it remains in itself historical, like the names of "Hampton" and "Cary" in *Epigrammes* CXXVI. It refers to a world outside the poem, existing in identifiable time and place, in which the poet and Lady Wroth live.

By claiming that his sonnet, unlike other "*Muses* praise," will "but say you are / A Sydney," Jonson defines a kind of poetry which celebrates an ideal existing in the temporal world. Yet he is not arguing that his poetry merely copies that living perfection, for paradoxically his own poem does not, as he wittily pretends, "but say you are / A Sydney." It literally surrounds that name with "praise," of a distinctly literary character, which derives from and yet simultaneously establishes the meaningful associations of the name. The "praise" and "a Sydney" each have significance and authority and yet they conform to and enhance each other as embodiments of the same ideal:

My praise is plaine, and where so ere profest,
  Becomes none more then you, who need it least.

This final declaration defines the difference between his "plaine" poetry and that of other "*Muses* praise," while also distinguishing it from poems like Sidney's twenty-eighth sonnet, which ends with the poet's claim, itself admittedly a self-conscious posture, to eschew the elaborations of other writers:

But know that I in pure simplicitie,
  Breathe out the flames that burne within my heart,
  Love onely reading unto me this art.

Sidney's "pure simplicitie" is said to be divinely inspired by "Love" which transforms him into a prophetic voice,[16] his tongue purified by fire, so that he can without profanation "Breathe" forth the sacred name of "Stella." Like the lover sighing the name of Laura in *Canzoniere* 5, he is the instrument of a mythological god and the worshipper of a celestial lady whose "art" is a miraculous gift matching the ideal of supernatural "Love," at once his feeling, his beloved, and the deity who rules and instructs him.

Jonson, by contrast, claims here no heavenly inspiration for his "plaine" poetry, even pointedly renounces such a source, for the phrase "any *Muses* praise" is contrasted with simply "mine," not "my Muse's," and with "My praise" rather than "My Muse's praise." He is not the instrument of a supernatural power whose authority therefore depends upon a gift of miraculously purified "art," but a poet whose discrimination of what is praiseworthy derives from his familiarity with "the great" in the historical and social world that produces "a Sydney" as the living embodiment of his ideal. He is also, despite his opening hyperboles, finally not a lover worshipping his celestial lady, but a poet who adopts that role for compliment while speaking as the moral equal of his aristocratic subject, whose "praise" therefore derives further authority from its disinterestedness. What he pronounces is not the truth which "Love" inspires him to find in his own "heart," but what he can "see" and rightly value in the society in which he lives. His role as poet is therefore different from Astrophil's, as the final couplet expresses by its rejection of the hyperbolic, religious, and metaphorical language of the Petrarchan lover in favor of an apparently direct statement, closer to the style at the end of "The Good-morrow" or the valedictions "of Weeping" and "Forbidding Mourning," which makes his compliment to the lady seem "plaine" matter of fact.[17] His "praise . . . where so ere profest" can be seen to be true by any reader capable of recognizing how it "Becomes" the human embodiment of the ideal which it defines, the living representative of what it means to be "a Sydney."

Jonson's manipulations of the expectations evoked by the presence of a speaker seeming to adopt the conventional role of the poet in love are even richer in implications for his definition of his own poetry in *Epigrammes* LXXVI. Although this is not a sonnet, it explicitly invites comparison with Petrarchan love poetry by claiming to concern the speaker's search for "What kinde of creature I could most desire, / To honor, serue, and loue; as *Poets* vse," and by closely paralleling in its larger development and in verbal detail the opening sonnet of *Astrophil and Stella*.[18] Here a comparison to this particular poem, not merely to a conventional type, is clearly demanded, and the fame of Sidney's sequence ensured that Jonson's readers would make the comparison.

Astrophil and Stella begins with a narrative devised as an argument to illustrate the poet-lover's true source of "Invention":

> Loving in truth, and faine in verse my love to show,
> That the deare She might take some pleasure of my paine:
> Pleasure might cause her reade, reading might make her
>   know,
> Knowledge might pitie winne, and pitie grace obtaine,
>   I sought rit words to paint the blackest face of woe,
> Studying inventions fine, her wits to entertaine:
> Oft turning others' leaves, to see if thence would flow
> Some fresh and fruitfull showers upon my sunne-burn'd
>   braine.
> But words came halting forth, wanting Invention's stay,
> Invention, Nature's child, fled step-dame Studie's blowes,
> And others' feete still seem'd but strangers in my way.
> Thus great with child to speake, and helplesse in my throwes,
>   Biting my trewand pen, beating my selfe for spite,
>   'Foole,' said my Muse to me, 'looke in thy heart and write.'

Jonson's speaker tells a parallel story about trying to write a poem, ending, like Astrophil's, with a message from his Muse, of a similarity wittily designed to define large differences:

> On Lvcy Covntesse of Bedford
> This morning, timely rapt with holy fire,
>   I thought to forme vnto my zealous *Muse*,
> What kinde of creature I could most desire,
>   To honor, serue, and loue; as *Poets* vse.
> I meant to make her faire, and free, and wise,
>   Of greatest bloud, and yet more good then great;
> I meant the day-starre should not brighter rise,

Nor lend like influence from his lucent seat.
I meant shee should be curteous, facile, sweet,
    Hating that solemne vice of greatnesse, pride;
I meant each softest vertue, there should meet,
    Fit in that softer bosome to reside.
Onely a learned, and a manly soule
    I purpos'd her; that should, with euen powers,
The rock, the spindle, and the sheeres controule
    Of destinie, and spin her owne free houres.
Such when I meant to faine, and wish'd to see,
    My *Muse* bad, *Bedford* write, and that was shee.

Like Sidney's sonnet, Jonson's poem begins as if it were going
to be the author's account of his efforts to express his "love" in
verse. The speaker portrays himself in the traditional state of the
poet "rapt" with the "holy fire" of divine inspiration and purified
passion, like Petrarch in *Canzoniere* 5, or Astrophil at the conclusion of Sonnet 28,[19] invoking a Muse to write of an adored
lady "as *Poets* vse." Yet the fact that there is so much conscious
effort to do "as *Poets* vse," so much explicit comment on the
speaker's role as poet-lover, calls in question whether he actually
feels what his use of conventional language implies. He does not
sound as if he were "rapt" with flames of either divine inspiration or passionate feeling, for there is something down-to-earth
and practical about being "timely rapt" just "This morning"
when he was getting ready to write a poem. There is also
calculation rather than rapture in "I thought to forme," similar
to Astrophil's self-interested plan to write:

    Loving in truth, and faine in verse my love to show,
    That the deare She might take some pleasure of my paine:
    Pleasure might cause her reade, reading might make her
        know,
    Knowledge might pitie winne, and pitie grace obtaine,
        I sought fit words to paint the blackest face of woe.

Yet the intention of Jonson's speaker is not to "show" his feelings
"in verse" in order to persuade the lady to grant him "grace";
there are no hints that he is driven to write as a means of allevi-

ating "paine," or that he is, despite apparent control, in need of "pitie." His plan is disinterested; his tone detached, almost impersonal; his "deare She" a "kinde of creature." Even his "desire" is deliberately emptied of "fire" by being equated with an earnest wish "to honor, serue, and loue" according to the correct formula, "as *Poets* vse." His wit, unlike Sidney's, does not seem humorously to admit, or even lay claim to, the presence of conflicting feelings.

Lines 5 through 16 then expand the fundamental differences between Jonson's speaker, as he thought of himself "This morning," and the figure of the poet-lover which he was dutifully aspiring to become. This poet did not "in truth" feel himself to be a worshipper or servant seeking "grace" of the sovereign lady, but a creator with power "to forme" a "creature" according to his "desire," perhaps as Pygmalion created the statue of Galatea who became the living object of his passion. His repetitions of "I meant to make her faire . . . I meant . . . I meant . . . I meant . . . " insist on the clarity of his intentions, the assurance of his standards, the power he believed that he commanded to shape a human being, to frame the very "soule" he "purpos'd her." He felt his godlike art extending to the design of the universe, for in granting supremacy to his creation he "meant the day-starre should not brighter rise," and to the control of "destinie" which he would allow the lady to spin for "her owne free houres." This poet assumed miraculous power to create a mythological "creature," combining "each softest vertue" with a "manly soule," and therefore worthy of his supremely discriminating "desire."

Because these lines, describing a past intention which may or may not have been fulfilled, are parallel in position to Astrophil's story of his frustrated search for "fit words" in "others' leaves" instead of drawing inspiration from Stella's image in his "heart," Jonson's reader is led to expect his poet to discover how he also looked to the wrong source for what he sought. Indeed, in the final couplet such expectations seem to be met. This Muse, though less insolently than Astrophil's, seems to chide the speaker for wrong-headed or at least unnecessary efforts, as Phoebus corrects the "Bold head" in *Epigrammes* CXXVI, by teaching him the simplicity of his true task. Instead of trying, so elaborately and self-consciously, to "faine" a fictitious "creature" who would exemplify his ideal, he should merely record the fact that it is already embodied in the Countess of Bedford. The Muse therefore seems to mock the speaker's posturing as a godlike creator and to suggest that his true role is "To honor, serue, and loue" a lady, "as *Poets* vse." This conclusion, among other interpretations, is certainly intended as a playful means of enhancing Jonson's compliment to his subject, and is supported by the truly handsome description given her in the poem, which makes her worthy of honor, service, and love.

The parallel with Sidney's sonnet points to such a reading of the last line, which would at the same time make the message of Jonson's Muse a humorous critique of the lesson to Astrophil as Jonson's poem perceives it. His becomes, by pointed contrast, an admonition to the poet to seek inspiration outside of the demanding confines of his own "desire." His Muse urges the poet's disinterested recognition of the ideal existing independently in the human and social world rather than in his own "heart." This recommendation to the poet is made especially pointed by the advice of the Muse to write "Bedford" rather than "Lvcy." For "Bedford," like "Sydney" and "Cary" in the two epigrams discussed, is the lady's family name and therefore identifies her as existing in time and place outside the poem, like the poet who set out to write it "This morning." It is a name with a wealth of historical associations developed by the poet's language but is in itself neither literary nor metaphorical. Whereas "Lvcy," though also the actual first name of the Countess, has metaphorical implications from its Latin root, *lux*, implications used by Jonson hyperbolically in the couplet which opens—and with slight variation concludes—*Epigrammes* XCIIII, also to the Countess of Bedford:

Lvcy, you brightnesse of our spheare, who are
Life of the *Muses* day, their morning starre!

And again in *The Forrest* XII: "that other starre, that purest
light, / Of all Lvcina's traine; Lvcy the bright."

In *Epigrammes* LXXVI, however, he pointedly refrains from
calling his subject by her Christian name, as in the sonnet he
avoids naming Lady Wroth as Mary, although according to the
etymological account by Jonson's teacher, William Camden, in
his *Remains Concerning Britain*, that name bore the meaning of
"exalted."[20] He perhaps alludes to this etymology in the phrase,
"the great / And glorie of them all," and certainly evokes the
Christian name of the Countess of Bedford in LXXVI by referring to the "day-starre" lending "influence from his lucent seat."
Yet those allusions seem to emphasize still more the point of
"Bedford" appearing where their presence would lead the reader
to expect "Lvcy." For to invoke his ideal as "Lvcy" in the last line
would allow her transformation by the Muse into a metaphorical figure such as he perceives Stella to be in Sidney's sonnet,
whereas to celebrate "Bedford" is to insist on her actuality outside the mythological world created by the language of his
poem. This interpretation of the command bidden by the Muse
is supported by the contrast with the imperative delivered to
Astrophil, as well as by some of the obvious resemblances
between the use of "Bedford" here and the functions of the name
"Sidney" explored in the sonnet "To Mary Lady Wroth," or the
substitution of "Cary" for "Daphne" in *Epigrammes* CXXVI.

Jonson wittily complicates the final contrast with Sidney's
conclusion, however, by his speaker's earlier reference to "my
zealous *Muse*," to whom he would "forme" his ideal. This way
of introducing the classical convention not only casts the Muse
in the role of anxious listener rather than inspiring teacher, but
also suggests by "zealous" that he may be over-eager, officious,
a busy-body, a fanatic moved by exaggerated enthusiasm. The
possibility that Jonson might play such a joke on the traditional
figure of the Muse is supported by his practice in a number of

other poems in which the goddess of poetic inspiration is presented in distinctly human and fallible guises.[21] If, then, in the epigram "On Lvcy Covntesse of Bedford" Jonson is making jokes at the expense of his Muse in similar fashion, it is there described as "zealous" in some playfully derogatory senses, and its intrusion in the last line may be recognized as absurdly unnecessary interference, perhaps even as misguided.

The message of the Muse is superfluous because of course the speaker does not need the reminder that he should "*Bedford* write," for it is obviously from observing that lady that he has derived his criteria for the perfect "kinde of creature" described in a poem already entitled "On Lvcy Covntesse of Bedford." His Muse does not, like Astrophil's (according to his humorously exaggerated account), release him from speechless frustration, but merely "bad" him set down what he already intended, as the title proves.

The chiding of the Muse is misguided as well as unnecessary, however, for it implies that the word "Bedford" alone conveys all that the speaker had attempted to "faine" by the godlike power of his art. What the Muse therefore fails to recognize is that while the associations of the name do provide the poet with his idealizing language, yet it is that art which establishes the meaning and value of those associations. "My *Muse* bad, *Bedford* write, and that was shee" defines a relationship between subject and "praise" closely parallel to that implied in the closing couplet of the sonnet "To Mary Lady Wroth":

> My praise is plaine, and where so ere profest,
> Becomes none more then you, who need it least.

For the referents of the pronouns in the final phrase, "that was shee," are deliberately ambiguous to allow for two interpretations: "that ideal creature whom I intended to invent and actually described in the course of recounting my intentions, turned out to be a recognizable description of the Countess of Bedford"; and, simultaneously, "the Countess of Bedford can be seen to conform perfectly to the ideal woman described in my poem."

The poet's "praise" therefore "Becomes" its subject in the sense that it enhances it, as becoming adornment brings out the essential beauty of its wearer, [22] establishing by its distinct nature as poetry the significance and worth provided by the name "Bedford." The poem also "Becomes" the living, human representative of its ideal in another sense, by itself embodying the identical perfection, so "that was shee."

The mockery from the Muse of the poet's godlike image of himself is then not wholly justified, for by these simultaneous interpretations the poet is both recorder and creator, his power that of maker as well as mirror, his poem at once history and feigning. He is not divinely inspired by the "holy fire" of vision descending from the supernatural world, and yet his mythologized description of the ideal transcends the limits of the temporal and social world. For his lines "On Lvcy Covntesse of Bedford" make the particular, historical embodiments a generalized representative of perfection existing "This morning" in his "thought" but for readers of all times in his poem.

This definition of his poetry is actually explicated in another poem where true praise is again embodied in the subject's name, *The Vnder-wood* LII, Jonson's reply to the painter Burlase, who had idealized him in a flattering portrait:

My Answer
The Poet to the Painter
Why? though I seeme of a prodigious wast,
I am not so voluminous, and vast,
But there are lines, wherewith I might b(e)'embrac'd.

'Tis true, as my wombe swells, so my backe stoupes,
And the whole lumpe growes round, deform'd, and droupes,
But yet the Tun at *Heidelberg* had houpes.

You were not tied, by any Painters Law,
To square my Circle, I confesse; but draw
My Superficies: that was all you saw.

Which if in compasse of no Art it came
To be describ'd (but) by a *Monogram*,
With one great blot, yo'had form'd me as I am.

But whilst you curious were to have it be
An *Archetype*, for all the world to see,
You made it a brave piece, but not like me.

O, had I now your manner, maistry, might,
Your Power of handling shadow, ayre, and spright,
How I would draw, and take hold and delight.

But, you are he can paint; I can but write:
A Poet hath no more but black and white,
Ne knowes he flatt'ring Colours, or false light.

Yet when of friendship I would draw the face,
A letter'd mind, and a large heart would place
To all posteritie; I will write *Burlase*.

The definition of poetry as distinct from painting, presented as
if it were the main argument here, is actually no more seriously
intended than the poet's complimentary differentiation between
Burlase's artistic "Power" and his own relative lack of skill. For
while the poet is, of course, in one sense confined to "black and
white" ink on paper, he has the "Colours" of rhetoric by which
he may as readily as any painter portray his subject in "flatt'ring
. . . or false light." The true distinction argued by the poet is
between the kind of art seeking to present an "Archetype," here
implied to be an idealized abstraction which does not correspond
to its subject, "a brave piece, but not like" the living man it
claims to portray, and the kind of portrait the speaker "would
draw" in the last stanza. He "will write *Burlase*," as the Muse in
Epigrammes LXXVI "bad" the poet simply "*Bedford* write." That
is, he will designate his subject as a particular individual,
identifying him in his poem by the name which differentiates
him as a living human being whose portrait can be compared for
its veracity to his actual person. Yet the poet's praise does not
consist only of the name, as he playfully pretends here and in the
epigrams on Lady Wroth and the Countess of Bedford, but in the
qualities derived from the associations of that name, "A letter'd

All in War with Time

mind, and a large heart." These do themselves represent a kind of "Archetype," of friendship, but one for which he jokingly claims greater validity than the "brave" portrait by Burlase, because this "Archetype" is truly "like"—is embodied in—its subject, the living man, Burlase. The two are equated in his kind of poetry, in which the praise "Becomes" the subject as "the face" which he "would draw" of "friendship" becomes the poem celebrating Burlase, a human being living in the actual historical time shared by the fat and aging poet, whose picture—not idealized but concretely drawn—is also included in the poem, yet eternized "To all posteritie" in his literary portrait.

Jonson's poems of praise differ from Donne's celebrations of perfectly realized love in the *Songs and Sonets* by typically insisting on the speaker's identity as a poet celebrating his ideal in verse to a public audience of readers, using a language which idealizes by generalizing, even mythologizing, individuals and events, and which therefore in these ways seems to resemble more closely the style associated with conventional eternizing verse than that of Donne's characteristic love poems. Such a conclusion would in some ways fit "Her Triumph," as well as many of Jonson's complimentary verses to aristocratic ladies, although these differ from sonnet literature because their titles refer by family name to living individuals and because the posture of the poet-lover is consciously used as a literary device not intended to express the private feelings of a lover for his beloved.

Yet concerns shared with Donne rather than with the Petrarchan sonneteers are defined by the fact that in other poems, such as the sonnet to Lady Wroth and the epigrams praising Mrs. Cary and the Countess of Bedford, Jonson pointedly manipulates language with effects closer to those of Donne's poems. Often by his use of historical names but also by locating his speaker in some specified time, like "This morning," or place such as "Hampton," he denies a separation of the timeless world created by the power of art from the temporal world, where he finds particular embodiments of the ideal. These may include categories—Jonson's "the great, / And glorie of them all" or Donne's "all States, and all Princes"—yet do not cease to be particular or physical. We have seen this authority exercised in the poems built around historical names, and even in a way in "Her Triumph," where the mythologized lady exists in a pastoral world which is nevertheless tangible and concrete, precisely described by physical sensations of sight, touch, and smell which give it a kind of sensual immediacy (not intended by Marlowe's "valleys, groves, hills and fields, / Woods, or steepy mountain") as well as generality. With similar effects in two others of Jonson's best-known poems, "To Penshvrst" and "Inviting a Friend to Svpper," he places his speaker, identified as himself like the speaker in "My Answer" to Burlase, in a concretely pictured setting which he occupies as a poet celebrating its values. But these are experienced by the speaker in such nonliterary acts as eating liberally in the great hall at the Sidneys' home or drinking wine from the Mermaid Tavern. Jonson's speakers, like Donne's, therefore assert a kind of factual validity for their observations or arguments, and so also for their power as poets. They claim accuracy for their ability to "See" and rightly appreciate the things of this world, a very different kind of authority from that asserted most radiantly by the poet-lover in Shakespeare's Sonnet 18, which "giues life" to a miraculously transformed poetic world. The claims for their speakers—Jonson's poets and Donne's lovers—are not less assured, perhaps in the poems discussed, than those of conventional eternizing verse, but they are different in kind, and both Jonson and Donne, we have seen, characteristically identify their distinct kind by the ways in which their speakers differ from eternizing poet-lovers.

Jonson's choice to begin his second volume of shorter poems, *The Forrest*, with one called "Why I Write Not of Love,"[23] suggests an attempt to differentiate himself from other poets by his avoidance of the whole subject, and it is indeed true of Jonson's volumes of shorter poems that they are the first major collections of such verse by an English writer who began work in the 1590s to concern themselves more with other subjects.²⁴ Yet his declaration to "Write Not of Love" is proved untrue of five among the fifteen poems that make up the volume of *The Forrest*, for the opening poem itself, as well as three songs "To Celia" and one entitled "That Women Are Bvt Mens Shaddowes" contradicts his claim, and in *Epigrammes* and *The Vnder-wood* there are also a number of poems, such as "Her Triumph" and the epigrams to Mrs. Cary, Lady Wroth, and the Countess of Bedford, representing Jonson's most characteristic achievement, that treat in some fashion "of Love."

Typically they do so by means which defy the expectations of readers who would presuppose that a poet must inevitably write about love or who would demand an explanation when he does not, readers who therefore assume a conventional equation of poet and lover, if not lover and poet. These assumptions, and the simple identification they imply between versifying and being "in love," are broadly satirized in the opening lines of *The Vnder-wood* XLII, called "An Elegie":

> Let me be what I am, as *Virgil* cold;
>> As *Horace* fat; or as *Anacreon* old;
> No Poets verses yet did ever move,
>> Whose Readers did not thinke he was in love.
> Who shall forbid me then in Rithme to bee
>> As light, and active as the youngest hee
> That from the Muses fountaines doth indorse
>> His lynes, and hourely sits the Poets horse?
> Put on my Ivy Garland, let me see
>> Who frownes, who jealous is, who taxeth me.

The speaker makes fun of himself but also satirizes other poets and readers, whom he accuses of automatically identifying the conventional posture of the poet-lover with honesty of feeling and whom no poet can "ever move" who does not conform to such expectations. He makes other jokes, too, at the expense of writers who assume such a role by ready means,[25] donning the costume of a poet by crowning themselves with an "Ivy Garland" as a guarantee of their sincerity, which will make them successful poets and therefore formidable lovers, worthy of "frownes" from those "jealous" of their mythological charms and powers, who would not feel threatened by the fat, old man undisguised in verse.

Jonson's interest in such a distinction between the living poet and the versified figure of the conventional poet-lover is most often expressed, as here in the satirical opening of *The Vnderwood* XLII, by his creation of a speaker who identifies himself as an aging poet or lover, a device which he did not invent but adapted to his own concerns. The ultimate source for the figure of the aging poet in love was perhaps Horace's "Ode the First. The Fourth Booke," called "To Venus" in Jonson's translation in *The Vnder-wood* LXXXVI:

> *Venus*, againe thou mov'st a warre
> Long intermitted, pray thee, pray thee spare:
> I am not such, as in the Reigne
> Of the good *Cynara* I was: Refraine,
> Sower Mother of sweet Loves, forbeare
> To bend a man, now at his fiftieth yeare
> Too stubborne for commands so slack:
> Goe where Youths soft intreaties call thee back.

Jonson was also familiar with a poem by Anacreon, to which his satirical elegy alludes, where the poet identifies himself as an aging lover:[26]

> On Himself
>
> The women say, Anacreon, you are old. Take a mirror and behold the hairs no longer there; and your forehead is bare. But whether there are hairs or they are gone, I know not; but this I know, that it becomes the more for an old man to play at what is pleasant, by how much the nearer is the period of fate.

In poems by DuBellay, and occasionally in English sonnets, the lover also refers to himself as old,[27] but these references are not

All in War with Time

characteristically used in Jonson's manner as a device for contrasting the actual, flesh-and-blood poet living in time with the conventional figure of the poet-lover mythologized by art. Shakespeare's Sonnet 22, for example, using the kind of language associated with eternizing claims among the lower-numbered sonnets, develops the speaker's reference to being "ould" as an illustration of the facts of temporal experience which the love celebrated in his poem has miraculous power to alter or contradict:

My glasse shall not perswade me I am ould,
So long as youth and thou are of one date,
But when in thee times forrwes I behould,
Then look I death my daies should expiate.
For all that beauty that doth couer thee,
Is but the seemely rayment of my heart,
Which in thy brest doth liue, as thine in me,
How can I then be elder then thou art?

The "elder" lover is transformed into "youth" by the Petrarchan metaphor of exchanging hearts, itself a paradox true to the speaker's feelings despite its contradiction of the physical confinements and separations of living, human bodies growing old in a mutable world.

Jonson uses a speaker who describes himself to be aging, as a way of contrasting the poet living in time and place with the poet versified, in a playfully complimentary verse-letter, *The Vnder-wood* LVI:

Epistle
To My Lady Covell

You won not Verses, Madam, you won mee,
    When you would play so nobly, and so free.
A booke to a few lynes: but, it was fit
    You won them too, your oddes did merit it.
So have you gain'd a Servant, and a Muse:
    The first of which, I feare, you will refuse;
And you may justly, being a tardie, cold,
    Unprofitable Chattell, fat and old,
Laden with Bellie, and doth hardly approach

His friends, but to breake Chaires, or cracke a Coach.
His weight is twenty Stone within two pound;
    And that's made up as doth the purse abound.
Marrie the Muse is one, can tread the Aire,
    And stroke the water, nimble, chast, and faire,
Sleepe in a Virgins bosome without feare,
    Run all the Rounds in a soft Ladyes eare,
Widow or Wife, without the jealousie
    Of either Suitor, or a Servant by.
Such, (if her manners like you) I doe send:
    And can for other Graces her commend,
To make you merry on the Dressing stoole,
    A mornings, and at afternoones, to foole
Away ill company, and helpe in rime
    Your *Joane* to passe her melancholie time.
By this, although you fancie not the man,
    Accept his Muse; and tell, I know you can,
How many verses, Madam, are your Due!
    I can lose none in tendring these to you.
I gaine, in having leave to keepe my Day,
    And should grow rich, had I much more to pay.

Here the speaker's division of himself into two contrasting figures, "a Servant, and a Muse," jokes about the grotesquely wide disparity between the poet in the too solid flesh and his etherialized literary presence, and proclaims his own freedom from the confinements of either figure, since he speaks with as much comic detachment of the "Unprofitable Chattell, fat and old" as of the mercurial Muse who is "nimble, chast, and faire."

This humorously exaggerated impersonality about "the man" as well as "his Muse" further declares his freedom from the conventional role of poet-lover always identified—as in the speaker's declared intention in *Epigrammes* LXXVI "To honor, serue, and loue; as *Poets* vse"—with his position as servant to a sovereign mistress elevated above him. For Jonson's speaker here is no more seriously represented as the lady's servant than as the Muse, herself personified as a kind of attendant, a lady-in-waiting. The speaker's actual identity and relationship to the lady is shown, not by the mock titles of "Servant" or "Muse," but by his easiness in addressing "My Lady Covell," using her real name rather than a mythological or metaphorical title; by the polite social deference of "Madam" combined with playful humor; by the intimacy implied in references to private games and in his familiar view of her in her "Dressing" room on concretely imagined "mornings" and "afternoones," not in a mythological firmament. The tone is as calculatedly distant from that of the Petrarchan poet-lover serving in his verse a celestially elevated lady as the speaker's manner of addressing the lady in Donne's "The Relique."

These poems might imply a definition of the nature and power of poetry contradictory to the one explicated in the "Answer" to Burlase, for they seem deliberately to emphasize the disparity between the fat, old writer and his stylish portrayals of himself in his verse, "as light and active as the youngest hee" in other poetry. This would admit his art to be "a brave piece, but not like me," and therefore to imply a cynically arbitrary relationship, calculated like "flatt'ring Colours, or false light," between the idealizing language sanctioned by literary convention to use about himself in poetry and the realities of his actual experience, which is stubbornly physical and yet ephemeral.

Some such disparity between "the Language, and the Truth" is a satirical concern of part one of "A Celebration of Charis in Ten Lyrick Peeces." The speaker is again presented as an aging poet in love, here with humorous acknowledgment of the traditional view derived from Ovid's *Amores* I, ix, that it is "unseemly for the old man to love":

His Excuse for Loving

Let it not your wonder move,
Lesse your laughter; that I love.
Though I now write fiftie yeares,
I have had, and have my Peeres;
Poëts, though divine, are men:
Some have lov'd as old agen.
And it is not always face,
Clothes, or Fortune gives the grace;

Or the feature, or the youth:
But the Language, and the Truth,
With the Ardor, and the Passion,
Gives the Lover weight, and fashion.
If you then will read the Storie,
First, prepare you to be sorie,
That you never knew till now,
Either whom to love, or how:
But be glad, as soone with me,
When you know, that this is she,
Of whose Beautie it was sung,
She shall make the old man young,
Keepe the middle age at stay,
And let nothing high decay,
Till she be the reason why,
All the world for love may die.

The speaker's "Excuse for Loving" at the inappropriate age of "fiftie" seems at first to be the argument that "Poëts, though divine, are men," a playfully casual reference to the revered theory of supernatural inspiration, which then becomes a broad joke in the suggestion of the next line that their "divine" power is proved in the capacity of poets to love at "fiftie yeares" or at a hundred.

His real "Excuse," however, is expanded in lines 9 through 12:

And it is not always face,
Clothes, or Fortune gives the grace;
Or the feature, or the youth:
But the Language, and the Truth,
With the Ardor, and the Passion,
Gives the Lover weight, and fashion.

This aging poet, like the speakers in the satirical elegy and the "Epistle. To My Lady Covell," defends his freedom to bely the facts of his years, "face, / Clothes, or Fortune." Like them, he calculatedly assumes in his verse the conventional posture of the literary suitor which, by contrast with his actual person, "Gives the Lover weight, and fashion." The word "weight," referring in one sense to the number of pounds acceptable in a would-be lover, recalls the descriptions of the fat old poet in the satirical elegy, the epistle and the "Answer" to Burlase.[28] It also describes an element of literary style, such as Jonson admired in the writing of his teacher, William Camden—"What weight, and what authoritie in thy speech!"—and in the work of "most weighty Savile":[29]

> Where breuitie, where splendor, and where height,
>   Where sweetnesse is requir'd, and where weight.

It is this quality which makes style judicious and convincing, and therefore particularly useful to an aspiring poet-lover who would seduce the lady, above all to one who is old and fat and therefore in need of verbal "weight" to make him presentable by erasing from him the ugly marks of time.

The contrast between the two meanings, the gross bodily "weight" that serves only to "breake Chaires," and the "weight" of style which can persuade, here presumably by disguising the old man as a suitably slim, youthful lover, points to the disparity between the poet in the flesh and his self-portrait in verse. By so doing it emphasizes here, with conscious exaggeration, the self-interest in his theory of "Language." This motive is further underlined by the virtual identification of "weight" or persuasiveness with "fashion" or modishness, an equation elsewhere attacked by Jonson in a prefatory sonnet praising the style of Nicholas Breton:[30]

> Thou, that wouldst finde the habit of true passion,
>   And see a minde attir'd in perfect straines;
> Not wearing moodes, as gallants doe a fashion,
>   In these pide times, only to shewe their braines.

The speaker's "Excuse" is that it is not actual fact but "Language" which "gives the grace," in the sense of persuading the lady to grant him "grace," or "sexual favor," and also with the meanings of endowing the poet-lover with "grace" as a miraculous gift of inspired language and as "gracefulness" in the figure he paints himself to be. This argument, with the puns on "weight" and "grace" referring to both corporal and stylistic qualities, derives from a comparison traditional to literary criticism between style and the human body, a metaphor which Jonson elaborates at length in a passage of *Timber: or, Discoveries*. The first poem to Charis parodies the comparison itself, and also the theory of "Language" as a true image of the "man," which Jonson seriously argues here and elsewhere in his writings:[31]

> *Language* most shewes a man: speake that I may see thee. It springs out of the most retired, and inmost parts of us, and is the Image of the Parent of it, the mind. No glasse renders a mans forme, or likenesse, so true as his speech. Nay, it is likened to a man; and as we consider feature, and composition in a man; so words in Language: in the greatnesse, aptnesse, sound, structure, and harmony of it. Some men are tall, and bigge, so some Language is high and great . . . . Some are little, and Dwarfes: so of speech it is humble, and low, the words poore and flat; the members and *Periods*, thinne and weake, without knitting, or number. The middle are of a just stature. There the Language is plaine, and pleasing: even without stopping, round without swelling; all well-torn'd, compos'd, elegant, and accurate. The vitious Language is vast, and gaping, swelling, and irregular; when it contends to be high, full of Rocke, Mountaine, and pointednesse: as it affects to be low, it is abject, and creeps, full of bogs, and holes . . . . The next thing to the stature, is the figure and feature in Language: that is, whether it be round, and streight . . . or square and firme . . . every where answerable, and weighed. The third is the skinne, and coat. . . . After these the flesh, blood, and bones come in question. Wee say it is a fleshy style, when there is much *Periphrasis*, and circuit of words; and when with more then enough, it growes fat and corpulent . . . It hath blood, and juyce, when the words are proper and apt. . . . but where that wanteth, the Language is thinne, flagging, poore, starv'd, scarce covering the bone; and shewes like stones in a

sack. Some men, to avoid Redundancy, runne into that; and while they strive to have no ill blood, or Juyce, they loose their good. There by some styles, againe, that have not lesse blood, but lesse flesh, and corpulence.

The argument of the prose passage that "*Language* most shewes a man," better than any "glasse renders a mans forme, or likenesse," is wittily adapted in "His Excuse for Loving" to the aging poet's self-interest in disguising his figure by "grace" of "Language" to obtain "grace" of the lady. His intention is to exploit "Truth" to procure her "Beautie," which has miraculous power comparable with that of his poetry to alter the facts of temporal experience:

She shall make the old man young,
Keepe the middle age at stay,
And let nothing high decay,
Till she be the reason why,
All the world for love may die.

Like the beauty of the friend in Shakespeare's Sonnet 22, who can transform the "elder" lover into "youth," Charis can "make the old man young." This miraculous power to arrest time and decay is described in sweeping hyperboles reminiscent of Petrarchan verse, whose metaphors, such as the exchanging of the lovers' hearts, transcend the limits of physical reality by paradoxical assertion of emotional truth. But the source of Charis' more than human power is hinted to be itself physical; like the "divine" nature of poets, it derives from extraordinary sexuality.

Such bawdy suggstions of unusual sexual endowments and prowess, both the lady's and the aging lover's, are even louder in the conclusion of part nine, "Her Man Described by Her Owne Dictamen." There Charis mockingly pretends to portray for "Ben" the conventional young lover who would be acceptable to her in his stead. Her conclusion is in agreement with the poet's argument that it is "not always face, / Clothes, or Fortune" which seduce. At the same time she also rejects with a broad joke his theory that it is "Language" which "gives the grace." For having described in refined detail "what Man would please me," she concludes that she may after all choose to "rest" with her sexually satisfying lover:

> Such a man, with every part,
> I could give my very heart;
> But of one, if short he came,
> I can rest me where I am.

The last joke argues for the supremacy of physical fact over disembodied fancy, and therefore of fat, old "Ben" over the youth mythologized in Charis' description as a Petrarchan lover, "Eye-brows bent like *Cupids* bow." She is made to prefer the actual, living poet because as a flesh-and-blood man he "for love may die" in the punning sexual sense, whereas the literary lover perpetuated as an ideal image can never "die."

These poems, by appearing to sanction the calculated disparity between the writer's versified self-portrait and the facts of his actual experience, seem to argue a definition of poetry contradictory to the ideal posed by the speaker in his "Answer" to Burlase. Yet they propose this definition only satirically. For they explicitly point to the inaccuracy as well as the self-interest—and in Charis' view, the sexual inadequacy—of the mythologized portraits of the poet-lover, and by doing so they give his actual, nonversified bodily presence "weight" in both senses of the pun. For they insist on the reality of his physical existence and desires, which remain unaltered by the gift of "grace" in all its meanings, and also their descriptions of the fat, old poet who must not appear in verse are of course incorporated into the very poems which mockingly pretend to disguise or banish him.

Therefore, although these poems satirically define poetry as "flatt'ring Colours, or false light," they actually use the figure of the aging poet as a device to defend more seriously the kind of poetry the speaker argues for in the "Answer" to Burlase. For the presence of that figure, whose experience extends beyond the world of the poem—like the historical names of Cary, Sidney, Bedford, Burlase—prohibits a separation of an idealized literary world from the physical, historical world.

Jonson's poet-lover, himself actually called by his real name, or rather by its familiar abbreviation, Ben,[32] not appearing as an Astrophil or in the form of a swan, includes love among a lifetime of other experiences, of which writing a poem about love is one. This act, like the immediate situations in which Donne's lovers address their mistresses, occurs in time and place, which are kept "at stay" in the poem, as are Charis' middle-aged lovers, but not excluded from it. These poems therefore define their own nature and power by the way they contrast "Ben," growing gross and old in time's passage, with the figure of the Petrarchan lover arrested permanently in youth, whose "fashion" is humorously assumed by the historical one for the occasion of writing his poem.

The title of the first poem in *The Forrest,* "Why I Write Not of Love," which sounds like the preface to a direct, manly explanation of the poet's intention, is actually a joke about itself similar to *The Vnder-wood* XXIX, called "A Fit of Rime Against Rime," since the poem, while disavowing its matter, in fact concerns more than one meaning "of Love." In this way it also resembles the poems which present the figure of an aging poet in love, while claiming to disguise or exclude him:

Why I Write Not of Love
Some act of *Loue's* bound to reherse,
I thought to binde him, in my verse:
Which when he felt, Away (quoth hee)
Can Poets hope to fetter mee?
It is enough, they once did get
Mars, and my *Mother,* in their net:
I weare not these my wings in vaine.
With which he fled me: and againe,
Into my ri'mes could ne're be got
By any arte. Then wonder not,

That since, my numbers are so cold,
When *Loue* is fled, and I grow old.

Rather than ignoring or dismissing the subject of chief interest to English lyric poets, the poem makes a comment on it which is also, as we have found true of many other poems by Jonson, a reflection on traditional ways of representing it in verse. Its inclusion of such a characteristic comment can partly explain why Jonson placed the poem first in *The Forrest*, why he might have thought it to be suitable as an introduction to his volume, in a position comparable to the addresses "To the Reader," "To My Booke" and "To My Booke-seller," placed at the beginning of his volume of *Epigrammes*.

The poem seems on first reading to be a playful little fable portraying "Loue" in the familiar mythological form such as Jonson uses for compliment in *Epigrammes* CXIIII:

To Mrs. Philip Sydney

I must beleeue some miracles still bee,
    When Sydnyes name I heare, or face I see:
For Cupid, who (at first) tooke vaine delight,
    In meere out-formes, vntill he lost his sight,
Hath chang'd his soule, and made his obiect you:
    Where finding so much beautie met with vertue,
He hath not onely gain'd himselfe his eyes,
    But, in your loue, made all his seruants wise.

The fable in "Why I Write Not of Love" might be merely such a slight entertainment if it were not for the frame constructed for it, which alters the seemingly light-hearted tale, with surprisingly powerful effects. The very disparity between the elegant simplicity and ease with which the poet tells his little story and the ultimate force given the poem by its conclusion expresses Jonson's attitudes here toward "Love" and how poets write about it.

Although the poem creates a first impression of a graceful fable paying playful tribute to classical and Petrarchan models, even the seemingly simple, two-line introduction compresses hints of the complexity of attitudes toward human feeling and its portrayal in poetry which emerges at the end of the poem:

Some act of *Loue's* bound to reherse,
I thought to binde him, in my verse.

This couplet is so neat, the first line so frankly offered as if in explanation of the second, that its ironies are almost hidden by the speaker's blandness. Only the slightest touches cause the reader to question his apparent openness by closer attention to these seemingly transparent lines: the irregular stress in an other-wise metrically regular couplet, causing a heavy accent to fall on "bound," and the added emphasis given to this irregularity by the repetition of sound and meaning in "binde." The casual phrase "bound to," suggesting the poet's eagerness or his dutiful sense of obligation to tell his mythological tale, also contains a metaphor, which the irregular stress emphasizes, of bondage. He is not only an earnest story-teller but a prisoner or slave "bound" by the necessity of recounting "Some act of *Loue's*," perhaps be-cause of the exigencies of his role as poet, for he identifies "my verse" as the imprisoning fetter with which he "thought to binde" love. Perhaps he is also "bound" by the demands of readers to whom it is necessary to give an apology for "Why I Write Not of Love" because they expect the poet inevitably to "reherse" the story of "Loue's" acts. The choice of the verb "reherse," with its close rhyme with "verse," helps to describe this sense of the speaker's bondage. He is forced not simply to "tell," although the verb "reherse" could also have that neutral meaning, but to "re-tell," to "recite" over and over again some story, no matter which, so long as it recounts "Some act of *Loue's*."

This hint that the speaker is "bound" by the conventionality of the poet's role is enlarged in the contemptuous reply he at-tributes to Cupid in the tale itself:

Can Poets hope to fetter mee?
It is enough, they once did get
Mars, and my *Mother*, in their net.

Cupid equates the speaker with all "Poets," not to be differentiated in their ineffectual attempts to capture "Loue." He scorns them as "they," a gang of enemies whose individual efforts—"they once"—are representative of all. He escapes from the speaker, merely one among "Poets" who, because they are poets, artisans like Vulcan, the crippled and elderly husband of Venus, cannot come closer to "Loue" than by weaving a "net" to catch Cupid's amorous mother, as the cuckolded old, lame god captured Venus and Mars (a myth to which Ovid also alludes in the same poem in which he asserts that it is "unseemly for the old man to love").[33]

The concluding address to the reader, like the opening couplet, is also offered with disarming simplicity, as a comment on the effect of the episode narrated in the poem. With the first two lines, they make a frame for the fable, spoken by the poet who recited it, but they are not part of his mythological tale. They are said to the readers who have required the explanation "Why I Write Not of Love" which the fable supposedly provided:

> Then wonder not,
> That since, my numbers are so cold,
> When *Loue* is fled, and I grow old.

The picturesque mythological figure has escaped on his airy wings, and that marks the end of the "act of *Loue's*" which the poet was "bound to reherse." He has paradoxically succeeded in fulfilling that bond, and so has, within the limits of his invented myth, triumphed over "Loue"; and yet that success is called in question, the triumph overshadowed by his final words, "and I grow old." Suddenly the poet speaks, as it were, in his own voice, as a man, out of his personal experience. He is no longer totally identified with his role as rehearser of "verse," no longer simply a representative of "Poets," but an individual human being who is writing but also living and therefore aging and suffering.

The effect of this last phrase is to alter the primary meaning of

"Loue" in the poem. It is no longer chiefly the name for a playful mythological creature, but becomes seriously for the first time a term for human emotion which the aging poet feels has deserted him. If "*Loue* is fled," then his old age is empty, of sexual pleasure—the "act" of love in which Vulcan caught Venus and Mars—but also of affection and tenderness. In his life outside his "arte" he does not triumph over love but is abandoned by it to the lonely realities of aging and dying.

The speaker's last words infuse his explanation of "Why I Write Not of Love" with unexpected sadness, making his playful little fable seem not only an entertainment for his readers but a device for containing or controlling his own feelings by his "arte." They also comment on the nature of that "arte." The poet is expected to "reherse" a story about "Loue" in a pleasing mythological form. By doing so he can manipulate it in such a way as to demonstrate his control over it even if his fable recounts the escape of Cupid from his verse. The paradoxical nature of that triumph—capturing "Loue" in a story about failing to capture "Loue"—is itself a demonstration of the poet's power "in my verse." The last line, however, is spoken as if outside the poem, in recognition of the lover's helplessness to exert the power of "arte" in his own immediate experience, "When *Loue* is fled, and I grow old." This admission points to a distinction between himself as poet and as lover, and to a difference between his language about love as a writer who is "bound to reherse" what the conventions of love poetry dictate, and as a man speaking directly about his own feelings. The very reticence with which he phrases "and I grow old," as a quiet statement of fact, hints at the decorum necessary to his "arte," which would be shattered by less reserved expression of personal feeling. The implication is that perhaps a reason "Why I Write Not of Love" may be that raw, unmythologized feeling would escape or destroy the lover's efforts as poet to fetter it in "ri'mes" and "numbers." Love, its frustrations, betrayals, and desertions, are part of experience in the world of time and change which here remains divided from the world of "verse," its passing not arrested "By any arte."

The convention of the poet-lover as a literary device divided from the actual experience of loving is elaborated in *The Vnderwood* XXII. Here the speaker through the first seven stanzas praises a lady in a manner resembling the celebrations of beauty and virtue in "Her Triumph" and "On Lvcy Covntesse of Bedford." This manner the last stanza then casts in surprising perspective, with effects like those of the conclusion to "Why I Write Not of Love":

An Elegie

Though Beautie be the Marke of praise,
    And yours of whom I sing be such
    As not the World can praise too much,
Yet is't your vertue now I raise.

A vertue, like Allay, so gone
    Throughout your forme; as though that move,
    And draw, and conquer all mens love,
This subjects you to love of one.

Wherein you triumph yet: because
    'Tis of your selfe, and that you use
    The noblest freedome, not to chuse
Against or Faith, or honours lawes.

But who should lesse expect from you,
    In whom alone Love lives agen?
    By whom he is restor'd to men:
And kept, and bred, and brought up true.

His falling Temples you have rear'd,
    The withered Garlands tane away;
    His Altars kept from the Decay,
That envie wish'd, and Nature fear'd.

And on them burne so chaste a flame,
    With so much Loyalties expence,
    As Love, t(o)'aquit such excellence,
Is gone himselfe into your Name.

And you are he: the Dietie
　To whom all Lovers are designed,
　That would their better objects find:
Among which faithful troope am I.

Who as an off'ring at your shrine,
　Have sung this Hymne, and here intreat
　One sparke of your Diviner heat
To light upon a Love of mine.

Which if it kindle not, but scant
　Appeare, and that to shortest view,
　Yet give me leave t(o)'adore in you
What I, in her, am griev'd to want.

The lady to whom his "praise" is addressed is, like the admired
figure in "Her Triumph," a sovereign mistress with power to
"conquer all mens love," although here it is especially her "vertue" (only hinted in the other poem by the pastoral comparisons)
which makes her the beautiful representative of the ideal:

　To whom all Lovers are designed,
　That would their better objects find:
Among which faithful troope am I.

The speaker has "sung this Hymne," consisting of the first seven
stanzas, to elevate her in "triumph" for the "World" to "praise."
His intention as poet matches her achievement as "chaste"
embodiment of true love "restor'd to men," for his desire to
share this lady's perfection with mankind is virtuously disinterested, his position as only one among her "faithful troope" a
fitting tribute to her wide moral influence. As a writer he can
publicly voice his appreciation of this "chaste" lady without conflicting feelings, without confusion of motives, much as the poet
makes us "enjoy" the beauty of "Her Triumph" or as the speaker
in "On Lvcy Covntesse of Bedford" can "honor, serue, and loue"
a virtuous lady in his verse as other *"Poets* vse."

　The speaker's "Hymne" ends in the middle of line 30,
however, as the fable of "Why I Write Not of Love" is completed
before the poem itself ends. The poet then steps out of his liter-

ary role to speak "here" from his immediate experience as a man who, we discover, can publicly "adore" the lady in the poem while privately suffering from another kind of "Love":

Who as an off'ring at your shrine,
    Have sung this Hymne, and here intreat
    One sparke of your Diviner heat
To light upon a Love of mine.

Which if it kindle not, but scant
    Appeare, and that to shortest view,
    Yet give me leave t(o)'adore in you
What I, in her, am griev'd to want.

Because the word "Love" in Petrarchan poetry so often refers to the poet-lover's emotion as well as his beloved, the reader may first interpret the entreaty of stanza eight as a prayer that the speaker's feeling of "Love" may be as elevated as its "Diviner" object, who would be the "chaste" lady of his "Hymne." Yet in stanza nine, with the mention of "her," we learn that the speaker is now alluding to a woman not in the poem he has "sung," making "a Love of mine" refer to "her" as well as to his feeling. What he tells about "her" is first that she is "mine," which distinguishes her from the lady in the "Hymne," who is the object of "all mens love." They are further contrasted then by the speaker's confession that "I, in her, am griev'd to want" what he can "adore" in his poetic ideal, her chastity. According to this interpretation, "want" means "desire." The poet can "adore" in a versified lady the "vertue" which, in his beloved, causes him painful frustration. The moral values which easily win his affirmation and "praise" in literature he wryly perceives to be in conflict with his desires as a man in love.

A further division between the attitudes appropriate to the role of poet and the actual feelings of the speaker in his private experience of "Love" is allowed by the possibility that "want" can mean both "desire" and "lack." If the speaker is in this sense "griev'd to want" virtue in his mistress, then his prayer in stanza eight may be read as a plea that the lady in the poem will grant her "Diviner heat" to a woman of less "chaste a flame" so that she too will confine herself "to love of one," himself. This reading exposes further conflict in the speaker between the conventional posture of the poet assumed in his "Hymne" and his experience as a man living in the actual, physical world where celestial fire may "but scant / Appeare, and that to shortest view" amid the swiftly changing heats of bodily passion. For although as the poet in the "Hymne" he recognizes that only "vertue" is truly loveable, his capacity to grieve in private over an unvirtuous lady means that his feelings are not controlled by his literary values or his language. In verse he portrays himself as a celebrant who can only "adore" a virtuous lady, but as a man he cares and suffers for an unworthy woman. Like the conclusion to "Why I Write Not of Love," the simple brevity of his comment on the experience of loving hints at the impossibility, if not the impropriety, of portraying it in poetry which, as he defines it, is meant to promote the "triumph" of "vertue." The verbal play on "want," like the witty paradox of Cupid's flight from the poem that recounts it, seems an attempt to contain otherwise unadorned feeling by means which transform it into matter appropriate for poetry. Yet the final, crucial word "want" allows meanings which are conflicing or even contradictory. It therefore compresses within itself the lover's awareness of the confusion of motives and values he experiences in the physical, mutable world, yet which as poet, performing what he sees as his proper role—to "praise"—he must exclude from his "Hymne."

The conclusions or frames of both "An Elegie" and "Why I Write Not of Love" place the poet in a world outside his verse and therefore in space and time, as Jonson locates him in other poems by devices previously discussed, and as Donne's lovers are characteristically placed—by reminders of their immediate situations, of impending or remembered events, or, in "The Canonization," of increasing age in "My five gray haires." The final mention in "Why I Write Not of Love" that the poet grows "old" contrasts Jonson's speaker with a literary lover like Marlowe's "Passionate Shepherd," who exists with his beloved in a metaphorical landscape on a perpetual "May-morning" which grants them immunity to time. The speaker in "Why I Write Not of Love" could remain in such an unaging state if he did not step out of his mythologized tale in the last line, to speak of his experience in the passing world which the expectations of his readers would exclude from his "verse." The effect is different here from that of the references to fat, old "Ben" in other poems discussed. For it shows much more painful awareness of the ineradicable difference between the poet as a figure in his own verse, successfully manipulating his invented myths, and the living poet, helpless to control the flux of experience, growing old in lonely lovelessness.

The significance of this difference may be further explored in another of the poems which belie Jonson's claim to "Write Not of Love," *The Vnder-wood* IX. The title of this poem, "My Picture Left in Scotland," has an effect comparable to the phrase "I grow old" of locating the act of writing in the continuum of the speaker's temporal experience. The title gives a specificity of reference totally different in effect, for example, from the general category of pastoral to which Marlowe's title assigns "The Passionate Shepherd to His Love," but comparable to Jonson's "To His Lady, Then Mrs. Cary" and also many devices in Donne's *Songs and Sonets,* such as the lover's invitation in "The Blossome" to "Meet mee at London, then, / Twenty dayes hence." For Jonson's speaker, by announcing in the title that he has been to Scotland and has since come away, presumably to another unmythologized place, identifies himself in the first person as an individual with a personal history from which he speaks, as the poet in "Why I Write Not of Love" steps out of his fable to speak in the last line of that poem. Here the title directs the reader's response in ways distinct from what would be the effects of such a conventional title as "Complaint of a Louer Rebuked,"[34] which would place the speaker as well as the poem in a timeless literary category, and would define the range of expression decorous for such a figure. Jonson's title, by pointed contrast, announces that his poem will concern a particular experience of an individual person preceding the present moment "now" when he reflects on it in the following lines:

My Picture Left in Scotland

I now thinke, Love is rather deafe, then blind,
 For else it could not be,
   That she,
Whom I adore so much, should so slight me,
 And cast my love behind:
I'm sure my language to her, was as sweet,
   And every close did meet
  In sentence, of as subtile feet,
    As hath the youngest Hee,
 That sits in shadow of *Apollo's* tree.

Oh, but my conscious feares,
  That flie my thoughts betweene,
  Tell me that she hath seene
  My hundred of gray haires,
  Told seven and fortie years,
Read so much wast, as she cannot imbrace
 My mountaine belly, and my rockie face,
And all these through her eyes, have stopt her eares.

The poem begins with five lines which could almost be the opening stanza of a song entitled "Complaint of a Louer Rebuked," in which the speaker imagines himself the victim of Cupid because "That she, / Whom I adore" has rejected his "love." Yet if the first line seems conventional in its allusion to the traditional figure of Cupid, it actually describes an alteration of the convention, as the lover views it in the course of his changing experience. For the speaker once uncritically believed the traditional legend that "Love" is "blind," but "now" experience has forced him to revise his belief, because it failed him when he acted according to it, when he performed in the fashion appropriate to a follower of the "blind" god of "Love." This past performance he describes in the second group of five lines, having their own intricate pattern which sounds like a variation of the rhythms, alliteration, and assonance of the first five and repeats the rhyme sounds of lines 2, 3, and 4 in the final couplet:

> I'm sure my language to her, was as sweet,
> And every close did meet
> In sentence, of as subtile feet,
> As hath the youngest Hee,
> That sits in shadow of *Apollo's* tree.

Plaintively he describes how strictly he followed the rules for the poet-lover dictated by his belief in "blind" Cupid, and with what "sure" success he shaped his "language" to be as persuasively "sweet" and nimble as the "youngest" poet-lover. This comparison, although it is phrased in mellifluous cadences, containing pastoral and mythological associations "meet" for a love song, introduces the incongruous fact that this poet-lover is no longer young, except in the verses he addressed to the lady. There he portrayed himself as a conventional poet-lover, lightly tripping on "subtile feet"—like the cadences of his song—or reposing in eternal youth and leisure in the timeless landscape of a pastoral.

Yet the pun on "feet," like the double meaning of "weight" in the aging poet's "Excuse for Loving" Charis, stresses the difference between "feet" in poetry, which may be skillfully designed to persuade the lady, and the cumbersome "feet" of an aging lover who cannot compete in the flesh, as he attempts to do in "language," with the "youngest Hee, / That sits in shadow of *Apollo's* tree." The double meaning evokes a double "Picture." It paints an Arcadian scene of garlanded youths, singing and dancing or elegantly reposing in shady groves on some unchanging "May-morning," as in Marlowe's pastoral love song. At the same time it pictures that landscape with a no longer "youthful" poet resting in "shadow" which does not entirely hide his aging body.

The disparity between these two pictures is of course made more humorously incongruous but also sadder,[35] even more painful, by the last eight lines of the poem, which abandon the stanzaic pattern, the song-like cadences and soft *e* and *s* sounds, with the mythological allusiveness of the first ten lines. These changes in "language" mark the speaker's shift from describing his past efforts, when he acted as a true believer in "blind" Cupid, to uttering his present "feares," which are "conscious" in the archaic sense of "inwardly aware," perhaps even "guiltily privy to," with a private knowledge contrasted—with "but"—to what he presented publicly in verse:

> Oh, but my conscious feares,
> > That flie my thoughts betweene,
> > Tell me that she hath seene
> > My hundred of gray haires,
> > Told seven and fortie years,
> Read so much wast, as she cannot imbrace
> My mountaine belly, and my rockie face,
> And all these through her eyes, have stopt her eares.

His "conscious feares" paint a new "Picture" of the speaker, which is also a different kind of poem with a less intricate, song-like metrical and rhyme scheme, a coarser diction and harsher sound patterns, and one which he inwardly knows that the lady has "Read." In this verbal portrait he appears neither as the youthful lover of his own pastoral songs nor as the aging poet viewed from a distance "in shadow of *Apollo's* tree." Here he is seen and described in concretely observed detail which insists on his grossly physical nature. This description lifts him out of pastoral myth by precisely locating him in the passage of "seven and fortie years"—not the even fifty associated with the Horation convention of the aging poet—and by likening him to ugly objects in the natural world. The descriptive terms for "My mountaine belly, and my rockie face" are no longer "sweet," "meet" or "subtile." They are in fact very like the terms used by Jonson in the previously quoted passage from *Timber: or Discoveries* to describe "vitious Language" which is "vast, and gaping, swelling, and irregular; when it contends to be high, full of Rocke, Mountaine, and pointednesse."[36] The physical form which the lady has "Read" is a "vitious" corruption of nature, a work written in the ugly and "irregular" language of time, which does not mellow or enrich but lays "wast," made grimly humorous by the pun on "waiste" and "waste matter" or "waste land" (as in the "Answer" to Burlase). It is this work of time, the poem or "Picture" of the speaker's body, which he fears the lady cannot "imbrace" in the double sense of "accept" and "take in her arms." The hard and irreducible reality of his actual existence has destroyed the transforming power of "language." Myth has proved helpless to contradict or alter fact, and the "subtile feet" of poetry have not contained feeling, which can "flie" out of the poet-lover's control as it seems to erupt in the harsher, looser form of the last ten, unmythologized lines. There the poet breaks out of his pastoral song into present speech, as the speaker in the frame of "Why I Write Not of Love" steps out of his fable to address the reader from his actual experience. In both poems the sadness, even grimness, of the aging poet's existence is barely contained by the wit and grace of the poems themselves. When in the last line of "My Picture Left in Scotland" the speaker alludes once more to the myth of Cupid, stepping back into the poetic convention developed in the song-like beginning of his poem—"And all these through her eyes, have stopt her eares"—this seems to be not simply a playful turn of logic for the entertainment of the reader but an effort to control unmythologized feeling by picturing it in a form "meet" for poetry.

This concern for the relation between the power of poetry, which creates a timeless, regular, and decorous world, and the force of uncontrolled feeling in the world vulnerable to time and change, is at the heart of Jonson's most moving poem, *Epigrammes* XLV. There he writes "of Love," not in the particular senses defined by the traditions of verse to which his previously discussed poems are related, but as the most representative, inclusive, and painful of all human emotions.[37]

This poem, "On My First Sonne," begins with four lines combining the conventional "Farewell" of the classical epitaph with traditional Christian language of consolation:

> Farewell, thou child of my right hand, and ioy;
>   My sinne was too much hope of thee, lou'd boy,
> Seuen yeeres tho'wert lent to me, and I thee pay,
>   Exacted by thy fate, on the iust day.

Jonson uses the same argument in *The Vnder-wood* LXIII:

> To K. Charles, and Q. Mary.
> For the Losse of Their First-borne,
> An Epigram Consolatorie
> Who dares denie, that all first-fruits are due
>   To God, denies the God-head to be true:
> Who doubts, those fruits God can with gaine restore,
>   Doth by his doubt, distrust his promise more.
> Hee can, he will, and with large int'rest pay,
>   What (at his liking) he will take away.
> Then, Royall Charles, and Mary, doe not grutch
>   That the Almighties will to you is such:
> But thanke his greatnesse, and his goodnesse too;
>   And thinke all still the best, that he will doe.
> That thought shall make, he will this losse supply
>   With a long, large, and blest posteritie!
> For God, whose essence is so infinite,
>   Cannot but heape that grace, he will requite.

The epitaph "On My First Sonne" adds to this doctrine that God only "lent" the child to its human parents and therefore may justly take it away, the equally traditional argument of lines 5 through 8:

>   For why
> Will man lament the state he should enuie?
> To haue so soone scap'd worlds, and fleshes rage,
>   And, if no other miserie, yet age?

The same combination of Christian consolations is contained in lines 77 through 84 from *The Vnder-wood* LXXXIII, to the bereaved parents of Lady Jane Pawlet:

> Goe now, her happy Parents, and be sad,
>   If you not understand, what Child you had.
> If you dare grudge at Heaven, and repent

T'have paid againe a blessing was but lent,
And trusted so, as it deposited lay
   At pleasure, to be call'd for, every day!
If you can envie your owne Daughters blisse,
   And wish her state lesse happie then it is!

If in the two consolations to other bereaved parents these arguments seem unconvincing, the reason may be in part a modern
reader's skepticism or uneasiness about the persuasiveness of the
arguments themselves, but more pertinently some distaste for
the complacency with which the poet seems to educate the
anguished parents in their proper feelings. For the same traditional arguments do not jar falsely in *Epigrammes* XXII:

On My First Daughter

Here lyes to each her parents ruth,
Mary, the daughter of their youth:
Yet, all heauens gifts, being heauens due,
It makes the father, lesse, to rue.
At six moneths end, shee parted hence
With safetie of her innocence;
Whose soule heauens Queene, (whose name shee beares)
In comfort of her mothers teares,
Hath plac'd amongst her virgin-traine:
Where, while that seuer'd doth remaine,
This graue partakes the fleshly birth.
Which couer lightly, gentle earth.

The "ruth" admitted in the first line, the necessity to restrain
grief hinted throughout by the avoidance of the first person, the
delicacy of the myth placing the child's soul in the heavenly
train, the tenderness of the father's final farewell, all make the
doctrinal arguments seem less difficult to reconcile here with
personal feeling than when they are delivered as moral lessons
by the poet to other mourners.

In "On My First Sonne," however, the traditional consolations are unconvincing, not because of a failure in Jonson's
tone, but because the epitaph is itself concerned with the inadequacy of conventional language to control the painful force of

human feeling in the face of "age" and death:

On My First Sonne

Farewell, thou child of my right hand, and ioy;
   My sinne was too much hope of thee, lou'd boy,
Seuen yeeres tho'wert lent to me, and I thee pay,
   Exacted by thy fate, on the iust day.
O, could I loose all father, now. For why
   Will man lament the state he should enuie?
To haue so soone scap'd worlds, and fleshes rage,
   And, if no other miserie, yet age?
Rest in soft peace, and, ask'd, say here doth lye
   Ben. Ionson his best piece of *poetrie.*
For whose sake, hence-forth, all his vowes be such,
   As what he loues may neuer like too much.

Because the exclamation—"O, could I loose all father, now"—interrupts the official arguments against grieving, it denies their consolatory power for the speaker in the act of reciting them. The biblical and classical formulations, which have logical validity when applied to the emotions of representative "man" for a generalized "state" of mortality, cannot contain his individual feelings. These arguments would perhaps convince him if he "could . . . loose all father, now" in the sense of escaping his actual human relationship to the child, which would be to exempt himself from individual suffering as the moralistic poet in the two consolatory poems to other parents seems to be free of it.

In another sense, to "loose all father, now" suggests the speaker's longing to break out of the controlling conventions of epitaph poetry and biblical language used in the first four lines, as he actually does in the exclamation, letting "loose" the feelings which the decorum of his poem fails to contain. Yet the cry, "O, could I," implies that he would but cannot let "loose" his feelings, which are either unutterable or at least incapable of inclusion in the language of poetry. He is therefore compelled to return to a generalized, public manner deriving its authority from its traditional acceptance, and making possible the rhetorical questions which predict a conventional response:

> For why
> Will man lament the state he should enuie?
> To haue so soone scap'd worlds, and fleshes rage,
>   And, if no other miserie, yet age?

The speaker here seems to assent to this argument, although perhaps not so much because of its traditional weight as for his awareness of his own present "miserie" and "age," which at least his son will never have to experience.[38] He therefore appears to have made some adjustment of his individual feelings to the conventions of epitaph poetry and Christian prayer:

> Rest in soft peace, and, ask'd, say here doth lye
> Ben. Ionson his best piece of *poetrie.*

For the first time in this epigram, the speaker identifies himself as a poet, with power to triumph over mortality in his eternizing art. By transforming his son—using a pun on the Greek meaning of "poet" as "maker"[39]—into the metaphor of "his best piece of *poetrie,*" he has lifted him out of timebound human experience and endowed him with an immortal voice. The dead boy has, by the power of the speaker's art, become a poem which can "say" forever the name of its creator. In this eternizing conceit both poet and child-transformed-into-poem seem to have "scap'd" the temporal world and therefore the pain of separation by death.

Yet the speaker's metaphorical language has simultaneously transformed the boy-poem into a tombstone marking the buried body of the child with a message that can only mock the father, whose efforts in verse cannot save the life of his son. The eternizing conceit immortalizes "Ben. Ionson his best piece of *poetrie,*" but not the living relationship between parent and child which no art can rescue from mortality. In order to eternize his son, he has had to "loose" his fatherhood, has had to identify himself wholly with the role of poet, to speak no longer as a parent. This loss or renunciation is shown by his avoidance, after the one outburst of feeling, of the pronouns "my," "me," "I," "thou," "thee," so prominent in the first five lines, and by the exclusion of terms for their human bonds, "Sonne," "child," "father," or of any tender epithet such as "lou'd boy." If he has eternized the child, that achievement depends on his attempted renunciation of their living, human relationship and his exclusion of personal feeling. This accomplishment is expressed in the final couplet of the poem. By comparison with the grieving intimacy of the opening line—"Farewell, thou child of my right hand, and ioy"—it is severely impersonal and restrained, in the use of "his" and "what" to replace "I" and "thee," and in the reduction of "what he loues" to the meanness of "may neuer like." The effect of such severity is to seem cramped or contorted more than controlled:

> For whose sake, hence-forth, all his vowes be such,
> As what he loues may neuer like too much.

Like the frame of "An Elegie," these lines point to the division between the feelings and values acceptable in verse and the speaker's private experience. They call in question the triumph of the eternizing conceit and the consolatory power of the poet's conventional language. What he appears to have recognized is that he must "loose" in the sense of "be deprived of" all fatherhood to rescue his child by mythologizing him in a poem. Furthermore, to achieve that transformation he must not let "loose" his expressions of love or "miserie," but must control them in a poetic language which is not capable of containing the full force of painful human feeling. To write an epitaph, he must identify himself wholly with his role as poet, as in the "Epitaph on S(alomon) P(avy)" to be discussed,[40] offering traditional consolations to "man." To do so he must strip himself of the actual human relationships and private emotions he experiences outside of art, in the mutable world where eternizing "poetrie" cannot hold back "age," with its inevitable "miserie," or death.

Like "Why I Write Not of Love," "An Elegie," and "My Picture Left in Scotland," this epitaph presents a poet speaking out of his immediate experience in the historical and social world about a division between that world and his art, which must mythologize his actual experience in order to represent it in poetry. These poems therefore locate the poet as an individual in time and place whose act of writing is in a continuum of other experiences which its conventional, generalized, or mythological language makes a not wholly successful effort to control. Unlike other poems by Jonson of the kinds previously discussed, these contrast the actual poet with his presentation in verse in order to mark a division between experience in the world subject to time and change and loss, and its rendering in poetry. These poems therefore leave the reader with a painful awareness of what their art has been made to exclude.

By creating such an effect they point to a deliberate imposition of limits necessary for poetry, which allows the possibility that its authority may be in some ways arbitrary. In this respect they imply attitudes toward experience and its portrayal by the poet different from those which other poems by Jonson share with either Donne's *Songs and Sonets* or the eternizing sonnets of Shakespeare. These implied attitudes we shall find argued in more radical terms and to more extreme conclusions in poems by Marvell.

4
Marvell

The exploration—in Shakespeare's sonnets, in Donne's *Songs and Sonets* and in Jonson's verse—of the struggle in poetry between love and time, contributed its fullness to Marvell's best known poem, "To His Coy Mistress." The special glamor and assurance, the urbanity and energy, the sense of vastness charged with intensity which the poem unmistakably creates, even on first reading, is enhanced when it is set in the context of earlier poetic explorations which it includes, absorbs, and recreates.[1] The poem incorporates the wealth offered to a greatly gifted writer by the body of verse previously discussed, which of course also included richly various connections among particular poems as well as adaptations of the traditions of classical, Italian, and French love poetry. Marvell's poem seems a climax to the fusion of poetic conventions with the questioning, transforming, parodying, or rejecting of those conventions common to many of Shakespeare's sonnets and to much of the love poetry of Donne and Jonson. Furthermore, like the literature from which it grows, "To His Coy Mistress" deliberately evokes the reader's awareness of its relationship with this body of poetry, and, in a manner especially characteristic of Marvell's own writing, it does so by pointed allusions to some particular poems, on which it seems explicitly to comment, with as strongly shaping effects as Jonson created by the close parallels between his poem "On Lvcy Covntesse of Bedford" and the opening sonnet of *Astrophil and Stella*.

Marvell's title places his poem in the category of persuasions to love, such as Astrophil desired to write that he might "grace obtaine" from the lady, while his first line relates the form of that persuasion to other such poetry in which the lover struggles to assert his power over the "World" and "Time":

To His Coy Mistress

Had we but World enough, and Time,
This coyness Lady were no crime.
We would sit down, and think which way
To walk, and pass our long Loves Day.
Thou by the *Indian Ganges* side
Should'st Rubies find: I by the Tide
Of *Humber* would complain. I would
Love you ten years before the Flood:
And you should if you please refuse
Till the Conversion of the *Jews*.
My vegetable Love should grow
Vaster then Empires, and more slow.
An hundred years should go to praise
Thine Eyes, and on thy Forehead Gaze.
Two hundred to adore each Breast:
But thirty thousand to the rest.
An Age at least to every part,
And the last Age should show your Heart.
For Lady you deserve this State;
Nor would I love at lower rate.
  But at my back I alwaies hear
Times winged Charriot hurrying near:
And yonder all before us lye
Desarts of vast Eternity.
Thy Beauty shall no more be found;
Nor, in thy marble Vault, shall sound
My ecchoing Song: then Worms shall try
That long preserv'd Virginity:
And your quaint Honour turn to dust;
And into ashes all my Lust.
The Grave's a fine and private place,
But none I think do there embrace.
  Now therefore, while the youthful hew
Sits on thy skin like morning dew,
And while thy willing Soul transpires
At every pore with instant Fires,

Now let us sport us while we may;
And now, like am'rous birds of prey,
Rather at once our Time devour,
Than languish in his slow-chapt pow'r.
Let us roll all our Strength, and all
Our sweetness, up into one Ball:
And tear our Pleasures with rough strife,
Thorough the Iron gates of Life.
Thus, though we cannot make our Sun
Stand still, yet we will make him run.

The title identifies the speaker as a lover addressing the lady to whom he offers an argument against "This coyness." That phrase identifies the situation in which he is speaking, and makes his persuasion a direct response to her protestations of real or feigned reluctance. The poem therefore has the immediacy and privacy provided by the situations typical in Donne's *Songs and Sonets.*

His manner of speaking after this explanatory opening couplet identifies him as a lover who is also a poet, or who would apparently be willing to adopt that role, "Had we but World enough, and Time." As an alternative to their actual situation, he describes himself and the lady resting or wandering in "our long Loves Day," which, like "each May-morning" in Marlowe's pastoral persuasion, seems to be offered as an imagined ideal transcending the limits of time and place, here spanning the "World" from the "Ganges" to the "Humber" and "Time" from "the Flood" to "the last Age." He is portrayed in the posture of the poet-lover reclining beside the river where he has retired to "complain," the term for one genre of Petrarchan verse, or in the act of inventing "praise," the formal name for another sort of poetry, here incorporating both the blazon, in which each "part" of the lady's beauty receives its appropriate compliment, and the eternizing poem in which "the last Age should show your Heart" to those future readers existing at the end of time.

Because these lines are cast in the conditional tense—emphasized by the opening "Had we," followed by many repetitions of "would" and "should"—the speaker playfully disavows the poetry he is in the act of writing, pretending that he "would" like to or "should" (perhaps in the sense of "ought to") "complain," "praise," and eternize but is prevented from doing so by the limitations of "World enough, and Time." Yet because his disavowal is only playful, because he does permit himself leisure to invent an elegant and unhurried pastoral setting in which the lady may be eternally admired, he seems less helpless in subjection to time than he pretends. Also suspect, therefore, are his claims for the manner in which he would choose to "love" if time granted him the power of choice:

> For Lady you deserve this State;
> Nor would I love at lower rate.

The deference of the title, "Lady," and the acknowledgment of her desert, the connotations of majesty, sovereign power, permanence and order in "State" are wittily at odds with "rate," which would be taken to mean simply "rate or speed of time passing" if it were not described as "lower." This adjective makes "rate" part of a financial metaphor in which the "praise" counted out by the poet for each "part" of the lady is his contribution to a bargain, while hers must be to sell her favor once the "rate" is raised to the deserved height.

The lover's fanciful alternative to their real situation, therefore, at the same time that it acknowledges the attraction of leisured and opulent poetic persuasion by parodying the conventions of this poetry, emphasizes what he sees as their cynical self-interest, especially by including all the numbering reminiscent of lines from Jonson's translation of Catullus in *The Forrest* VI:[2]

> Kisse, and score vp wealthy summes
> On my lips, thus hardly sundred,
> While you breath. First giue a hundred,
> Then a thousand, then another
> Hundred, then vnto the tother
> Adde a thousand . . .

The bargaining implied by Marvell's metaphor of the "lower rate," as well as the extravagant literalness of assigning specified numbers of years to each "part" recalls poems like "Loves Infiniteness," in which Donne's speaker, with apparent sincerity and in a matter-of-fact tone, drives the implications of a conventional metaphor to absurdly literal conclusions, as the first stanza illustrates:

> If yet I have not all thy love,
>   Deare, I shall never have it all;
> I cannot breath one other sigh, to move,
>   Nor can intreat one other teare to fall.
> All my treasure, which should purchase thee,
>   Sighs, teares, and oathes, and letters I have spent,
> Yet no more can be due to mee,
>   Then at the bargaine made was ment.
> If then thy gift of love were partiall,
> That some to mee, some should to others fall,
>   Deare, I shall never have Thee All.

The speaker's offering "To His Coy Mistress" of his parody of poetic "praise" points, like Donne's, to the self-serving uses of its conventions, but also to their prurience, by the arrangement of details in the anatomical order characteristic of the blazon, an example of which is contained in lines 13 to 42 of Jonson's fifth poem in "A Celebration of Charis." There the poet-lover composes a series of compliments which Cupid mistakes for a description of Venus:

> So hath *Homer* prais'd her haire;
> So, *Anacreon* drawne the Ayre
> Of her face, and made to rise,
> Just above her sparkling eyes,
> Both her Browes, bent like my Bow.
> By her lookes I doe her know,
> Which you call my Shafts. And see!
> Such my Mothers blushes be,
> As the Bath your verse discloses
> In her cheekes, of Milke, and Roses;
> Such as oft I wanton in!

And, above her even chin,
Have you plac'd the banke of kisses,
Where, you say, men gather blisses,
Rip'ned with a breath more sweet,
Then when flowers, and West-winds meet.
Nay, her white and polish'd neck,
With the Lace that doth it deck,
Is my Mothers! Hearts of slaine
Lovers, made into a Chaine!
And betweene each rising breast,
Lyes the Valley, cal'd my nest,
Where I sit and proyne my wings
After flight; and put new stings
To my shafts! Her very Name,
With my Mothers is the same.
I confesse all, I replide,
And the Glasse hangs by her side,
And the Girdle 'bout her waste,
All is *Venus:* save unchaste.

By following the same direction as Jonson's "praise," stripping it of elaboration beyond the naming of increasingly seductive parts, and ending with the enthusiastic exclamation, "But thirty thousand to the rest," Marvell's lover makes almost as broad a joke as Donne's in "Loves Progress," who argues in similar detail against the conventional view that such "Progress" should begin "at the face" in favor of those who, because they "Rather set out below; practise my art." The parodic "art" of Marvell's speaker, like Donne's, reveals the titillating effects of the kind of "praise" for which his mistress bargained; like Jonson's, it makes fun of the refined attempt to disguise that prurience by placing the highest "rate" on the poet's power to show posterity her "Heart" in his immortal verse as "Ben" makes the high point of his blazon the chastity of Charis. These revelations, of course, make questionable the speaker's commitment to the role of the poet-lover he should adopt if only the exigencies of his actual experience would permit.

The kind of poetry parodied in this first part, although it must have some appeal for the speaker who, however playfully, indulges in it, clearly has greater attraction for the lady, who seems to equate "love" wholly with eternizing "praise," whereas he certainly does not accept this equation. For the imagined ideal in which the speaker claims he would participate if his actual situation were not subject to passing time, while elegant and easy, is portrayed as eternally unfulfilled. It is a "long Loves Day" with no night of love to follow, a timeless poetic state to be enjoyed only by such wholly literary figures as the "Passionate Shepherd" and his beloved in Marlowe's song. Because the speaker in "To His Coy Mistress" phrases this image in a conditional form, as an alternative to his immediate situation, he makes a distinction between himself as a man in love and the mythologized poet-lover he "would" become in the complaining, praising, and eternizing poems which he claims insufficient time to write. In those verses he could exercise a poet's power to arrest time in a world without the limitations and confinements imposed by physical existence and therefore also without compelling desires, but in actual experience he cannot.

In the second part of the poem he again begins by pressing the argument that time rather than love sets the limits of human experience. Because "But" introduces these lines as an alternative in opposition to the first passage, it seems to predict that the lover will make a counter-argument to his first conditional fantasy by speaking out in his own person, not as a mythologized poet-lover. The brutal sexual joking about worms, the degradation of "love" to "Lust" and "dust," the fear and horror evoked in the speaker by his vision of the future, all contrast with his earlier, elegant fantasy by their seemingly realistic toughness. Yet in this second part he presents another imagined setting in which again he and the lady exist as conventional figures in an eternizing poem:

> But at my back I alwaies hear
> Times winged Charriot hurrying near:
> And yonder all before us lye
> Desarts of vast Eternity.
> Thy Beauty shall no more be found;

> Nor, in thy marble Vault, shall sound
> My ecchoing Song: then Worms shall try
> That long preserv'd Virginity:
> And your quaint Honour turn to dust;
> And into ashes all my Lust.
> The Grave's a fine and private place,
> But none I think do there embrace.

He is again a poet-lover whose "ecchoing Song" sounds forever in celebration of the lady. It is "ecchoing" in the sense of "unending" but also "repetitive" and "imitative" and most meanly "reverberating" outside the "marble Vault" in which she lies buried while the poet-lover remains alive. This is an unmistakable "ecchoing" of language conventional to such eternizing poems as Shakespeare's Sonnet 55:

> Not marble, nor the guilded monument,
> Of Princes shall out-liue this powrefull rime.

Yet this language is used here to remind the lady of poetry's powerlessness to save her from physical death, as the noblest tomb will fail to protect her body from decay. Like the first imagined setting, this is in its own way a literary image of a world in which "Times winged Charriot," a mythologized sun, is forever "hurrying near" but perpetually—"alwaies"—arrested in its passage. It is a world of "vast Eternity" evoked by the speaker's art, endlessly unfulfilled like "our long Loves Day" but more static and more frighteningly empty, arid as deserts, cruelly lifeless and confining as a "marble Vault" or by implication as the kind of poem for which such a memorializing monument is a conventional metaphor. In this passage the lover has therefore again composed for the lady the verses he claimed to have no time to write, here also parodying conventions of eternizing and *carpe diem* poetry, exploiting especially their threatening possibilities. Again he uses them to expose, though with much fiercer brutality, the inadequacy of "love" eternized in verse where poet-lovers sing to dead ladies, "But none I think do there embrace."

Having exploited by his parody the threatening implications of eternizing art, such as Shakespeare used in sonnets like 104—"Ere you were borne was beauties summer dead"—in which the poet or his "Song" outlives the beloved, after having earlier exposed what he saw as its cynical self-interest and prurience, the speaker in the last section of the poem seems to abandon all its poses. "Now" he speaks from his actual situation as a man living in the present, passing moment which he must persuade the lady to enjoy with him immediately, not in a poem:

> Now therefore, while the youthful hew
> Sits on thy skin like morning dew,
> And while thy willing Soul transpires
> At every pore with instant Fires,
> Now let us sport us while we may;
> And now, like am'rous birds of prey,
> Rather at once our Time devour,
> Than languish in his slow-chapt pow'r.
> Let us roll all our Strength, and all
> Our sweetness, up into one Ball:
> And tear our Pleasures with rough strife,
> Thorough the Iron gates of Life.
> Thus, though we cannot make our Sun
> Stand still, yet we will make him run.

The tenses here are no longer conditional or future but imperative—"Let us"—like the urgings of the lover in "The Goodmorrow," pointing neither to "our long Loves Day" nor to "vast Eternity" but to "Now," which the speaker repeats with mounting urgency. No longer does he create a mythologized world in which he is the languishing poet-lover forever promising to rescue the beautiful lady from devouring time, whose power they can escape only in his art. He specifically casts aside those conventional roles by inverting the language associated with them:

> Rather at once our Time devour,
> Than languish in his slow-chapt pow'r.

The verb "languish" is the formulaic term for the behavior of the

Petrarchan lover,[3] such as he portrayed himself to be earlier, stretched by the riverside to "complain." He is not composing verses to the lady or imagining that he will do so, but directly addressing her and in language not conventional to eternizing poetry. His images are harsher, more physical, more violent. They define a relationship no longer Petrarchan, for they break down the vast separation—he by the humble "Humber" while she wanders beside the more exotic "Ganges"—of the languishing lover from the remote and stately mistress by describing them together in the same images. They are "like am'rous birds of prey" or like a besieging army or perhaps a cannon "Ball" crashing "Thorough the Iron gates of Life."[4]

Because he is not composing verses which transform the limits of the "World and "Time," he must find a new way to take command over them, to make them serve his argument, conform to his feelings. To do so he adopts verbal tactics like those of the lover in "The Good-morrow" whose greeting, "And now good morrow to our waking soules," has the effect of summoning the immediate present, as if at his beckoning and with his lordly permission. Here the speaker's reiterations of "Now" seem to make the present moment arrive because he wills it, as his simile "while the youthful hew / Sits on thy skin like morning dew" asserts the conformity of nature's cycles, of fresh day and season, to the lady's "youthful" beauty and his own young desires. Furthermore, these lines emerge as the conclusion to a carefully developed logical and rhetorical argument[5]— "Now therefore"—which suggests, as was implied earlier by his allowance of time to write what he claimed not "enough" leisure to compose, that he has from the beginning felt less helpless than he admitted in his subjection to time. Indeed, the fact of the limits imposed by time which he lamented—one hears genuine longing for the spacious leisure of "World enough, and Time"—has all along been made to justify his argument for making love, not composing poems. Paradoxically, therefore, the exigencies of experience which he credited with power to prevent him from idealizing his "love" in verse were already shaped in conformity with his nonpoetic intentions.

The logical and rhetorical pattern which emerges with "Now therefore" does not have the kind of effects characteristic of the syllogistic "When . . . When . . . When . . . Then . . . And" construction of such poems as Shakespeare's Sonnet 15. For here the logic and rhetoric are not invented by a poet to create a timeless order in his poem where his love can live forever, but are designed by a lover to exploit the ephemeral quality of experience for more immediate and self-serving ends. Rather than intending to arrest time, his argument to this point means to insist that it is rapidly passing. It therefore derives its authority, not from the miraculous power of art, but from an apparently realistic admission of the facts of physical existence, supported by the tough and frankly sexual character of the images, which are themselves rapid and fragmentary here, in keeping with his sense of racing with speeding moments.

His syllogistic argument, therefore, like his images, is the persuasive device of a lover expressing the immediate urgency of his desires, not the invention of a poet-lover like Marlowe's "Passionate Shepherd," creating a literary ideal to "delight" the "mind" of the lady. Nor is it a lesson from a disinterested teacher of the accumulated wisdom of the *carpe diem* and *carpe florem* traditions, like the speaker in Herrick's best known persuasion poem, which contains many details suggesting Marvell's familiarity with its particular embodiment of those traditions:[6]

To the Virgins, to Make Much of Time
Gather ye Rose-buds while ye may,
    Old Time is still a flying:
And this same flower that smiles to day,
    To morrow will be dying.

The glorious Lamp of Heaven, the Sun,
    The higher he's a getting;
The sooner will his Race be run,
    And neerer he's to Setting.

That Age is best, which is the first,
   When Youth and Blood are warmer;
But being spent, the worse, and worst
   Times, still succeed the former.

Then be not coy, but use your time;
   And while ye may, goe marry:
For having lost but once your prime,
   You may for ever tarry.

The suggestive resemblance of "Gather ye Rose-buds while ye may" to "Now let us sport us while we may" points out important differences, not only the passionate engagement of Marvell's lover in his imperatives but his avoidance of idealized pastoral language comparing love-making to picking "Rose-buds." We are reminded that in "our long Loves Day" he did not imagine his lady gathering flowers but more worldly "Rubies," and that therefore his supposedly idealized pastoral fantasy lacks the innocent health of his now more frankly physical language. That is, the comparison "the youthful hew / Sits on thy skin like morning dew"[7] is the only natural detail in the poem which has the genuinely unworldly innocence of pastoral while referring to the physical fact that the "Coy" lady's body is revealing her desires "At every pore with instant Fires."

If his invitation, "Now let us sport us while we may," could be a deliberate revision of Herrick's line,[8] it is certainly an echo of some lines from another translation of Catullus by Jonson in *The Forrest* V:

Come my Celia, let vs proue,
While we may, the sports of loue;
Time will not be ours, for euer:
He, at length, our good will seuer.
Spend not then his giufts in vaine.
Sunnes, that set, may rise againe:
But if once we loose this light,
'Tis, with vs, perpetuall night.

Marvell's lover has greatly intensified the physical, sexual qualities of the "sports of loue," by mentioning the nearness of "every pore" of the lady's body (a device which insists on the immediacy of her presence like Donne's metaphors of eyes reflecting faces), by his comparisons to "am'rous birds of prey" and especially to the "Ball" tearing "Thorough the Iron gates of Life," an image which seems intentionally indefinite and yet decisively not a metaphor for writing a poem. That is, the wording allows the interpretation that the lovers together will break through the "gates" which confine "Life" within their bounds, and so will emerge into something which is not "Life" (implying a pun on "dying"), or that they will break into the "gates" which contain "Life" and so together will fully enter it, or that their passage through the "Iron gates" is the substance "of Life" itself. The difficulty of deciding among these possibilities suggests that they may be intended simultaneously, but what is unmistakably meant by the metaphor is that the process by which the lovers realize any or all of these possibilities is physical and sexual. Their achievement is in the flesh, not in poetry, and it takes place in passing time, not in eternizing art:

Thus, though we cannot make our Sun
Stand still, yet we will make him run.

This is the lover's conclusion "To His Coy Mistress" and also Marvell's comment on his own poem in relation to others in which a lover struggles in contest with time. It again recalls Jonson's translation of the classical admonition to seize the day:

Sunnes, that set, may rise againe:
But if once we loose this light,
'Tis, with vs, perpetuall night.

For if Marvell's lovers, who cannot arrest the sun, "will make him run," either by chasing him closely from behind, or racing at his side or with him "hurrying" at their backs, they will escape "perpetuall night" by remaining forever within the light of his beams. This is the argument of Donne's speaker in "The Anniversarie," whose "love hath no decay" because it is metaphorically the sun in the lovers' world:[9]

> This, no tomorrow hath, nor yesterday,
> Running it never runs from us away,
> But truly keepes his first, last, everlasting day.

It is also essentially similar in kind to the conclusion of the lover in "The Sunne Rising,"[10] although Marvell seems playfully to criticize the argument of that poem by making his own lover's triumph include the admission that "we cannot make our Sun / Stand still," whereas Donne's lover offers it "ease" in resting with him:

> Shine here to us, and thou art every where;
> This bed thy center is, these walls, thy spheare.

Yet the argument of "The Sunne Rising," we have seen, depends ultimately on the lover's acceptance of the physical limitations of his situation, on his adaptation of the sun's rising and continuing presence to his own needs and desires, so that he seems to control it by his language, which has itself been made to conform to, not alter, fact. In this way, it works according to the same essential pattern as the argument of Marvell's lover, and derives its authority from the same kind of apparent adjustment to the realities of the physical, temporal world, or conformity to its laws of operation. The lover's metaphor at the end of "To His Coy Mistress" does not claim miraculously to arrest the passage of time within the permanent world of the poem, but likens the lovers' feelings to the motions of the sun, and by that device, which is not a promise to eternize in poetry, asserts for those feelings the power and permanence of the natural order.

Marvell's "To His Coy Mistress" seems a culmination of the traditions of poetry discussed earlier, and even a deliberate comment on its relation to individual poems within that body of verse. For these reasons and also because the poem is in many important ways a unique achievement within the body of Marvell's own poetry, it is tempting to construct an argument that, as the full flowering of a line of poetic exploration, "To His Coy Mistress" exhausted, for Marvell at least, that wealth of literary suggestion.[11] Such a theory would place the poem at the beginning of Marvell's career as a poet, a theoretical convenience for which there is no known factual support, and would define the differences between it and his other poems with related concerns as "developments" or "declines" from the kind of poem it defines itself—through varying relationships with other poetry—to be.

Since there is no biographical, editorial or other historical evidence for such a chronological arrangement,[12] all that can be said is that while Marvell concerned himself in a number of other poems with the contest between love and time, and with earlier presentations of that struggle in poetry, yet these other poems are essentially, some even radically, different from "To His Coy Mistress." These differences do not explain when or why Marvell came to write what is now his most famous poem, but they do demonstrate it to be uncharacteristic in many of its deepest assumptions. These are much closer to some characteristic attitudes of both Donne and Jonson toward the nature of poetry and its relation to experience in the "World" and in "Time" than the assumptions in other poems by Marvell. The very existence of such fundamental inconsistency is an unexplained characteristic of Marvell as a poet, and one which further differentiates him from both Donne and Jonson in their love poems.

The devices which insist that the speaker in "To His Coy Mistress" is a lover directly and intimately addressing the lady whose physical nearness has a shaping influence on his argument, devices which help to define its affinities with Donne's immediate and private kind of love poem, are themselves rare in Marvell's own poetry.[13] Much more characteristically he speaks in a manner closer to Jonson's as a poet contemplating his subject and interpreting it for an audience of readers:

The Picture of Little T. C. in a Prospect
of Flowers

I

See with what simplicity
This Nimph begins her golden daies!
In the green Grass she loves to lie,
And there with her fair Aspect tames
The Wilder flow'rs, and gives them names:
But only with the Roses playes;
           And them does tell
What Colour best becomes them, and what Smell.

II

Who can foretel for what high cause
This Darling of the Gods was born!
Yet this is She whose chaster Laws
The wanton Love shall one day fear,
And, under her command severe,
See his Bow broke and Ensigns torn.
           Happy, who can
Appease this virtuous Enemy of Man!

III

O then let me in time compound,
And parly with those conquering Eyes;
Ere thy have try'd their force to wound,
Ere, with their glancing wheels, they drive
In Triumph over Hearts that strive,
And them that yield but more despise.
           Let me be laid,
Where I may see thy Glories from some shade.

IV

Mean time, whilst every verdant thing
It self does at thy Beauty charm,
Reform the errours of the Spring;
Make that the Tulips may have share
Of sweetness, seeing they are fair;
And Roses of their thorns disarm:
           But most procure
That Violets may a longer Age endure.

But O young beauty of the Woods,
Whom Nature courts with fruits and flow'rs,
Gather the Flow'rs, but spare the Buds;
Lest *Flora* angry at thy crime,
To kill her Infants in their prime,
Do quickly make th' Example Yours;
      And, ere we see,
Nip in the blossome all our hopes and Thee.

The title itself recalls Jonson's practice of insisting on the actual, historical existence of his subject—here identified only as "Little T. C.," perhaps in imitation of Jonson's "Epitaph on S(alomon) P(avy) a Child of Q. El(izabeths) Chappell"[14]—while calling attention to the portrayal of that living subject in art, here the "Picture." Jonson's kind of poetry, perhaps even specifically "Her Triumph," is also recalled by the opening imperative—"See"—directing an audience to attend while the poet begins to create a myth—"with what simplicity / This Nimph begins her golden daies!"—which will interpret its historical subject to the public. The immediacy of "See" and the particularity of "This Nimph" are given a kind of distance or "Prospect" by the poet's mythologizing language (as in "Her Triumph") which places the child "there" in the "green Grass" as a subject for contemplation like one of the flowers rather than as a participant in an immediate situation. This effect is not altered when he begins to address her at the end of stanza three, since his language is obviously not phrased for infant comprehension but for a sophisticated audience of readers. Her position in the poem is therefore comparable to that of the child in Jonson's *Epigrammes* CXX:

> Epitaph on S(alomon) P(avy) a Child
> of Q. El(izabeths) Chappell
>
> Weepe with me all you that read
>   This little storie:
> And know, for whom a teare you shed,
>   *Death's* selfe is sorry.

'Twas a child, that so did thriue
　　In grace, and feature,
As *Heauen* and *Nature* seem'd to striue
　　Which own'd the creature.
Yeeres he numbred scarse thirteene
　　When Fates turn'd cruell,
Yet three fill'd *Zodiackes* had he beene
　　The stages iewell;
And did act (what now we mone)
　　Old men so duely,
As, sooth, the *Parcæ* thought him one,
　　He plai'd so truely.
So, by error, to his fate
　　They all consented;
But viewing him since (alas, too late)
　　They haue repented.
And haue sought (to giue new birth)
　　In bathes to steepe him;
But, being so much too good for earth,
　　Heauen vowes to keepe him.

Marvell's use of "Picture" and "Prospect" in his title with his opening "See" have effects comparable to Jonson's device of the introduction or frame which emphasizes his poetic intention to shape experience—here the death of the child-actor—into a "little storie" in which the reader can "know" the just and decorous feeling—"a teare"—properly evoked by the poet's interpretation of the event. Marvell's "See" also introduces a "storie" about "Little T. C." as "This Nimph begins her golden daies!" His speaker, too, invents a myth which interprets the meaning of the child to the reader, but it is one which has very different implications from Jonson's.

Jonson's "storie" teller, whose Olympian power enables him to interpret the emotions of personified Death, Heaven, Nature, the Fates, creates a myth which ultimately eternizes the boy, whose "good" is cherished in "Heauen" and in the epitaph itself, which proclaims his continuing existence in the present tense of the final lines:

But, being so much too good for earth,
   Heauen vowes to keepe him.

"Heauen" will "keepe" the child forever in the sense of "retain possession" of him, but also with the meaning of "tenderly guard and sustain" that the verb still has in the Anglican liturgy, for example in the closing prayer for the Burial of a Child:

May Almighty God, the Father, the Son, and the Holy
Ghost, bless you and keep you, now and for evermore. *Amen.*

The poem creates a moral explanation of fact which it presents as an interpretation by the poet of the true order of the universe in which events like the untimely death of the boy-actor can be interpreted as part of that larger design. By totally identifying with the role of mythologizing poet, and by rigorously excluding uncontrolled and private feelings—for he invites his public audience to "Weepe with me" a decorous, single "teare"—he has succeeded in eternizing the child in this poem. It does not allow a painful sense of the limits of such poetic power over time and feeling to intrude on the conventions of the epitaph, as that sense so powerfully and expressively breaks "loose" in the epitaph, "On My First Sonne." [15]

Marvell's speaker in "The Picture of Little T.C." is also a poet who grants his readers the benefit of his extraordinary power to interpret the living child by seeing into her future and predicting the feelings of the god of "Love" who "shall one day fear" this girl, even now recognized by the speaker to be the "Darling of the Gods." Although in stanza three he speaks as a poet who is a future lover of the girl, one of the aspiring "Hearts" over which she, mythologized as Diana, will (like the lady in "Her Triumph") "drive" her triumphant chariot, this posture is pointedly adopted, as Jonson's speaker in a poem like "To His Lady, Then Mrs. Cary" assumes the same conventional role, for the literary occasion and for social compliment as the poet retires at a distance to admire and praise:

Let me be laid,
Where I may see thy Glories from some shade.

It is his manner of using his mythologizing power, and its implications for the relation of the poem to the world outside of poetry, which differentiates Marvell's art here from Jonson's.

The poet's description in the first stanza of the child as he can
"See" her at the present moment is transformed by his language
into a pastoral poem in which she "loves to lie" on all her
"golden daies" in a landscape where the grass is always "green"
and full of flowers:

I

See with what simplicity
This Nimph begins her golden daies!
In the green Grass she loves to lie,
And there with her fair Aspect tames
The Wilder flow'rs, and gives them names:
But only with the Roses playes;
        And them does tell
What Colour best becomes them, and what Smell.

While the speaker describes her in the language of a poet,
metaphorically transforming her into one of the flowers by the
comparative "And there with her fair Aspect tames / The Wilder
flow'rs" as if she were one of the tamer, he at the same time
differentiates her from them by assigning her the powers of
naming and interpreting.[16] This perhaps makes him a kind of
God and the child like unfallen Adam, to whom his Maker
granted the gift of naming all the creatures, or like Milton's Eve
whose special task was to give names to the flowers.[17] At the
same time it also assigns her the art of a poet who "names" as the
speaker has named her a "Nimph," who "only with the Roses
playes," for they are the conventional flowers of poetry to which
"fair" ladies are most frequently compared, who can "tell / What
Colour best becomes them" as he has chosen to surround her
with literary "golden" or "green" which "becomes" her childish

"simplicity" in the sense of "best suiting" and also "transforming it" into pastoral innocence.

The speaker is therefore a poet making a timeless setting for a mythologized "Nymph," and the child is like a poet ordering and interpreting nature, rendering it civilized and comprehensible. Both forms of poeticizing are made to seem innocent and enhancing here, largely by the conventional associations with the decorous literary language of this stanza, which nevertheless hints at complications of attitude within its conventionality. Such suggestions are contained in the word "begins," introducing the possibility of change, and the somewhat ambiguous line, "But only with the Roses playes." This wording allows the innocent notion that she chooses "only" them for playmates because the other flowers are too wild, but also more ominously that she "only with the Roses playes" in the sense of "toys with" or "teases" as one with power to torment or harm them. These details in the first stanza raise questions about the validity of the speaker's mythologizing poetry and about the innocence of the child's poetic activity which "tames," "names" and "playes" with nature in ways that may change its "Aspect" or even harm or destroy it.[18]

The suggestion in "begins" that the speaker's art is falsifying because it cannot, despite its pastoral idealizing, arrest the passage of the child's "golden daies," is developed in stanzas two and three, which with playful hyperboles predict how her "fair Aspect" will change, becoming the cruel beauty of the lady in Petrarchan poetry who perhaps "playes" with her lovers instead of roses. The fact that she, and the poet who imagines himself among her future victims, exist "in time," not in an unchanging literary landscape, is underlined by that phrase and by the opening of stanza four:

> Mean time, whilst every verdant thing
> It self does at thy Beauty charm,
> Reform the errours of the Spring;

> Make that the Tulips may have share
> Of sweetness, seeing they are fair;
> And Roses of their thorns disarm:
> But most procure
> That Violets may a longer Age endure.

Again the poet returns here to pastoral language, although now it is acknowledged as only an interlude, "Mean time," which has no power to perpetuate the child's "simplicity." Again he seems to grant her the gift of poetry which creates an idealized "Spring" purified of such natural imperfections as Shakespeare's eternizing poet reformed in the "eternall Sommer" of Sonnet 18, and which corrects the disparity troubling in other Shakespearean sonnets between the "fair" appearance of flowers and their lack of "sweetness." She is to renew the Garden of Eden itself, removing all conflict and danger from the natural world so that "Roses" need not protect themselves with the weaponry of their "thorns," a conventional metaphor for the imperfection of fallen nature as in Shakespeare's Sonnet 35, "Roses haue thornes, and siluer fountaines mud." The speaker here seems to encourage, even instruct, the child in her poetic transformations of nature, which coincide with his own pastoral "Picture" in stanza one, and which would alter nature by idealizing it and "most" of all by eternizing it, arresting the passage of time with magical "charm," in order "That Violets may a longer Age endure."

In the last stanza, however, he cautions her and either consciously or unknowingly also himself who practiced the same idealizing and eternizing art in stanza one, about the dangers inherent in such poetic interference with the processes of nature:

> But O young beauty of the Woods,
> Whom Nature courts with fruits and flow'rs,
> Gather the Flow'rs, but spare the Buds;
> Lest *Flora* angry at thy crime,
> To kill her Infants in their prime,
> Do quickly make th' Example Yours;

And, ere we see,
Nip in the blossome all our hopes and Thee.

With what sounds like another revision of Herrick's line,
"Gather ye Rose-buds while ye may," in "Gather the Flow'rs, but
spare the Buds," he points out the selfish destructiveness of her
imaginative alterations of nature. He also reminds her that if her
power to "Reform," "Make," and "procure" a world shaped
according to her ideal distinguishes her from natural creatures, it
nevertheless cannot rescue her from their common mortality.
Her attempts to eternize nature cannot insure her own immortality. She exists "Mean time" with "every verdant thing" to which
she is compared by the poet, who pointedly refuses to eternize
her in the final stanza:

Lest *Flora* angry at thy crime,
To kill her Infants in their prime,
Do quickly make th' Example Yours;
        And, ere we see,
Nip in the blossome all our hopes and Thee.

Rather than perpetuating her as an image in a timeless poetic
world, he invents a myth—the revenge of Flora—to threaten her
with the fact of her own vulnerable life, and creates a
metaphor—"Nip in the blossome"—reminding her of the
mortality she shares with the flowers which her poetic
subjections, like devouring time itself, would destroy. Instead of
admonishing her, in the manner of other poets, to "Gather ye
Rose-buds," he calls that activity a "crime." Rather than shaping
her experience into a myth which would establish her in an
eternal order, as Jonson's places the boy-actor forever in
"Heauen," Marvell invents a myth which subjects the child to
time and death, both as a human being who is unlike flowers and
as a natural creature who shares their existence in an imperfect
and mutable world.

The effects of this conclusion are to insist on the distortions
and limitations of the kind of poetic transformations of nature

which the speaker indulges in at first but then criticizes. It points to their destructiveness, their selfishness, and ultimately their ineffectuality as efforts to alter experience in the temporal world. In these effects the conclusion of "The Picture of Little T.C." expresses attitudes resembling those in many of Shakespeare's sonnets in the second half of the collection, where the speaker exposes as false the eternizing metaphors in which the friend conceives of his own beauty and power. Of course Marvell's poem has none of the bitterness and disgust of such sonnets, since "Little T.C." can only playfully be imagined to hold the attitudes toward nature and her own relation to it that are actually the poet's attribution, and therefore can only teasingly and tenderly be cautioned or corrected for them. Yet because her imaginative behavior toward the flowers is a prediction of her cruelty to her lovers as Petrarchan lady, a connection is established between threatening poetic power and dangerous conceptions of personal "command" over other human beings. This makes the criticism of eternizing verse in Marvell's poem closer in these respects to Shakespeare's than to Jonson's or Donne's.

Yet there is implied in the speaker's way of using myth in the conclusion to "The Picture of Little T.C." another view of the power of poetry which differentiates Marvell's from that of all the poets previously discussed. By the speaker's sudden introduction of Flora in the last stanza, inventing a myth to threaten the girl with her own mortality, he suggests an arbitrariness in his poem altogether different from the claims made by Jonson for his "little storie" of the death of the child-actor. For Jonson presents his poem as a mythologized version of factual history which interprets the moral design of the universe. Far from being an arbitrary invention of the poet, it is presented as an account of the hidden workings of Death, Heaven, Nature and the Fates, and derives its authority from its claims as poetry to interpret the otherwise inscrutable operations of these great powers in the historical world. To support these claims its mythological narrative is sustained so that it includes the whole "storie," containing within itself a sequence of causes and effects that have a kind of internal coherence and consequence something like the terms in a logical proposition.

Marvell's speaker, on the other hand, introduces his myth of Flora only as he needs it to "make th' Example" of his subject:

> But O young beauty of the Woods,
> Whom Nature courts with fruits and flow'rs,
> Gather the Flow'rs, but spare the Buds;
> Lest *Flora* angry at thy crime,
> To kill her Infants in their prime,
> Do quickly make th' Example Yours;
>   And, ere we see,
> Nip in the blossome all our hopes and Thee.

This is not an assertion of the moral workings of the universe but a way of phrasing a possibility, "Lest *Flora*," a speculation about what might happen "ere we see." By introducing it in this manner, the speaker seems to call attention to the fact that he is inventing myth, along with other poetic devices, to conform to his conception as the child subjects nature to her desires. Both forms of poetic activity are not only shown to have the distorting or limiting effects attributed to conventional eternizing verse in other poems previously discussed, but they are also revealed as willful, dependent on the needs of the poet rather than conforming to the design of the universe which it is the traditional role of poetry to interpret.

The uses of myth in "The Picture of Little T.C.," by contrast with Jonson's epitaph, therefore imply the possibility that poetic language is essentially arbitrary. The effect of such a suggestion is to make the reader uneasy about the authority of the speaker who uses such language, and who, like his invention—the revenge of Flora— can "quickly make th' Example" which he, perhaps in revenge against the cruelty of figures such as "T.C." will become in his prediction, desires us to see.[19] For, as we have noticed, in the beginning of the poem his own language transforms nature in ways very similar to those attributed to the heedless "simplicity" of the child. Yet instead of developing a new moral attitude in the course of the poem which would demand a different kind of language, even in the last stanza, where his cautionary myth seems intended to educate "Little T.C." (and his readers) in a new awareness of the dangers in poetic abuses of nature, his own language still betrays his earlier attitude. For in the last line he acts metaphorically upon "Little T.C." in precisely the way he has warned her not to treat nature, by allowing Flora the power to "Nip in the blossome all our hopes and Thee." This is not to "spare the Buds" but to "kill" one of her "Infants," to which he has earlier likened the child, "in their prime." His own power in creating this final metaphor is as dangerous to "Little T.C." as her command over the flowers or over "Hearts that strive." His lessons to the child and the reader have not been able to "Reform the errours" of the poetic mind continually shaping the world to its desire. The reader is therefore led to question whether Marvell is not fully in control of the poem's implications or whether he has deliberately created a speaker whose own language, either knowingly or unconsciously, illustrates the inescapable force of that desire.

The likelihood that Marvell intended some playful criticism of the poet-lover as well as of his subject in "The Picture of Little T.C." is strengthened if that poem is set beside "The Garden." The comparison is suggested by obvious resemblances between the speakers, similar in their witty urbanity, their ironic detachment, their joking assumption of postures conventional to the figure of the poet-lover whom they do not seriously intend to imitate. A more pointed comparison to be made here, however, is that in "The Garden" the speaker also makes fun of habits of mind and language which manipulate, threaten, even annihilate, the matter upon which they work, while demonstrating these habits in his own poem. For among the multiple lines of argument, the many metaphorical designs in "The Garden," those relevant to this discussion are the speaker's witty attacks on violations of the natural world by the human mind.[20] These he represents as the tendency of men to reduce nature to symbol, myth, and metaphor while his own language works upon it with similar effects.

In the first two stanzas the speaker detaches himself in elegant leisure from the "uncessant Labours" of "men," represented by their contest for "the Palm, the Oke, or Bayes":

I

How vainly men themselves amaze
To win the Palm, the Oke, or Bayes;
And their uncessant Labours see
Crown'd from some single Herb or Tree.
Whose short and narrow verged Shade
Does prudently their Toyles upbraid;
While all Flow'rs and all Trees do close
To weave the Garlands of repose.

II

Fair quiet, have I found thee here,
And Innocence thy Sister dear!
Mistaken long, I sought you then
In busie Companies of Men.
Your sacred Plants, if here below,
Only among the Plants will grow.
Society is all but rude,
To this delicious Solitude.

Human vanity is seen in the world's preference for the active rather than the contemplative life, for "busie Companies of Men" rather than pastoral "Solitude," shown by the supreme value placed on crowns woven of "the Palm, the Oke, or Bayes" above "all Flow'rs and all Trees." "All" represents various and abundant natural life, plants allowed to "grow" and renew themselves by the fertility implied in "do close," a verb meaning "draw together," especially in sexual union. By contrast, the coveted "Palm," "Oke," and "Bayes" are "single" plants, torn from their natural setting and therefore from their processes of growth and renewal. They are wrought into crowns, symbols designed to immortalize human power, which endow them with an arbitrary meaning, which imply a hierarchy of values in nature actually imposed on it by "Society," which reduce the perpetuity, abundance, and variety of the natural world to a "short and narrow verged Shade."

The speaker allies himself on the side of the plants, which "upbraid" other men for their vanity. He is superior to them because he recognizes their follies, dismissing them as "all but rude" intruders, whereas his more mannerly respect for nature makes him at home in its civilized order. Yet for all his decorous appreciation, there are hints even here that he participates in a milder form of their symbolic manipulations of nature. For he sees "all Flow'rs and all Trees" woven into "Garlands of repose," which while not rudely torn from their natural setting or cheapened by being singly individuated, yet are nevertheless shaped by his interpretation into another symbol of human values, as are the "sacred Plants" of "Innocence" and "quiet," whom he courts as "Fair" ladies. To be sure, he allows them to remain "among the Plants," but at the same time his language transforms them into personified abstractions. Like the speaker in "The Picture of Little T. C.," his verbal treatment of nature hints from the beginning what later stanzas increasingly betray, that he shares to some degree the very attitudes his poem criticizes.

This tendency is more pointedly shown by his mock-Petrarchan and mock-Ovidian joking in stanzas three and four:[21]

III

No white nor red was ever seen
So am'rous as this lovely green.
Fond Lovers, cruel as their Flame,
Cut in these Trees their Mistress name.
Little, Alas, they know, or heed,
How far these Beauties Hers exceed!
Fair Trees! where s'eer your barkes I wound,
No Name shall but your own be found.

IV

When we have run our Passions heat,
Love hither makes his best retreat.
The *Gods*, that mortal Beauty chase,
Still in a Tree did end their race.
Apollo hunted *Daphne* so,
Only that She might Laurel grow.
And *Pan* did after *Syrinx* speed,
Not as a Nymph, but for a Reed.

The speaker mocks those conventional lovers who prefer the "white" or "red," Petrarchan adjectives for the lady's complexion—like Charis' "cheekes, of Milke, and Roses"—to the greater "Beauties" of the garden, burlesquing lovers who, like him, boast that their beloveds are "as rare, / As any she beli'd with false compare."[22] He also scorns their "cruel" folly of immortalizing their ladies by cutting their names in the bark of trees. Yet the speaker himself then postures as such a figure, turning the trees metaphorically into "Fair" ladies whose names he will then adoringly carve. In this activity he also resembles Adam giving names to the creatures,[23] "Little T. C." to the flowers, and the poet to his subject. If he is in a sense less foolish than the lovers because he does not impose a "Mistress name" upon the trees, nevertheless he does transform them by his personification into ladies whom he can love, and "wound" them by carving their own names, thereby identifying them in words which may be as arbitrarily imposed as "Neæra, Chloe, Faustina, Corynna."[24] He is therefore capable of abusing nature to satisfy his own desires, even while he teases the lovers for such activity. He shows himself to be both unlike and like them, and also the gods in stanza four, who resemble him in their amorous preference for trees over "mortal Beauty," and whose desire is expressed in transforming power like his own and like the lovers': the gods turn women into trees. This power is here associated with the "Flame" of love and also with art. For the god of poetry "hunted *Daphne* so, / Only that She might Laurel grow," the plant symbolic of his art, "And *Pan* did after *Syrinx* speed, / Not as a Nymph, but for a Reed" on which to sound his music.[25] The gods therefore turn "mortal Beauty" into immortal song. These associations point to further resemblances between the gods and the speaker whose poem retells their myths, but also between their hunting and chasing and the vain efforts of men striving "To win the Palm, the Oke, or Bayes," the "Laurel" being the tree from which is plucked the symbolic crown of "Bayes."

The poet is implicated in his own joking by these multiple resemblances between his verbal acts and the "uncessant Labours" of ambitious men, "Fond Lovers," and especially the amorous gods of poetry, to whom he is further likened by his sensual, even erotic intimacy—"Insnar'd with Flow'rs"—with natural objects in stanza five:

What wond'rous Life in this I lead!
Ripe Apples drop about my head;
The Luscious Clusters of the Vine
Upon my Mouth do crush their Wine;
The Nectaren, and curious Peach,
Into my hands themselves do reach;
Stumbling on Melons, as I pass,
Insnar'd with Flow'rs, I fall on Grass.

After such preparation the reader may expect to find further signs of what the first two stanzas only delicately hint. In his descriptions of how his "Mind" and "Soul" act upon the garden, the speaker exhibits the very attitudes toward nature for which he has criticized other, less civilized men:

VI

Mean while the Mind, from pleasure less,
Withdraws into its happiness:
The Mind, that Ocean where each kind
Does streight its own resemblance find;
Yet it creates, transcending these,
Far other Worlds, and other Seas;

Annihilating all that 's made
To a green Thought in a green Shade.

VII

Here at the Fountains sliding foot,
Or at some Fruit-trees mossy root,
Casting the Bodies Vest aside,
My Soul into the boughs does glide:
There like a Bird it sits, and sings,
Then whets, and combs its silver Wings;
And, till prepar'd for longer flight,
Waves in its Plumes the various Light.

VIII

Such was that happy Garden-state,
While Man there walk'd without a Mate:
After a Place so pure, and sweet,
What other Help could yet be meet!
But 'twas beyond a Mortal's share
To wander solitary there:
Two Paradises 'twere in one
To live in Paradise alone.

Even without the casually limiting "Mean while," or the deflating satirical comment of stanza eight, the glamorous language of six and seven contains hints of its distorting power, in itself and in its connections with the first five stanzas.

"The Mind" is engaged in the activity of an artist as it "creates, transcending these, / Far other Worlds, and other Seas." "These" may refer to things growing in the garden but also to the ideas or images within the "Mind," resembling "each kind" of creature existing outside itself in the natural world.[26] The "other Worlds" created by the "Mind" are therefore different from the natural world, recalling the symbolic, metaphorical and mythical transformations of it in earlier stanzas. These "Far other Worlds, and other Seas" have their own energy and vastness, and yet the invention of them is at once creative and destructive:

Annihilating all that 's made
To a green Thought in a green Shade.

The image is beautifully satisfying to the "Mind" and yet "Annihilating" has the inescapable meanings of "reducing" or even "utterly destroying," confining or razing "all that 's made," either by the poet's "Mind" or by God or nature, to a single "green Thought in a green Shade." This resembles the "short and narrow verged Shade" to which human symbols reduce "all Flow'rs and all Trees," and also the impositions of their "Passions heat" upon nature by the "Fond Lovers," the gods and the speaker himself. The implied conformity between the "Mind" which makes a "green Thought" and the "green" of the garden depends solely on the speaker's manipulation of language. For a "Thought" can be "green" only in some abstract sense, like "fresh" or "innocent,"[27] for example, whereas a "Shade" can be "green" only in color. Combining the two by means of metaphor, the speaker "creates" a satisfying "resemblance" which may not exist in fact outside his "Mind" or poem.

Even the beautiful language of the seventh stanza hints at its own limits and distortions. The "Soul" transcends the mortal world "like a Bird" and like a poet who "sings" of "other Worlds," and yet it does not escape its own self-love. Its activity divested of the body is beautifully vain as it "whets, and combs its silver Wings," as if it had taken upon itself another physical form to admire. In this form it continues to act upon the natural world as it "Waves in its Plumes the various Light." The metaphor implies control achieved by another kind of verbal manipulation. That is, according to the most obvious facts of the physical world, a bird might be said to "Wave its Plumes in the various Light." The speaker's poetic inversion of "in" makes us perceive those facts differently, picturing the bird as if altering the light by the motions of its wings. According to this metaphorical perception, the poet's "Soul" as bird is the manipulator of nature, as the "Mind" had previously reshaped it to "a green Thought in a green Shade" (which in nonmetaphorical language would be phrased something like "a fresh thought of a green

shade"). These verbal acts are alike in involving the speaker's
disturbance of nature to make it conform to his ideal. Together,
however beautiful, they suggest some loss or diminution, by
hinting that the "various Light" of the natural world is somehow
reduced in a metaphor of "a green Shade." If the "Mind" and
"Soul" are like a poet, they make "other Worlds" than nature
which are beautifully distorted reorderings of it in poetry. These
resemblances are supported by the recognizably conventional
nature of the phrase "a green Shade" and also of the simile of the
poet as a bird.[28]

A final hint of the limits or distortions of poetic power comes
in the last stanza where the speaker no longer "Withdraws" into
"The Mind" but appreciatively describes the actual garden
around him, for an audience of readers acknowledged by his use
of "we":

How well the skilful Gardner drew
Of flow'rs and herbes this Dial new;
Where from above the milder Sun
Does through a fragrant Zodiack run;
And, as it works, th' industrious Bee
Computes its time as well as we.
How could such sweet and wholsome Hours
Be reckon'd but with herbs and flow'rs!

The "skilful Gardner" praised by the speaker, who "drew" a
sundial by planting "flow'rs and herbes" in the pattern of the
"Zodiack," is yet another representation of man reordering nature for his own needs. His "Dial" is like the crowns of leaves
braided into symbols to immortalize human power, like the
"Garlands of repose" and other metaphors imposed on the
garden by the poet, including his personification here of "th' industrious Bee." The speaker perceives the activity of this natural
creature to be humorously like the "uncessant Labours" of
"busie" men and also like himself since it "Computes its time as
well as we." Yet the pun on "time," the common seventeenth-
century spelling of "thyme," points out that the poet is again

fabricating a "resemblance" as the gardener has constructed a "Zodiack."[29] For "time" remains to the bee merely the growing plant itself, while for the speaker it has been transformed into an abstraction, like a number on a clock-face, by which passing "time" is "reckon'd" in the symbolic order designed by the gardener. The fact that the gardener is a conventional type of the poet, as in Shakespeare's Sonnet 15, and that "th' industrious Bee" has a long literary history, supports these parallels.[30]

The speaker's reorderings of nature within his own "Mind" attempt to control it like the floral "Dial":

Where from above the milder Sun
Does through a fragrant Zodiack run.

Unlike the lovers in "To His Coy Mistress," who will "make" their sun "run" by pacing themselves to its motions, this artist has shaped nature in an abstract, symbolic design so that the sun seems to "run" according to his plan while actually following its own remote motions. The result is a "sweet and wholsome" construct, as satisfying to the "Mind" as the "fragrant Zodiack" is to the senses. The "Dial" is as delightful a reordering of nature to conform to man's desire as "The Garden." The creation of the "skilful Gardner" represents Marvell's poem, but also conventional eternizing verse, even poetry itself, by its efforts to impose its own design on the mutable world.

If in "The Garden" as well as in "The Picture of Little T. C." the speaker exhibits in his own language some version of the very attitudes he criticizes, the likelihood is stronger that Marvell intended such exposure, as a playful means of showing the limits of the human "Mind" irresistibly shaping nature to satisfy its desire for control over the "World" and "Time." The fact that the speakers in these two poems are sophisticated and urbane, that their language is wittily calculated in its imitations of conventional love poetry, suggests that Marvell meant them to be aware of their own participation in these limits. As poets they seem to be knowing about the arbitrary nature of their own

inventions. They may therefore have a tentative kind of authority, not as Olympian interpreters of the true moral order of the
universe, like the poet in Jonson's epitaph on the child-actor.
The poets in "The Picture of Little T. C." and "The Garden" are
ultimately to be trusted only for their witty skepticism about the
authority of poetry itself.

In "The Mower's Song" Marvell created a speaker who is
comical or absurd without being witty, who reveals delusions
for which he claims authority recognizable to the reader as false.
This figure's distortions and abuses of the world outside his own
"Mind" are exposed by the ways in which the poem, unknown to
the mower himself, burlesques conventional eternizing verse:

The Mower's Song

I

My Mind was once the true survey
Of all these Medows fresh and gay;
And in the greenness of the Grass
Did see its Hopes as in a Glass;
When *Juliana* came, and She
What I do to the Grass, does to my Thoughts and Me.

II

But these, while I with Sorrow pine,
Grew more luxuriant still and fine;
That not one Blade of Grass you spy'd,
But had a Flower on either side;
When *Juliana* came, and She
What I do to the Grass, does to my Thoughts and Me.

III

Unthankful Medows, could you so
A fellowship so true forego,
And in your gawdy May-games meet,
While I lay trodden under feet?
When *Juliana* came, and She
What I do to the Grass, does to my Thoughts and Me.

Marvell

But what you in Compassion ought,
Shall now by my Revenge be wrought:
And Flow'rs, and Grass, and I and all,
Will in one common Ruine fall.
    For *Juliana* comes, and She
What I do to the Grass, does to my Thoughts and Me.

And thus, ye Meadows, which have been
Companions of my thoughts more green,
Shall now the Heraldry become
With which I shall adorn my Tomb;
    For *Juliana* comes, and She
What I do to the Grass, does to my Thoughts and Me.

This "Song" is the complaint of a poet-lover, whose conventional posture is assumed only mockingly, or playfully and occasionally, by the speakers in "To His Coy Mistress" and "The Picture of Little T. C.," only at moments by the poet in "The Garden." Like Marlowe's "Passionate Shepherd" this speaker is a pastoral figure, but here a mower whose daily intimacy with nature takes a more obviously destructive form, of which we are told in the title and reminded by the unvarying part of the refrain, "What I do to the Grass." His relation to nature—as mower, as poet, and as lover—is developed in ways resembling the speaker's treatment of "Little T. C." while distinguishing him from the poet-lovers in other, earlier poems—for example, from Sidney's Pyrocles in a short lyric from book two of *The Countess of Pembroke's Arcadia*.

Here Sidney's lover has retired to complain by the side of a brook where with a willow stick he writes in the sand these verses:[31]

Over these brookes trusting to ease mine eyes,
(Mine eyes even great in labour with their teares)
I layde my face; my face wherein there lyes
Clusters of clowdes, which no Sunne ever cleares.

In watry glasse my watrie eyes I see:
Sorrowes ill easde, where sorrowes painted be.

My thoughts imprisonde in my secreat woes,
With flamie breathe doo issue oft in sound:
The sound of this strange aier no sooner goes,
But that it dooth with *Echoe's* force rebound
 And make me heare the plaints I would refraine:
 Thus outward helps my inward griefes maintaine.

Now in this sande I would discharge my minde,
And cast from me part of my burdnous cares:
But in the sandes my paynes foretolde I finde,
And see therein how well the writer fares.
 Since streame, aier, sand, mine eyes and eares conspire:
 What hope to quench, where each thing blowes the fire?

As in "The Mower's Song," where the speaker laments the loss
of what was "once" the relation of his "Mind" to nature, Sidney's
poet-lover no longer enjoys his former pastoral "ease" in the
natural world. What he now finds in nature is born—"Mine eyes
even great in labour"—of his disordered senses, darkened by
"Clusters of clowdes, which no Sunne ever cleares." This creation of his "inward" sufferings is "painted" on nature, by his reflected image in the brook—"In watry glasse my watrie eyes I
see," by the sound of his "plaints" which "with *Echoe's* force
rebound," and above all by his poem which "in the sandes my
paynes foretolde." These impositions by "the writer" upon
nature are distortions which he can recognize although "imprisonde" by them, which "conspire" only with his desire:

 Since streame, aier, sand, mine eyes and eares conspire:
 What hope to quench, where each thing blowes the fire?

Implied is an "inward" disorder that is actually measured by the
"outward" order represented in the fundamental, substantial,
and permanent existence of the natural elements—water, air,
earth—out of which he has composed his complaint.[32] The
unquenchable "fire" of his passion is only "inward"; however
powerful its flames, they burn in his "thoughts" and in the poem

which records them, but cannot consume the "streame, aier, sand" existing ultimately undisturbed in their natural and permanent state.

Marvell's poet-lover also laments the destruction of his former "Thoughts" of oneness with nature, conveyed in the first stanza by "once" and the shift from past to present tense in the refrain:

> My Mind was once the true survey
> Of all these Medows fresh and gay;
> And in the greenness of the Grass
> Did see its Hopes as in a Glass;
> When *Juliana* came, and She
> What I do to the Grass, does to my Thoughts and Me.

It is this shift in tense, and the rather awkwardly blunt phrasing of "What I do to the Grass," in contrast to the pastoral personifications preceding the refrain, which jar upon the poet-lover's conventionally elegiac tone. Forced to think of what he does literally "do" to the "Grass" as mower, the reader must question the speaker's claims to former sympathy with the natural world.[33] If his "Mind was once the true survey" of nature, he may boast of a conformity with the pastoral scene, as a map corresponds with its territory, while suggesting a kind of proprietary measuring as in a "survey" of one's estate, even a calculating "survey" to estimate the readiness of the grassy fields for mowing. These suggestions make his choice of "fresh" and "gay" and his identification of "greenness" with "Hopes" seem callous, his comparison of the "Grass" to a reflecting "Glass" an absurd metaphor which ignores the actual properties of nature, turning it into a mere reflection of his "Hopes." That is, Pyrocles' metaphor depends on the physical fact that brooks literally can mirror a face bending over them, although his "inward" disorder expressed in his "watrie eyes" enables him to "see" only projections of his own "Sorrowes." Whereas grass cannot actually reflect at all, but must be transformed into an abstraction (like a "green Thought") existing only in the poet-lover's "Mind"— "greenness" perhaps in the sense of "young growth or expectation"—in order to become the "Glass" reflecting the mower's "Hopes." The added meaning of "greenness" as "raw or naïve immaturity" points to the ludicrous lack of awareness in the mower's claims. His metaphor, by its absurdity, is exposed as a more willed and deluded distortion than the feelings "painted" on nature by Sidney's helpless poet-lover, who would "see" otherwise if he were not "imprisonde" by his "woes." The mower's language, therefore, is shown to have more dangerous possibilities, strengthened in the multiple suggestions of the refrain:

When *Juliana* came, and She
What I do to the Grass, does to my Thoughts and Me.

By admitting here his activity as mower, excluded from his earlier deluded memories of sympathy with nature, he reminds the reader that as the lady's cruelty kills his "Thoughts" of living in harmony with the pastoral world where meadows are always "fresh and gay" and the grass ever green, so he destroys nature for his own uses. Furthermore, "What I do to the Grass" can refer not only to his mowing but also to his imaginative activity in the first four lines, where as poet he has metaphorically distorted nature to reflect his image of himself, the way the lady violates his feelings to comply with her image of her own power.[34] His roles of mower and poet are as cruel and dangerous in their effects as her "force to wound" in the role of Petrarchan mistress, such as the poet predicted that "Little T. C." would become.

The division brought by Juliana between his "Thoughts" and the "Medows" is elaborated in stanzas two and three in language which seems to shift the poet-lover's blame for his loss from the cruel lady to nature's own lack of sympathy:

II
But these, while I with Sorrow pine,
Grew more luxuriant still and fine;
That not one Blade of Grass you spy'd,
But had a Flower on either side;

When *Juliana* came, and She
What I do to the Grass, does to my Thoughts and Me.

III

Unthankful Medows, could you so
A fellowship so true forego,
And in your gawdy May-games meet,
While I lay trodden under feet?
When *Juliana* came, and She
What I do to the Grass, does to my Thoughts and Me.

The implied personification in his earlier choice of "fresh and gay" is developed in the way the blades of grass are individuated as if they were people and then expressly accused of "Unthankful" betrayal. This development intensifies by comic exaggeration the sense of the speaker's imposition upon nature of his own sulky feelings—of resentment, desertion, anger, self-pity, and sentimentality—especially in recalling with specious nostalgia "A fellowship so true" between a mower and grass.

This grotesque heightening of his self-delusion with the deepening of bad feelings projected upon nature is expressed progressively in each refrain. In stanza two, "What I do to the Grass" refers, in addition to the act of cutting it down, to his verbal activity in the stanza itself. There he has separated his feelings from the meaner emotions he attributes to the grass, as Juliana proudly withholds herself from the speaker. In stanza three, the same phrase can describe his haughty contempt for the grass or his personifying of nature which further separates it from himself since he is now prostrated as nonhuman grass "trodden under feet" of the vulgar dancers. Both interpretations allow parallels with the lady's treatment of the poet-lover.

The refrain changes in the last two stanzas, bringing the occasion of the speaker's suffering into the continuous present and making explicit, with "For," the causal connection between her cruelty to him and his projection of desire for "Revenge" upon the flowers and grass:

IV

But what you in Compassion ought,
Shall now by my Revenge be wrought:
And Flow'rs, and Grass, and I and all,
Will in one common Ruine fall.
　For *Juliana* comes, and She
What I do to the Grass, does to my Thoughts and Me.

V

And thus, ye Meadows, which have been
Companions of my thoughts more green,
Shall now the Heraldry become
With which I shall adorn my Tomb;
　For *Juliana* comes, and She
What I do to the Grass, does to my Thoughts and Me.

His revenge is achieved through his action as a mower who cuts down the grass, behavior analogous to his poetic activity. For his "Mind" has "wrought"[35] out of the meadows reflections or, by personification, "Companions of my thoughts more green," once again denying the separation between himself and nature which, by the deliberately destructive act of the speaker's revenge, now participates with him in a grotesquely clumsy "fall" from the pastoral to the mortal world.[36]

Yet if he has in one sense verbally pulled the grass down with him in his "fall," denying it that immunity from decay and death which it had seemed to enjoy by growing "more luxuriant and fine" while he diminished, at the same time he also distinguishes himself from it by his human and distinctively poetic powers. For of the dead grass he can make the "Heraldry" which will "adorn" his "Tomb," the verb "to adorn" being a conventional term for the poet's art, as in line 8 of Marvell's "The Coronet," and the "Tomb" a familiar metaphor for eternizing verse.

The wreath of dead grass, resembling the symbolic crowns of "the Palm, the Oke, or Bayes," which he makes into adornment is therefore also a metaphor for this kind of poetry, since heraldry on a tomb is a symbolic language which interprets for posterity the identity of the person to whose memory the monument is dedicated. His revenge on the grass is therefore "wrought" by first killing it and then transforming it metaphorically into "Heraldry" which will eternize him while the grass itself is dead. In this activity he will "do" to nature what the lady "does" to him, murdering it, subjecting it to his pride (only the mighty and well-born are buried in tombs adorned with heraldic insignia), and triumphing over it by making its death eternize him, as Juliana also proudly uses the poet-lover's art to immortalize her power over him in this "Song."

The mower in this revenge triumphs over "Unthankful" nature by transforming it into poetry, but in order to do so he has robbed it of its natural identity as well as its life. In subjecting it to his desires, as lover and as poet, he has inevitably distorted and destroyed the natural world, in the arrogant fashion that the lady's image of her power has violated his identity. This makes his deluded "Thoughts" more damaging than those of Sidney's poet-lover, which keep him "imprisonde" without actually interfering with nature itself, for reflected images, echoed sounds, even words written in sand, do not permanently deface or interrupt the "outward" order of nature.[37] Whereas the mower has used his language to alter the grass, once a natural creature but by his art transformed into "Heraldry," no longer "green" or living and growing, no longer natural or subject to time, but dead artifice. Implied is a final joke played on the mower, however. For in the poet-lover's apparently triumphant imposition of his "Mind" over nature it is ultimately and despite all his efforts, the grass which has the final revenge. In the form of "Heraldry" the wreath of dead grass identifies the figure entombed to be a mower who cut it down, and only for that destructive act will he be remembered after his death in his own immortal "Song."

As in "The Picture of Little T. C.," the activities of the poet are

compared to the dangerous power of the cruel mistress and condemned, but here the condemnation, while more obviously
funny, is also harsher in two important respects. For in the poet's
advice to "Little T. C." there is a strong likelihood that he is conscious of its application also to his own poetic distortions, that
like Sidney's lover—though more humorously—he sees how he
may be shaping nature falsely according to his own feelings. By
contrast, the delusions of the mower only intensify in the course
of the poem until his destructive "Thoughts" finally include him
without alternative in "one common Ruine." His projection of
feelings on the natural world involves only self-pity, excluding
the possibility of self-knowledge. Furthermore, the condemnation of the mower is harsher also because his images of nature
lack the genuine delight that both "Little T. C." and her inter-
preter take in the natural world and their idealizations of it. The
mower's images of nature are more naïvely and narrowly sub-
jected to his feelings, with the result that their essentially
arbitrary quality emerges far more absurdly. In the conclusion,
when the poet-lover transforms grass into "Heraldry," the wil-
fulness of this act, without tender appreciation of natural growth
and beauty, seems far more brutal than the behavior of "Little
T. C." toward the flowers or the metaphorical treatment of her
by the poet. The greater destructiveness of the mower's verbal
activity may also be measured by contrast with the witty metamorphoses of nature perpetrated by the lover of trees in "The
Garden," whose poetry, like the creation of the "skilful
Gardner," reorders nature without killing its growth or sweetness. By contrast, the poet-lover whose art is ultimately defined
by his role as mower is condemned for his brutality, without his
knowledge, by his own eternizing "Song," made from the grass
which his power has wilfully cut down. The authority of this
speaker is unquestionably undermined by the comic exaggerations and distortions of his language which burlesque a conventional complaint, such as Pyrocles', and by the joke ulti-

mately played on him by his own poem. The arbitrariness of its language, for which he claims eternizing power, destroys that claim to miraculously alter and transcend the natural world which it merely violates.

Some of the more radical implications for Marvell's view of poetry, suggested in these discussions of "The Picture of Little T. C.," "The Garden," and "The Mower's Song," emerge still more strongly if they are used as a kind of context in which to read another poem, "The Unfortunate Lover," related to these in different and sometimes oblique ways. This poem is extraordinarily peculiar, in the sense of original but also strange,[38] yet within the context of these other poems it can be seen to resemble them in its burlesque of poetic conventions, especially those of eternizing verse, as a means of exposing the essential arbitrariness of poetic language:

The Unfortunate Lover

I

Alas, how pleasant are their dayes
With whom the Infant Love yet playes!
Sorted by pairs, they still are seen
By Fountains cool, and Shadows green.
But soon these Flames do lose their light,
Like Meteors of a Summers night:
Nor can they to that Region climb,
To make impression upon Time.

II

'Twas in a Shipwrack, when the Seas
Rul'd, and the Winds did what they please,
That my poor Lover floting lay,
And, e're brought forth, was cast away:
Till at the last the master-Wave
Upon the Rock his Mother drave;
And there she split against the Stone,
In a *Cesarian Section*.

III

The Sea him lent these bitter Tears
Which at his Eyes he alwaies bears.
And from the Winds the Sighs he bore,
Which through his surging Breast do roar.
No Day he saw but that which breaks,
Through frighted Clouds in forked streaks.
While round the ratling Thunder hurl'd,
As at the Fun'ral of the World.

IV

While Nature to his Birth presents
This masque of quarrelling Elements;
A num'rous fleet of Corm'rants black,
That sail'd insulting o're the Wrack,
Receiv'd into their cruel Care,
Th' unfortunate and abject Heir:
Guardians most fit to entertain
The Orphan of the *Hurricane.*

V

They fed him up with Hopes and Air,
Which soon digested to Despair.
And as one Corm'rant fed him, still
Another on his Heart did bill.
Thus while they famish him, and feast,
He both consumed, and increast:
And languished with doubtful Breath,
Th' *Amphibium* of Life and Death.

VI

And now, when angry Heaven wou'd
Behold a spectacle of Blood,
Fortune and He are call'd to play
At sharp before it all the day:
And Tyrant Love his brest does ply
With all his wing'd Artillery.
Whilst he, betwixt the Flames and Waves,
Like *Ajax,* the mad Tempest braves.

VII

See how he nak'd and fierce does stand,
Cuffing the Thunder with one hand;
While with the other he does lock,
And grapple, with the stubborn Rock:
From which he with each Wave rebounds,
Torn into Flames, and ragg'd with Wounds.
And all he saies, a Lover drest
In his own Blood does relish best.

VIII

This is the only *Banneret*
That ever Love created yet:
Who though, by the Malignant Starrs,
Forced to live in Storms and Warrs;
Yet dying leaves a Perfume here,
And Musick within every Ear:
And he in Story only rules,
In a Field *Sable* a Lover *Gules*.

The title predicts a complaint like "The Mower's Song" in which the tormented speaker laments what the lady's cruelty "does" to his feelings. But the figure identified as the lover here is first presented in the third person—"my poor Lover"—as the hero of the poet's narrative, occupying stanzas two through seven with a frame composed of the introductory and concluding stanzas. Within the story of his "Unfortunate" adventures this figure speaks in his own voice only the enigmatic lines at the end of stanza seven: "a Lover drest / In his own Blood does relish best." Whatever absurdities this declaration ultimately conveys, it has initially neither the tone nor the substance of a conventional lover's complaint. Like the narrative itself, it places the figure in the category of "a Lover," without any mention of the lady whose power to wound may perhaps be the force which draws his "Blood." It prescribes for him a posture which is more assertive than languishing, expressed in a tone more boastful than plaintive. Like the poem of "The Unfortunate Lover" itself, what the protagonist in its narrative "saies"

All in War with Time

invites comparison with a Petrarchan complaint at first by large divergences from its conventions.

The story which the poet tells of "my poor Lover" is a tale crammed with wild adventures, including a shipwreck, an unnatural birth attended by "forked streaks" of lightning and "ratling Thunder," adoption of the orphaned child by beasts of prey, a duel with Fortune and a final struggle with the elemental weapons of "angry Heaven." To emphasize the epic qualities of the story, the poet recounts the spectacular birth of the protagonist "in a *Cesarian Section,*" a term having antique, heroic associations as well as medical, and describes him as he "Like *Ajax,* the mad Tempest braves." The opening lines also direct attention to the heroic proportions of his "Unfortunate Lover" by means of contrast with another kind of lover:

> Alas, how pleasant are their dayes
> With whom the Infant Love yet playes!
> Sorted by pairs, they still are seen
> By Fountains cool, and Shadows green.

The easy and passive pastoral state of these lovers, resembling "The Garden" and the landscape in which "Little T. C." plays with the flowers, points up by contrast the violent and hostile world into which the "poor Lover" is born and must battle for survival, preparing for the heroic proportions of his story.

These epic outlines of the narrative contain details which invite comparison as well as contrast with the conventional love complaint. For the landscape of the heroic world is composed of a Petrarchan lover's metaphors. In stanza three:

> The Sea him lent these bitter Tears
> Which at his Eyes he alwaies bears.
> And from the Winds the Sighs he bore,
> Which through his surging Breast do roar.

His "Tears" and "Sighs," part of the "stocks intire" of the Petrarchan lover, are here not said to be imposed in images upon the landscape, as in Pyrocles' complaint. Nor are they expressed precisely in the form of the public demonstrations of feeling which Donne's lovers contemptuously reject in "A Valediction: Forbidding Mourning"—"No teare-floods, nor sigh-tempests move"—or in "The Canonization":

What merchants ships have my sighs drown'd?
Who saies my teares have overflow'd his ground?

Rather than overflowing on the natural world like the feelings of the speaker in Donne's "Twicknam Garden," who complains of being "Blasted with sighs, and surrounded with teares," this lover's "Tears" and "Sighs" are willingly "lent" him by the elements themselves, turning his "surging Breast" into a stormy seascape comparable in proportions to the natural world.

Again in stanza five there is a similar confusion among inward and outward elements:

They fed him up with Hopes and Air,
Which soon digested to Despair.

The apparently external existence and equation of "Hopes" and "Air" here are not attributed, as in Sidney's complaint, to the imposition of the lover's feelings upon nature but seem to derive from the dominance of his heroic passion over the very elements and order of the world, making them conform to his sufferings. In the same stanza the verbal paradoxes which conventionally characterize the Petrarchan lover's feelings are also given external causes which then act upon the hero's being:

And as one Corm'rant fed him, still
Another on his Heart did bill.
Thus while they famish him, and feast,
He both consumed, and increast:
And languished with doubtful Breath,
Th' *Amphibium* of Life and Death.

While in stanza six he is torn "betwixt the Flames and Waves" which are aspects of the natural landscape there and again in stanza seven:

From which he with each Wave rebounds,
Torn into Flames, and ragg'd with Wounds.

Because these heroic sufferings of the "Unfortunate Lover" are absurd magnifications of the Petrarchan lover's woes, the total absence of any mention of the lady who causes the "Wounds" from either the narrative which recounts his history, or from the one speech made by the "poor Lover" himself, is both hilarious and pointed. It is further emphasized by the contrast between him and the pastoral lovers of the opening stanza who are conveniently "Sorted by pairs," like animals in the Ark or like stockings, instead of battling hostile forces in a world occupied entirely alone.

The effect of this blandly accepted absence of the lady from the poem is to call in question the cause of the sufferings experienced by the hero. The narrative suggests that he is somehow born to be a "poor Lover" or that nature conspired "when the Seas / Rul'd, and the Winds did what they please" to make him suffer, or that it was the will of "angry Heaven." Yet these explanations are suspect because they seem to bear no necessary relation to the claim that he is a lover. They leave unanswered, or even unasked, the question, "Who does he love?" as does his own declaration that "a Lover drest / In his own Blood does relish best." What he seems to offer there, as some sort of self-justification, is actually revealing of a very different cause for his apparently unmotivated suffering than either the cosmic explanations given in the narrative or the lady's cruelty of which the Petrarchan lover complains. The hero identifies himself in the role of "a Lover" who is "drest" in a spectacular costume in which he "does relish best." The verb "relish" could mean "to enjoy" sensually or even sexually, "to please," and also "to sing a love song."[39] All three possibilities imply that the "Lover drest / In his own Blood" indulges in his suffering because it gives him pleasure and because it is an effective costume for the role he chooses to play and the ends it is designed to achieve.

What those ends might be is yet another question, since the omission of the lady, emphasized here by the fact that the verb "relish" has no object, seems to preclude the possibility that he has donned the costume of "a Lover drest / In his own Blood" in order to appease her cruelty or appeal to her pity, that he might "relish"—"enjoy," "please," "sing to"— her. He seems to embrace the part of "Unfortunate Lover" for the sheer pleasure of suffering or in order to become the hero of a universal "spectacle of Blood," a worthy opponent of Fortune in a duel fought before Heaven as interested spectator. Or his role is chosen to make him the important audience for whom "Nature to his Birth presents / This masque of quarrelling Elements." These suggestions are made even more preposterous by the hilarious possibility that he is "drest / In his own Blood" as a fowl is "drest" to furnish a banquet.[40] He is then a true "Lover" according to the "best" recipe, having been "fed . . . up" to the proper size for stuffing. He sees himself as "relish" for the universe which cruelly devours him, like the "Corm'rants," but also as "relish" for himself, "consumed, and increast" by the pleasures of his pain. Both his own spoken justification and the narrative of his "Unfortunate" adventures point to the motives of self-indulgence and self-aggrandisement for his assuming the role of "poor Lover."

These suggestions are supported and enlarged by the frame of the narrative, in which the poet introduces and makes his concluding comment on the "Unfortunate Lover." The first stanza, we have seen, presents the contrasting figures of loving "pairs" enjoying a "pleasant" pastoral world:

Alas, how pleasant are their dayes
With whom the Infant Love yet playes!
Sorted by pairs, they still are seen
By Fountains cool, and Shadows green.
But soon these Flames do lose their light,
Like Meteors of a Summers night:
Nor can they to that Region climb,
To make impression upon Time.

Taken as a whole and in the light of the succeeding narrative, this stanza points to a contrast between undifferentiated pastoral lovers, whose "Flames" are fleeting, and the heroic individual who can "climbe / To make impression upon Time," lines strangely close to Marvell's description in "An Horation Ode Upon Cromwel's Return From Ireland" of Cromwell, who "Could by industrious Valour climbe / To ruine the great Work of Time."[41] Here "To make impression upon Time" means both "to assault it"—like the figure of the eternizing poet-lover "all in war with Time"—and "to make Time take notice,"[42] both of which meanings describe the actions of the "poor Lover" in the narrative. The implication is that his self-aggrandisement is part of his effort to ensure that his own "Flames" will not "lose their light" but will burn forever in a timeless, incorruptible region beyond reach of sublunary lovers who fade "Like Meteors of a Summers night."

The concluding stanza implies that the struggles of the "Unfortunate Lover" have achieved this end, which is to elevate him above the mortal condition of "Th' *Amphibium* of Life and Death" by eternizing him in poetry:

> This is the only *Banneret*
> That ever Love created yet:
> Who though, by the Malignant Starrs,
> Forced to live in Storms and Warrs:
> Yet dying leaves a Perfume here,
> And Musick within every Ear:
> And he in Story only rules,
> In a Field *Sable* a Lover *Gules.*

By identifying the lover as a "Banneret," a grade of knighthood conferred on the battlefield, the poet attributes the lover's triumph to his heroic combat, which has taken place in the narrative and which has been appreciated by "Love," who has "created" the title in honor of his achievement. Yet because it is symbolized by the heraldic design of a crimson figure in a black ground ("Sable" and "Gules" are the terms for black and red in heraldry), recalling "a Lover drest / In his own Blood," there is more than a hint that the "Unfortunate Lover" has designed his own heraldry, like the poet-lover in "The Mower's Song," and that the "Love" which has "created" him a title is his own. This makes him, like the mower, the inventor as well as the hero of his own story, written and acted in order to eternize himself:[43]

Yet dying leaves a Perfume here,
And Musick within every Ear.

His success is won in "Storms and Warrs" which guarantee his importance because in his version of experience they were designed exclusively to test him or to punish him for his heroism by the "Malignant Starrs." This triumph over cosmic adversaries is recorded in the narrative in which he has mythologized himself, and is adorned forever by the heraldry of the "Lover" as he has symbolically elevated himself:

And he in Story only rules,
In a Field *Sable* a Lover *Gules*.

This reading of the conclusion makes the narrative of stanzas two through seven the lover's "Story" of himself, which the poet recounts with seemingly uncritical enthusiasm, apparently accepting his protagonist's self-image as representative or illustrative of "they" who can "climb, / To make impression upon Time." Within the narrative there are no author-comments conventional to heroic poetry which could explicitly distinguish the poet's view of the "Unfortunate Lover" from the one devised and acted out by that figure, although the wildly inflated proportions of the story prevent the reader from feeling uncertain about the poet's degree of seriousness here. For, in the narrative, details presented as mythologized events burlesque themselves by their literalness:

They fed him up with Hopes and Air,
Which soon digested to Despair.

Even comparisons seemingly designed by the poet to match the heroic magnitude of his subject, "Like *Ajax*, the mad Tempest braves," tend to deflate, as in this mythological allusion to a hero whose own madness caused his destruction by the gods.[44]

The frame of the last stanza, presented as the final interpretation by the poet of the narrative recounted in stanzas two through seven, also seems on the surface to accord with the hero's view of himself, while defining with even more comic effects than before a wide divergence from his attitudes. Especially telling are the poet's uses of "only" in the first and last couplets of stanza eight:

This is the only *Banneret*
That ever Love created yet.

The lines allow the hero's own interpretation that he is the unique creation of "Love," the supreme model, but also that he is "only" the first of such fictions "yet" invented, or—if the tone is sarcastic—the "only" such improbable creation ever so far thought of. The possibilities then remain that the lover is what he pictures himself to be, or he is not; or he is, and yet that image evokes an altogether different response in the poet than in the lover, who is the audience as well as creator and hero of his own history. These questions remain unanswered:

And he in Story only rules,
In a Field *Sable* a Lover *Gules.*

He "rules" alone, uniquely, supremely "in Story," or "rules" merely in "Story," or merely "rules" in the sense of dominating or pre-empting the hero's place "in Story." All these interpretations are allowed by the phrasing, and all acknowledge that he has succeeded in his effort "To make impression upon Time" by eternizing himself in the "Story" which the poet has recounted.

This achievement is itself open to ridicule, however, because the familiar metaphors in which it is expressed are included merely perfunctorily and with supreme irrelevance at the end of the poem:

Yet dying leaves a Perfume here,
And Musick within every Ear.

Because they are conventional to eternizing verse in which the poet dedicates his song to immortalizing his beloved, they are a final reminder that in "The Unfortunate Lover" the hero is both lover and self-loved. His "dying" creates the "Perfume"—perhaps the "relish" of an aromatic dinner[45] —and the "Musick" perpetuated in his own "Story," which has shaped all his experience, his world, even his "dying" itself, solitary like all his acts, to that ridiculous end.

The fundamental resemblances between the lover in this poem and the speaker in "The Mower's Song" consist in the ways they abuse language—the symbolism of heraldry—to create fictions which insure their escape from mortality in verse that can eternize them only when they are dead. Both figures are therefore presented as poets whose transformations of the world in accord with their desires are comparable to those of the lover, equally distorting, delusive, and ultimately destructive. Both, therefore, also resemble in some ways the poet of "The Garden," the figure of "Little T. C." and the speaker who interprets her.

"The Picture of Little T.C." suggests further connections with "The Unfortunate Lover" because both present a central figure about whom the poet tells a mythological story to an audience directed to "see" what he presents. Yet in neither does the poet have the kind of unquestioned authority of the speaker in Jonson's "Epitaph on S(alomon) P(avy)." In "The Picture of Little T.C." the poet perpetrates the kind of irresponsible acts in his own language against which he cautions the child in her play with the flowers. In "The Unfortunate Lover" the poet indulges himself in recounting, with evident "relish," the ridiculous "Story" in which the lover eternizes himself, even suggesting the possibility that it is the poet's own creation, since he gives the hero neither an historical nor a traditional literary name, but introduces him as "my poor Lover." This intrusion of himself, as author, with its show of proprietary condescension toward the hero of his "Story," precludes the Olympian blend of detachment and sympathy of Jonson's speaker in his "storie" of the child-actor. It also denies historical authenticity to his narrative, as well as the authority of traditional mythological interpretations. Instead it allows the possibility that the "Story" which eternizes the "Unfortunate Lover" is merely the arbitrary invention of the poet, or perhaps his amused retelling of the hero's inflated account of himself. Its absurdity demonstrates that poets' interpretations, like those of lovers, have neither inherent authority nor essential conformity to the realities outside their own constructs.

Such an interpretation makes "The Unfortunate Lover" a radical comment not only on the conventions of Petrarchan verse, but upon poetry itself. This concern the poem shares with "The Definition of Love," which is implicitly "about" the nature of poetic language, defining Marvell's attitudes toward it by detailed contrast with other poems where the speaker struggles to make his language control his experience in the world of time and change:

The Definition of Love

I

My Love is of a birth as rare
As 'tis for object strange and high:
It was begotten by despair
Upon Impossibility.

II

Magnanimous Despair alone
Could show me so divine a thing,
Where feeble Hope could ne'r have flown
But vainly flapt its Tinsel Wing.

III

And yet I quickly might arrive
Where my extended Soul is fixt,
But Fate does Iron wedges drive,
And alwaies crouds it self betwixt.

IV

For Fate with jealous Eye does see
Two perfect Loves; nor lets them close:
Their union would her ruine be,
And her Tyrannick pow'r depose.

And therefore her Decrees of Steel
Us as the distant Poles have plac'd,
(Though Loves whole World on us doth wheel)
Not by themselves to be embrac'd.

VI

Unless the giddy Heaven fall,
And Earth some new Convulsion tear;
And, us to joyn, the World should all
Be cramp'd into a *Planisphere*.

VII

As Lines so Loves *oblique* may well
Themselves in every Angle greet:
But ours so truly *Paralel*,
Though infinite can never meet.

VIII

Therefore the Love which us doth bind,
But Fate so enviously debarrs,
Is the Conjunction of the Mind,
And Opposition of the Stars.

The title of "The Definition of Love" is in its own way as initially misleading as "The Unfortunate Lover" for it too predicts a
poem in an altogether different mode. The title leads the reader
to expect a philosophical argument designed to establish a
general proposition, when instead the poem begins as the
complaint of a Petrarchan poet-lover whose song publishes his
"despair" to readers of love poetry. The absence here of a
defined situation or listener and the generalized, explanatory
language imply address to a public audience rather than intimate
speech or monologue.[46] This speaker does not even imagine himself addressing his complaint to his surroundings, like the
mower, but explains himself to the world at large, assuming its
interest in his sufferings.

Immediately the absurd juxtaposition of the title with the
lover's complaint calls in question the validity of his claims and

the authority of his language. For the title promises, not "A Lover's Complaint For His Love," but the impersonal "Definition" of the nature of love itself, yet the speaker immediately claims for his feelings a "rare" elevation and intensity, as well as a proud lineage, which would make them unique rather than representative.[47] These early signs of arrogance in the poet-lover, as well as his lack of the philosophical detachment predicted by the title, make his language suspect from the opening stanza:

My Love is of a birth as rare
As 'tis for object strange and high:
It was begotten by despair
Upon Impossibility.

Having been accustomed by Shakespeare and other sonneteers to understand the poet's "Love" as referring at once to his feeling and to his beloved, the reader makes that equation in the first line, only to learn in the second that the "Love" whose distinguished "birth" the speaker boasts is exclusively his own feeling. For this "Love" he makes aristocratic claims resembling those of the mower inventing a coat-of-arms for his tomb, or of the "Unfortunate Lover" whose "Birth" was celebrated with a courtly entertainment, a "masque." The beloved is mentioned only after, and as "object," meaning "that external entity toward which the feeling is directed," but also its "intention or goal."[48] Both these, as well as the grammatical meaning of "object," tend to submerge the human identity of the beloved, who is in fact never addressed as "you" or "thou," nor referred to by name or as "she." They make the poet-lover here—almost like the "Unfortunate Lover" who does not have even an "object" outside himself—seem far more interested in the nature, origins, and effects of his own feelings. The cerebral and introspective quality of his concern is also exaggerated by the use of the language of propagation—"begotten by despair / Upon Impossibility"—exclusively for abstractions of his own feelings. These are both mother and father of his "Love," which is therefore all the more pointedly self-begotten.

This self-absorption is enlarged in the next lines where the prominent and ambiguous placing of "alone" allows more than one reading. The primary one projects his "despair" as a supernatural force in the universe, generously devoting itself to his plight, like the elements which "lent" cosmic "Tears" and "Sighs" to the "Unfortunate Lover." The placing of "alone" also suggests that only to "me" above all others is granted a vision of such an "object strange and high," the choice of "strange" allowing the comic possibilities of "weirdly peculiar" and also "unfamiliar." The snobbish lover has therefore selected an "object" which may be "strange" to him, perhaps precisely because it is "rare" and "high":

Magnanimous Despair alone
Could show me so divine a thing.

Again the effect is to reduce the beloved to an abstract "object" or "thing" interesting chiefly as a means of elevating the lover's feelings to "divine" heights where his "extended Soul is fixt." This is perhaps his "object," resembling the self-elevating desire of the "Unfortunate Lover" to become the hero of a cosmic "masque" or "spectacle," or the central dish on the menu of a universal banquet. The phrase "extended Soul" itself, by grotesquely endowing the immaterial with body, attaches more impediments to the lover's desired spirituality than his boasts—"And yet I quickly might arrive"—would admit.

In both "The Mower's Song" and "The Unfortunate Lover" the destructive activities of the mind are associated with the poet's art and expressed in language which relates the speaker's misconceptions to poetic conventions by burlesquing them. Here the speaker's identity as a poet transforming the world according to his individual conceptions and desires is further defined by detailed verbal connections between his language and specific poems in which Donne's lovers attempt to preserve their feelings from destruction by establishing control in their language over the world of time and change.

Most obviously, stanzas five through eight of "The Definition of Love" seem to be a rebuttal of the lover's argument in "A Valediction: Forbidding Mourning." The "Two perfect Loves" in Marvell's poem operate by laws of nature which make their "union" impossible rather than inevitable, as Donne's lover argues in the last four stanzas of the "Valediction":[49]

> Our two soules therefore, which are one,
> Though I must goe, endure not yet
> A breach, but an expansion,
> Like gold to ayery thinnesse beate.
>
> If they be two, they are two so
> As stiffe twin compasses are two,
> Thy soule the fixt foot, makes no show
> To move, but doth, if the'other doe.
>
> And though it in the center sit,
> Yet when the other far doth rome,
> It leanes, and hearkens after it,
> And growes erect, as it comes home,
>
> Such wilt thou be to mee, who must
> Like th'other foot, obliquely runne;
> Thy firmnes makes my circle just,
> And makes me end, where I begunne.

Marvell's speaker explicates the opposite view that "Two perfect Loves" cannot transcend the divisions imposed by their separate identities in a changing and fragmented world. To point up his differences with Donne, Marvell uses a parallel development of a logical argument—"And therefore"— concluding with an extended formal comparison—"As Lines so Loves"—derived, like Donne's, from the impersonal, authoritative language of geometry:

> V
> And therefore her Decrees of Steel
> Us as the distant Poles have plac'd,

(Though Loves whole World on us doth wheel)
Not by themselves to be embrac'd.

VI

Unless the giddy Heaven fall,
And Earth some new Convulsion tear;
And, us to joyn, the World should all
Be cramp'd into a *Planisphere*.

VII

As Lines so Loves *oblique* may well
Themselves in every Angle greet:
But ours so truly *Paralel*,
Though infinite can never meet.

VIII

Therefore the Love which us doth bind.
But Fate so enviously debarrs,
Is the Conjunction of the Mind,
And Opposition of the Stars.

Yet Marvell's logic and demonstration, we shall see, are presented in ways which burlesque such an argument, so that their ultimate effect is to prove only their own arbitrariness and by implication, therefore, to attack the claims to authority of Donne's poetic language.

The assertion that Fate jealously "Us as the distant Poles have plac'd" assumes, as is also common in Donne's poetry (for example, in the comparison of the lovers' parting to "trepidation of the spheares" in the "Valediction"), a physical or specifically astronomical and geographical analogy for the relationship of the lovers. This analogy is used here to explain the inability of these two lovers to "close," a word for sexual union which, like "begotten . . . Upon," is absurdly at odds with the cerebral and self-absorbed character of the lover's language throughout the preceding stanzas. Yet the validity of the analogy is immediately questioned by the line following: "(Though Loves whole World on us doth wheel)." This echo of "The Sunne Rising" and "The Anniversarie" is placed and phrased so that it points to the astronomical metaphor as the speaker's arbitrary invention, not his discovery of a true analogy with the workings of the natural world (such as Donne's lovers present theirs to be). For it is not in *the* world, but only in "Loves whole World," which is "whole" because conceived to satisfy the shaping "Mind," that the lovers are "plac'd" apart as the poet describes. Significantly, there is no mention, as in Donne's "Valediction," of an actual parting or separation, of a physical absence or journey. This omission has comic effects like those produced by the total exclusion of the mistress from "The Unfortunate Lover." It encourages the literal-minded question: why *are* these lovers "Not by themselves to be embrac'd?" For it raises the possibility that the "Two perfect Loves" may not *in fact* be separated—for example, "on a divers shore." They seem almost to be divided by the poet-lover's own simile: "Us *as* the distant Poles have plac'd." These are the "Poles" of his mentally created "World," whose arrangement satisfies his sense of importance by providing a cosmic explanation of why the lovers are "Not by themselves to be embrac'd." Because the terms of this explanation are as exaggerated and self-elevating as the claims of the "Unfortunate Lover" to be opposed by universal forces, they seem to burlesque the complaint of the star-crossed lover.

The echo of Donne's poems undermines the authority of the speaker's astronomical and geographical comparisons in another way, because it is merely parenthetical and perfunctory:

And therefore her Decrees of Steel
Us as the distant Poles have plac'd,
(Though Loves whole World on us doth wheel)
Not by themselves to be embrac'd.

The lover seems far more interested in the "Impossibility" of his relationship than in the vision of love as a vast and passionate force evoked by the brief echo of two of Donne's most radiant poems. This absorption, with his grandiose excuses for failure to "close," hint that he may both cause and enjoy the thwarted nature of his "Love." He seems almost to welcome the argument, already suspected to be merely his own fabrication, that his "union" is fated not to be.

The conjunction "Unless" in stanza six introduces a catalogue of impossibilities that alone could allow the lovers to unite.[50] These take apart the "whole World" of his own creation and then rearrange it in a new metaphor recalling the "globe, yea world" of "A Valediction: of Weeping" and the "contracted" worlds of "The Sunne Rising," "The Good-morrow," and "The Canonization":

> Unless the giddy Heaven fall,
> And Earth some new Convulsion tear;
> And, us to joyn, the World should all
> Be cramp'd into a *Planisphere*.

In this first metaphor the lover shows himself willing, like the mower, to "ruine" the world to make it conform to his feelings. Its destructiveness is especially evident in his choice of "giddy" to describe the wheeling motion of his "Heaven," spoiling the possibilities of grandeur in "Loves whole World on us doth wheel." This lover imagines "Heaven" to be "dizzy," "sick," "mad," "foolish," "irrational," "stupid," "light-headed," "flighty," "inconstant." These impossibilities are the imposition of his own irresponsible feelings which, to achieve his "object"—supposedly "us to joyn"—willingly destroy the fabric of the world or forcibly reduce it (by the comic indignity of "cramp'd") to a "Planisphere." This kind of map is the projection of a sphere upon a plane, both flat and round,[51] and therefore a paradox contradictory to the facts of the physical world. By attributing irrationality to the motions of "Heaven" itself, he exposes his disbelief in the authority of analogies with a world containing within itself such imaginable disorder, such possibilities of violating logical and physical laws. By conceiving only impossible ways to achieve "union," he reveals at least disbelief if not disinterest in it as a reality, or perhaps even as an ideal.

Marvell's metaphors, because they include pointed adaptations from Donne's love poems, attribute his own speaker's delusive, distorting, and dangerous verbal power to Donne's language as well. What Marvell apparently sees as the falsity of its claims to authority, and therefore its essential lack of conformity to existence outside its own constructs, is especially exposed in the simile of stanza seven:

As Lines so Loves *oblique* may well
Themselves in every Angle greet:
But ours so truly *Paralel*,
Though infinite can never meet.

The "Loves *oblique*" are Donne's lovers in "A Valediction: Forbidding Mourning," which derives its conclusion that they can transcend the divisions of time and space by claiming the conformity of their feelings to demonstrable geometric figures:

Such wilt thou be to mee, who must
Like th'other foot, obliquely runne;
Thy firmnes makes my circle just,
And makes me end, where I begunne.

Marvell, by making his lover contrast loves "oblique" and "Paralel," shows how the same kind of analogy may be applied to demonstrate an opposite argument. The effect is not to establish the equal or greater authenticity of his speaker's language, but to suggest that Donne's lover is applying the seemingly impersonal and irrefutable demonstrations of logic and geometry to accomplish his "object" with as much wilfull distortion as the poet for whom "The Definition of Love" takes the form of a complaint.[52] He therefore denies the claims of Donne's speaker to achieve control over the flux of experience by adjusting his language in conformity to the facts of the physical world rather than by metaphorical transformations of them.

In the final stanza, without ceasing to order the world to satisfy his own feelings, Marvell's lover finally gives a definition of his "Love" which allows at least the possibility that he may recognize its distorting power:

. . . the Conjunction of the Mind,
And Opposition of the Stars.

The word "Conjunction" had the sexual meanings of "union," "marriage," "copulation," mocking the self-inclosed absorption of this "Love" which cannot "joyn" its "object" except in the "Mind." "Conjunction" was also the term for the union of elements in alchemy, altering the fabric of nature, making glitter out of dross. In astronomy it was used to describe the apparent proximity when viewed from the earth of actually distant celestial bodies. In grammar a "Conjunction" is a word which connects two otherwise separate clauses.

These possibilities of meaning for "Conjunction" call attention to the activity of the "Mind" connecting, transforming, uniting within itself, or in its language, a construct in "Opposition" to the world outside itself. With this world it has no essential conformity because it cannot discover true analogies between itself and that world, but can only invent them arbitrarily, as the poet's "Mind" in "The Garden" contrives the "resemblance" of "a green Thought in a green Shade." What the speaker calls "Love" is the conflict between the attempt of the "Mind" to create a "whole World" which would then provide such analogies, and the "Opposition of the Stars," operating by immutable laws in their own remote sphere, to such a delusive, distorting, and ultimately defeated effort.

This is the lover's "Definition" of his own "rare" feeling,[53] but even that claim to refinement and uniqueness—while designed by him to elevate himself above less aristocratic lovers—is ultimately a device used by Marvell for identifying him as a representative of a type also embodied in the mower, the "Unfortunate Lover," the lover of trees in "The Garden," the poet and the child in "The Picture of Little T. C." All these figures, we have seen, are variously cast in the role of the poet-lover by devices which resemble their mental constructs to the conventions of love poetry. Set in this context, the speaker's language in "The Definition of Love" is also specifically compared to Donne's in some of his most confident poems, and those most like Marvell's own "To His Coy Mistress," where he makes the largest claims for the power of his lovers to preserve their ideal against the threat of mutability. By using this comparison to point up the arbitrary nature of the language of his poet-lover and Donne's speakers, Marvell makes "The Definition of Love" a criticism of Donne's kind of poetry, much as "The Picture of Little T. C.," "The Garden," "The Mower's Song," and "The Unfortunate Lover" are designed to expose the delusive claims of conventional eternizing verse to transform the "World" and "Time" into the "Eternity" of art.

The nature of this criticism is Marvell's original contribution to the body of poetry to which his own poems discussed in this essay are richly, variously, and complexly related.[54] Implied in other poems but most pointedly argued in "The Definition of Love" is his view that this poetic tradition embodies the absurd efforts of the "Mind" to "Reform the errours" of the mutable world so that it will conform to its "Love" of itself, using an essentially arbitrary language which, in order to achieve this idealization, must distort, reduce, or even annihilate what it eternizes in poetry. It is perhaps because these poems imply by their burlesque language such a radical rejection of the tradition from which they grew that they are its last great embodiments.

5

Conclusion

The uses of the eternizing conceit in the lyric poetry of Shakespeare, Donne, Jonson, and Marvell embody each writer's struggle to define his own poems in relation to literary tradition. Their rich poetic inheritance, which each learned to use for his own ends, seems to have been represented for them by the convention of the poet's promise to confer immortality, the metaphoric assertion of artistic power common to their classical, Italian, French, and recent English predecessors. Perhaps it was the fact that this conceit was variously used by so many revered literary models that made its appeal to poets working in a period of vigorous literary assimilation, the later sixteenth century, when the love lyric, at least, seemed to have been born in their own language in the adaptations, imitations, and translations enthusiastically circulated in *Tottel's Miscellany*.

Shakespeare, most of all poets, was obsessed with the eternizing conceit, initially perhaps because it was the traditional embodiment of poetry's power to combat the transcience and decay that early haunted him in the "wide world and all her fading sweets." The boast that his art "giues life" that "shall not fade" recalls the promises of Petrarch and Ronsard, whose verses had proven themselves to be "eternall lines" in which the poets, even more triumphantly than their mortal loves, could escape universal decay. The metapor of the "rime" more "powrefull" than the "guilded monument, / Of Princes" attaches ancient associations of imperial might, law, civilization, to his own fight against "Deuouring time," endowing his personal struggle—"for loue of you"—with the enduring weight of poetic tradition.

The gradual transformation in Shakespeare's uses of the eternizing conceit in the collection of his sonnets numbered from 1 to 126 is among the most convincing signs that there is some loosely chronological direction to the grouping, and also that it is in some sense an autobiographical record. In approximately the first half of the collection the metaphor is used, with varying degrees of confidence,[1] in reinforcing the poet's hope to rescue his "loue" from "wastfull time." This use is Shakespeare's adaptation of a traditional definition of poetic power. Perhaps (we can speculate by analogy with his plays) because of his growing concern with other forms of power than time's waste of mortal beauty,[2] the eternizing conceit gradually becomes associated in the higher numbered sonnets with the power—sexual, social, political—exerted by the friend rather than by the poet "in war with Time." The power of the beautiful friend, which makes him seem to himself and to the poet unnaturally exempt from the ravages of time, is viewed with an increasingly painful mixture of passionate admiration, desire, frustration, horror, and fear, as a cruel and inhuman quality which the poet-lover must use his verse to unmask.

This shift in Shakespeare's use of the eternizing conceit, from a traditional means of defining poetic authority to a parodic attack on other kinds of power, seems to have originated in changing feelings about his friend, which ultimately dictated a different view of poetry. That is, the ideal "loue"—his feeling and his friend—which his eternizing poems are designed to celebrate becomes so painfully mixed, so cynically degraded that as a subject for poetry it demands at once concealment and exposure rather than enduring praise. The uses of the eternizing conceit in approximately the second half of Sonnets 1 to 126 act out that ironically double role for poetry. As parodies of poetic praise they both disguise and publicize. Their power is not expressed in the promise to immortalize the beautiful ideal but in their brutal insistence on his mortality. Their language does not transform the changing world into the "eternall lines" of art but perverts eternizing conventions to hint at secret and dangerous knowledge. The impulses behind their rejection of the traditional role of poetry seem to be profoundly personal, and the poems convey a sense of not fully disclosed, often murky private matter which distinguishes them from Shakespeare's eternizing sonnets and all other love poetry of the period.[3]

Donne's hostility to the conventions of eternizing poetry seems, by contrast, to be much more literary in origin. This is not to argue that his poems convey less conviction in rejecting traditional claims to poetic power, or that they are less passionate in feeling, or that they fail to convince when they dramatize private situations. Nor would it be accurate to describe the language of his finest and most characteristic *Songs and Sonets* as closer to the conventions of earlier love poetry. On the contrary, Donne's inventions are more experimental than Shakespeare's parodic sonnets, his claims to new sources of authority more innovative than Shakespeare's calculated perversion of poetry's traditional role. When Donne argues the power of his lover to give shape to experience by making his language conform to the facts of the timebound world rather than to alter them miraculously, he is newly defining poetry.

Yet this sense of discovering fresh sources of verbal power gives to many of Donne's love poems a radiance that makes them resemble Shakespeare's eternizing sonnets. Donne's express a belief in an almost magical efficacy of language to impose order on the flux of experience, even if its workings are said to be like those of natural, not miraculous forces. Although a radical reviser of literary conventions in the *Songs and Sonets*, he does not—like the poet-lover in Shakespeare's parodic sonnets—seem to have been disillusioned with the grand and enduring possibilities traditionally associated with poetry.

Jonson, more explicitly than either Shakespeare or Donne, identifies his own poems with literary tradition, claiming to find in the actual, present world living embodiments of the ideals celebrated by writers of all ages. With apparent ease he characteristically assumes the traditional posture of the poet, secure in his Olympian power to make discriminations, to deliver judgments, to interpret in verse a permanent moral design behind the shifting accidents of history. Yet his "authoritie"— a word occurring often in Jonson's poems[4]— is exerted within consciously imposed limits, implying a prescription for poetry close to his formula for the ideal "lines of life":[5]

In small proportions, we just beautie see:
And in short measures, life may perfect bee.

Beyond these limits set by decorum to achieve artistic control, as a number of his finest poems "of Love" acknowledge, are ranges of unruly experience and feeling where the poet's language is powerless to impose order on the painful changes and losses brought by time. His epitaph "On My First Sonne" (itself a reminder of how closely these men lived in their daily existence to scenes of mortality) most bitterly confesses the limits of literary language and convention. There the eternizing conceit mocks the father with its traditional power to confer life in a "piece of *poetrie*" which excludes "fleshes rage," "miserie," the "loves" of parents and children, all passionate human bonds and feelings, from its deathless words.

The radiant energy of the lover's language in "To His Coy Mistress," so consciously reminiscent of Donne's best *Songs and Sonets*, is no where else to be found in Marvell's lyric poetry. More characteristically his speaker is either a sophisticated and urbane observer, only playfully adopting the conventions of love poetry, or a lover whose complaints burlesque those conventions. In both kinds of poems Marvell displays a witty skepticism about his own language more radically critical than Jonson's sense of the limits of poetry. Marvell's distrust of poetic constructs as arbitrary impositions of the human mind implies that they distort rather than simply exclude. His view of poems as delusive reshapings of the world to conform with our desire for unchanging perfection is more distrustful than Jonson's attitude, more profoundly doubtful of the moral role traditionally claimed for poetry. It is an attitude utterly destructive of the promise of verse to transform its subject by miraculous power which will immortalize it, for it views the poet's reshapings of experience to be as self-interested, as distorted by desire as the fondest lover's.

Lyric poetry, while it may respond to such larger movements as the religious, political, philosophical, and scientific revolutions that transformed England in the seventeenth century, has most distinctly of all literary forms its own unique history, or histories, in which the shaping events are poems. The historical changes in love lyrics of this period are worked out in the individual poems discussed in these essays and in the multiple connections among them. Some direct causes for Marvell's wittily devastating criticisms of conventional love poetry are poems of Sidney, Shakespeare, Donne, and Jonson; while Marvell's own love poems are among the causes for the virtual disappearance of the eternizing conceit from English poetry. They mark the end of a period in literary history as well, perhaps, as in his own poetic development.[6] For Marvell is the last great writer of love poems in this tradition.

Notes

Index

Notes

1. Shakespeare

1. The simplest and least controversial among traditionally postulated divisions of the collection are: 1-126, mainly involving relations between the speaker and one or more young men; 127-152, mostly concerned with a woman or women; 153-154, which are loose translations of a Greek poem from the fifth century A.D.

2. For distinctions between sonnet sequences and collections, see C. L. Barber, "An Essay on the Sonnets," *The Sonnets of Shakespeare* (New York, 1962), pp. 7-11; L. C. Knights, "Shakespeare's Sonnets," *Elizabethan Poetry*, ed. Paul Alpers (New York, 1967), pp. 291-292; C. S. Lewis, *English Literature in the Sixteenth Century* (Oxford, Clarendon Press, 1954), pp. 327-328, 502-508.

3. The fact that the motif of a rival poet is used traditionally by Petrarchan poets is discussed by Hyder Rollins, ed., "The Sonnets," *A New Variorum Edition of Shakespeare* (Philadelphia, Pa., 1944), II, 292. All quotations from the sonnets are taken from the text printed in Volume I of this edition. Despite the difficulties presented to the reader by this unmodernized text, any form of modernization involves decisions of critical interpretation, often controversial, which are largely irrelevant to the argument of this essay, and might therefore distract from it. The reader who prefers to use a modernized text may compare where differences, especially of punctuation, alter meanings. However the *Variorum* text, which is that of the first edition of 1609, has itself no absolute authenticity since it is unlikely that Shakespeare prepared it for publication. The only changes I have made in the text are traditional emendations for obvious reasons of sense: "of" for "or" in Sonnet 65, line 12; "my" for "by" in Sonnet 54, line 14; "blanks" for "blacks" in Sonnet 77, line 10; a period removed from the end of line 7 of sonnet 126.

4. Terms like "earliest" and "first" in this chapter refer to the place of the sonnets in the numbered sequence as they appear in the 1609 edition, rather than to chronology of composition, although a reader familiar with Shakespeare's sonnets, narrative poems, and plays is likely to find that many of the lower-numbered sonnets from 1 to 126

seem closer to Shakespeare's writing known to belong to the years from 1592 to 1594, while many of those in the second half resemble more closely the language and concerns of plays written up to 1597, or even later. The only external evidences for dating are the mention of Shakespeare's sonnets in print by Francis Meres in 1598 and the appearance of Sonnets 138 and 144 in 1599 in *The Passionate Pilgrim*. The sonnets from 127 to 152 seem to be a medley of earlier and later compositions, apparently grouped together because most involve a woman. They are also different from the first group in that none is concerned with the attitudes and feelings associated with the promise of immortality in verse, nor are 153 and 154, for which reason these two groups have been omitted from this discussion.

5. Shakespeare's eternizing sonnets are grouped for discussion by a number of critics with whose interpretations this chapter fundamentally disagrees. Most extensive are Edward Hubler, *The Sense of Shakespeare's Sonnets* (New York, 1952); J. B. Leishman, *Themes and Variations in Shakespeare's Sonnets* (New York, 1966); J. W. Lever, *The Elizabethan Love Sonnet* (London, 1956), pp. 246-272. The word "eternizing," though graceless, is used throughout this book because it is the traditional term with which specific meanings have been associated and for which there is no substitute other than lengthy and repetitive explanation.

6. This observation is made by James Winny in *The Master-Mistress* (London, 1968), p. 62. Similar emphasis is given to the presence of the eternizing conceit in the dedication prefixed to the 1609 edition: "TO THE ONLIE BEGETTER OF THESE INSVING SONNETS Mr. W. H. ALL HAPPINESSE AND THAT ETERNITIE PROMISED BY OVR EVER-LIVING POET WISHETH THE WELL-WISHING ADVEN-TVRER IN SETTING FORTH."

7. For analysis of this sonnet concerned with structural questions, see Stephen Booth, *An Essay on Shakespeare's Sonnets* (New Haven, Conn., 1969), pp. 175-186, 209-214.

8. Syllogistic structure is discussed by J. V. Cunningham in "Logic and Lyric," *Tradition and Poetic Structure* (Denver, Colo., 1960), pp. 40-58. "When . . . Then" constructions among Shakespeare's sonnets are mentioned by Hubler, *The Sense of Shakespeare's Sonnets*, p. 25.

9. In Shakespeare's time "conceit" could mean "concept, conception," but could also refer to "a witty remark or idea, a clever act of deception, and the products of the artistic imagination" according to K. K. Ruthven, *The Conceit* (London, 1969), p. 1. For other uses of "conceit" in the sonnets see 26 and 108.

10. On the convention of the poet as gardener see Rosemond Tuve, *Elizabethan and Metaphysical Imagery* (Chicago, Ill., 1961), pp. 146-148.

11. The pun depends on such possible meanings of "stay" as "a suspension of action," "a check," "a cessation of progress," "a hindrance," "a duration," "a stationary condition," "a permanent state."

12. For other uses of "compare" as a literary term for formal poetic comparison see Sonnets 21, 35, and 130.

13. The resemblance is very strong between Sonnet 18 and the most famous passage from Sir Philip Sidney's *An Apology for Poetry*, ed. Geoffrey Shepherd (London, 1967), p. 100: "Only the poet, disdaining to be tied to any such subjection, lifted up with the vigour of his own invention, doth grow in effect into another nature, in making things either better than Nature bringeth forth, or, quite anew . . . . Nature never set forth the earth in so rich tapestry as divers poets have done; neither with pleasant rivers, fruitful trees, sweet-smelling flowers, nor whatsoever else may make the too much loved earth more lovely. Her world is brazen, the poets only deliver a golden." The influence of Sidney's *Apology* on Shakespeare is defended by Alwin Thaler, *Shakespeare and Sir Philip Sidney* (Cambridge, Mass., 1947).

14. This ambiguous line allows the meaning of "to time" as "in rhythm with time" as well as supporting the metaphor of being grafted "to time, becoming a living part of time."

15. The description of the kind of eternizing poem represented by Sonnets 15, 18, 19 and 65 is intended also to characterize—with appropriate modifications of detail—55, 60 and 63. On 81 and 107 see note 17.

16. The punctuation as quoted from the *Variorum* text, unlike many modernized versions, allows "meditation" to refer to what precedes or what follows, or both. Certainly this reading is not intended to suggest that the poem is a meditation in sonnet form, the description of some of Donne's sonnets given by Helen Gardner in "General Introduction," *The Divine Poems* (Oxford, Clarendon Press, 1966), pp. xl-lv. References to Donne's religious poetry are to this edition.

17. It is arguable that Sonnets 81 and 107 should be included in this list, but their self-pitying preoccupation with the poet-lover's "common graue" and "poor rime" makes them unlike the eternizing sonnets discussed, and closer in concern, tone, structure to Sonnets 71, 72 and 74. Certainly 81 resembles these more than it does the poems involving the rival poet, 78-80 and 82-86, which form a coherent group apparently

interrupted by 81. Similarly, Sonnet 73, although it mentions the speaker's death, seems an intrusion on the feeling of the three closely related sonnets surrounding it.

18. Sonnet 29 is discussed in contrast to Sonnet 120 later in this chapter.

19. See, for example, Sonnet 84 of Francis Petrarch, *Sonnets and Songs*, trans. Anna Maria Armi (New York, 1968), p. 139. Quotations from Petrarch are all taken from this translation. See also the sonnet from "The Countess of Pembroke's Arcadia," *The Poems of Sir Philip Sidney*, ed. William Ringler (Oxford, Clarendon Press, 1962), pp. 75-76. All quotations from Sidney's poetry are taken from this edition.

20. The most significant exceptions to the kind of poetry described as characteristic of many among approximately the first half of Sonnets 1 to 126 are 33, 34, and 35, a group which, uniquely among the lower-numbered sonnets, appears to concern a particular incident (which is not a conventional Petrarchan situation), although it presents it in ways significantly different from the devices of language devised for that purpose to be discussed later in this essay. For they employ formal and extended similes, a continuous present tense, sustained patterns of word-play and paradox, all devices which tend to impose a primarily rhetorical rather than a temporal pattern and have the effect of generalizing the incident, making it seem an illustration in the poet-lover's argument rather than chiefly a recounting of an episode as it happened in time. For further remarks on this group as exceptional, see nn. 28, 30, 31, and 50 in this chapter; Patrick Cruttwell, *The Shakespearean Moment* (New York, 1960), pp. 60-61; Knights, "Shakespeare's Sonnets," pp. 282-284.

21. The closeness of connection has been frequently noticed, though in different terms, between the eternizing sonnets and 64, as, for example, by Leishman, *Themes and Variations in Shakespeare's Sonnets*, p. 21.

22. Many of the lower-numbered sonnets such as 24, 27, 40, 42, 43, 46, and 47 discussed earlier in this chapter play on sound patterns which seem merely self-indulgent or mechanical and therefore do not have the kind of expressive significance attributed here to "Ruine . . . ruminate." But other devices of language in Sonnet 64 seem to support such an interpretation, much the way the reading given of Sonnet 30 in this chapter argues validity for similarily expressive (though playfully rather than bitterly mocking) use of alliteration and assonance.

23. For examples of "reflexive reference" and its relation to the con-

ception of the poem as a literary artifact, see Barbara Smith, *Poetic Closure* (Chicago, Ill., 1968), p. 150.

24. Divisions of the sonnets into different *kinds* of poetry are argued in various ways by Cruttwell in *The Shakespearean Moment*, pp. 1-38; Knights, "Shakespeare's Sonnets," pp. 274-297; John Crowe Ransome, "Shakespeare at Sonnets," *The World's Body* (New York, 1938), pp. 270-303.

25. Sonnet 54 is frequently grouped with previously discussed eternizing sonnets, for example, by Leishman in *Themes and Variations in Shakespeare's Sonnets*, p. 21; Lever, *The Elizabethan Love Sonnet*, p. 212; Winny, *The Master-Mistress*, p. 156.

26. Discussions of the metaphor of "ornament" are given in Tuve, *Elizabethan and Metaphysical Imagery*, pp. 61-78; Winny, *The Master-Mistress*, pp. 121-128.

27. "Fair" was not only the adjective most commonly used by other poets as well as by Shakespeare to express the Platonic-Petrarchan notion that outward loveliness is the expression of inward or spiritual beauty. It was also used as a noun referring to the lady in a conventional poet-lover's verse, as in Sonnet 21, line 4, or to beauty itself, especially beauty in nature, as in 18, line 7.

28. This distinction between kinds of "Canker bloomes" is illustrated with relevant quotations in the notes to the *Variorum* text, I, 144-145. Again the exception among the lower-numbered sonnets is the group consisting of 33, 34, and 35.

29. For related uses, see Sonnets 99, 111, and, as discussed later in this chapter, Sonnet 101. The context for such diction in Renaissance theory of the relation between poetry and painting is conveniently summarized by Tuve, *Elizabethan and Metaphysical Imagery*, pp. 50-60.

30. See Sonnets 35 and 99. Again, Sonnets 33, 34, and 35 are unique among the lower-numbered sonnets in employing the vocabulary of tainted nature common after 54 but employed earlier virtually only in this exceptional group.

31. The metaphor of the mask occurs earlier only in Sonnet 33. For remarks on sexual innuendo in the language of Sonnet 54 see Hilton Landry, *Interpretations in Shakespeare's Sonnets* (Berkeley, Cal., 1963), pp. 51-52.

32. Samuel Daniel, "Sonnets to Delia," *The Complete Works in Verse and Prose of Samuel Daniel*, ed. Alexander Grosart (London, 1885), I, 63. All quotations from Daniel are taken from this edition. For

discussions of Daniel's sonnets in relation to Shakespeare's, see Leishman, *Themes and Variations in Shakespeare's Sonnets,* pp. 78-85; F. T. Prince, "The Sonnet from Wyatt to Shakespeare," *Stratford-upon-Avon Studies* II (London, 1960), 24-26.

33. There is also perhaps an allusion to the doctrine of the odor of sanctity, here given a profane — even blasphemous — context (as it may also be given in Sonnet 94) but seriously used in such religious poems of the seventeenth century as George Herbert, "Life," *The Works of George Herbert,* ed. F. E. Hutchinson (Oxford, Clarendon Press, 1941), p. 94; "A Contemplation on Flowers," traditionally but erroneously attributed to Henry King according to Margaret Crum, ed., *The Poems of Henry King* (Oxford, Clarendon Press, 1965), p. 251. For sonnets using closely related flower imagery see especially 69, 70, 94, 95, 99, and 102. The pointed omission of any reference to their "substance" from the praise of the "Sweet Roses" in Sonnet 54 links it closely with the portrait of the friend in 53, with its opening question: "What is your substance, whereof are you made, / That millions of strange shaddowes on you tend?"

34. The vulgarity and fraudulence of cosmetics is a commonplace of Elizabethan poetry and a metaphor used especially frequently in Shakespeare's sonnets, especially in 21, 67, 68, 82, and 83.

35. See especially Sonnets 69, 70, 83, 93, 94, 102, 103, 105.

36. The vocabulary of this sonnet is clearly related to metaphors of painting cited in n. 34 above.

37. This pointed contrast depends on the Renaissance equation of "satire" with "harsh numbers." See, for example, Joseph Hall, "A Post-script to the Reader," appended to the 1597 edition of his "Virgidemiarum," *The Collected Poems of Joseph Hall,* ed. A. Davenport (Liverpool, 1949), p. 97: "It is not for euery one to rellish a true and naturall Satyre, being of it selfe besides the natiue and in-bred bitternes and tartnes of particulers, both hard of conceipt, and harsh of stile, and therefore cannot but be vnpleasing both to the vnskilfull, and ouer Musicall eare, the one being affected with onely a shallow and easie matter, the other with a smoth and currant disposition."

38. In 63 the vow is to "fortifie/Against . . . Ages cruell knife."

39. For a discussion of "illumination" see Tuve, *Elizabethan and Metaphysical Imagery,* pp. 30-31.

40. Sonnets 113 and 114 explicitly name the "deformedst creature" and "monsters" as parts of nature.

41. The appearance of the friend "To me" is further questioned by line 2: "For as you were when first your eye I eyde," with its ugly suggestion of furtive and prurient glances distorting what they see. This is another instance (see n. 22 on Sonnets 64 and 30) in which word-play could be dismissed as merely mechanical or, in this context, may be argued to express meanings supported by other language in the poem.

42. Sonnets sharing this vocabulary are cited in n. 33.

43. See especially Sonnets 77, 82, 83, 84, 103.

44. The only other sonnet in which the friend is called "Boy" is 126.

45. A sonnet closely related in subject and tone is 76, in which the conceit of the couplet seems designed in similar fashion as a parody of metaphors asserting the power of poetry in the struggle with time: "For as the Sun is daily new and old, / So is my loue still telling what is told."

46. Sonnet 1 of *Astrophil and Stella* is quoted in full in Chapter 3. Jonson uses "braines and hearts" in similar fashion as conventional synecdoches in "The Vnder-wood XXVIII," *Ben Jonson*, ed. C. H. Hereford and P. and E. Simpson (Oxford, Clarendon Press, 1954), VIII, 182. All quotations from Jonson are from this edition.

47. A similar reading of this sonnet, but one which finds it unsuccessful, is by Knights, "Shakespeare's Sonnets," pp. 296-297.

48. A detailed discussion of this poem, with a brief comparison to Sonnet 17, is given by William Empson, *Seven Types of Ambiguity* (London, 1947), pp. 133-138.

49. Sonnet 113 seems to describe the exhaustion of the natural world for the poet-lover, whose "eye" and "minde" are "Incapable of more repleat, with you."

50. The most prominent exceptions are again Sonnets 33, 34, and 35.

51. The editor of the *Variorum* edition scorns the view that this twelve-line poem was "deliberately placed" by Shakespeare as a "valedictory *envoi*" to the first group of sonnets, in I, 320. Although there is no evidence that Shakespeare himself arranged the poems in the order of the 1609 text, there is much internal evidence that some decisions about proximity and sequence were made. Therefore, the presence of the only non-sonnet, and the poem which most explicitly puts a stop to promises of immortality in verse, at the end of the series which explores the attitudes associated with that convention, seems deliberate. Its deliberate placing is also argued by Northrup Frye, "How True a Twain," *The Riddle of Shakespeare's Sonnets* (London, 1962), p. 39.

52. For similar uses of "minion" see, for example, "The Comedy of Errors," IV, iv, 63; "Cymbeline," II, iii, 46; "II Henry VI," I, iii, 87; "III

Henry VI," II, ii, 84; "Othello," V, i, 33; "The Tempest," IV, i, 98; "Twelfth Night," V, i, 128. All references to Shakespeare's plays are to *The Complete Works of Shakespeare*, ed. G. L. Kittredge (Boston, Mass., 1936).

53. A similar response to the tone of Sonnet 126 is made by R. P. Blackmur, "A Poetics for Infatuation," *The Riddle of Shakespeare's Sonnets*, p. 154.

2. *Donne*

1. *The Elegies and The Songs and Sonnets*, ed. Helen Gardner (Oxford, Clarendon Press, 1965), pp. 70-71. All quotations from Donne's love poetry are taken from this edition. Although the editor rearranges the poems for reasons given in her "General Introduction," she acknowledges on p. lxxxiii that the order in which they appeared in the first edition of 1633 "can be explained by reference to their appearance" in manuscripts prepared in Donne's lifetime and therefore possibly reflecting some of his own arrangements.

2. Edmund Spenser, "The Minor Poems," *The Works of Edmund Spenser*, ed. C. G. Osgood and H. G. Lotspeich (Baltimore, Md., 1947), II, 196.

3. Michael Drayton, "Idea," *The Works of Michael Drayton*, ed. J. W. Hebel (Oxford, Clarendon Press, 1932), II, 313.

4. This confidence associated with the eternizing conceit is mentioned by Leishman, *Themes and Variations in Shakespeare's Sonnets*, p. 68; Philip Martin, *Shakespeare's Sonnets* (Cambridge, England, 1972), p. 147.

5. One of Donne's most obvious departures from contemporary love poetry was his avoidance of the sonnet form. The title of his collection was given it by the editor of the second edition of 1635, who inverted the title of one manuscript collection, "Sonnetts and Songes," in imitation of the remarkably well-known volume of poems entitled *Songes and Sonnettes* but also called *Tottel's Miscellany*. See Gardner, "General Introduction," p. xlvii.

6. See also lines 17-18 of "Satyre II" and lines 1-7 of "To the Countesse of Salisbury. August. 1614," *The Poems of John Donne*, ed. H. J. C. Grierson (Oxford, Clarendon Press, 1951), I, 150 and 224. All quotations from Donne's epithalamions, satires, and verse epistles are taken from this edition.

7. See "Loves Infiniteness," "Loves Diet," "A Valediction: of the

Booke." Exceptions are "[Image and Dream]" (printed by Grierson as "Elegie X. The Dreame") and perhaps "His Parting From Her" (printed by Gardner as doubtful but by Grierson as "Elegie XII. His Parting From Her").

8. Donne's persuasion poems are characteristically constructed out of immediate situations as in "The Flea" and "A Lecture Upon the Shadow."

9. For a discussion of Donne's "situations" see Donald Guss, *John Donne, Petrarchist* (Detroit, Mich., 1966), pp. 112-123.

10. A detailed analysis of "The Good-morrow" is given by Clay Hunt, *Donne's Poetry* (New Haven, Conn., 1956), pp. 53-69.

11. For discussion of Shakespeare's Sonnet 7 see Chapter 1.

12. According to legend, seven Christian youths escaped the persecution under Decius by hiding in a cave where they fell into a sleep of miraculous length. See Gardner, "Commentary," p. 198.

13. Christopher Marlowe, "The Passionate Shepherd to His Love," *The Poems*, ed. Millar Maclure (London, 1968), pp. 257-258.

14. *Romeo and Juliet*, III, v, 7-10.

15. For other uses of "controules" see line 44 of "The Extasie" and line 17 of "A Hymne to Christ, at the Authors Last Going into Germany."

16. Donne associates "West" with death in the third stanza of "Hymne to God My God, in My Sicknesse" and in lines 9-12 of "Goodfriday, 1613. Riding Westward."

17. For other uses of this metaphor see, for example, "The Canonization," "Witchcraft by a Picture," "The Exstasie," "A Valediction: of Weeping."

18. Gardner follows Grierson in glossing these lines with a passage from Aquinas, in "Commentary," p. 199. Also implied by these lines is the popular belief that sexual intercourse ("dying") shortened the lifespan, referred to parenthetically in lines 24-25 of "Farewell to Love."

19. For a similar use of "busy" see line 8 of "To His Mistris Going to Bed" (printed by Grierson as "Elegie XIX. Going to Bed").

20. For remarks on connections between Shakespeare's sonnets and Donne's see Patrick Cruttwell, *The English Sonnet* (London, 1966), p. 28 and *The Shakespearean Moment*, p. 12.

21. See Chapter 1, n. 12.

22. Ovid, "Heroides and Amores," *The Loeb Classical Library*, trans. Grant Showerman (Cambridge, Mass., 1963), p. 373. All quotations from the "Amores" are taken from this translation.

23. See also "A Valediction: of My Name in the Window"; "A Vale-

diction: of the Booke"; "Song" ("Sweetest love"); "The Expiration"; "His Picture" (printed by Grierson as "Elegie V. His Picture"); "Image and Dream" (printed by Grierson as "Elegie X. The Dreame"); "His Parting from Her" (printed as doubtful by Gardner but as "Elegie XII. His Parting from Her" by Grierson); "On His Mistris" (printed by Grierson as "Elegie XVI. On His Mistris").

24. The interpretation given here differs fundamentally from that of Empson, *Seven Types of Ambiguity*, pp. 139-145.

25. For documentation of this popular doctrine see Gardner, "Commentary," p. 159. Similar imagery is used in "Song" ("Sweetest love") and "Witchcraft by a Picture."

26. Gardner prints in four-line stanzas "The Baite," "A Jeat Ring Sent," "The Undertaking," "The Exstasie," "A Feaver."

27. In lines 25-26 of "On His Mistris" (printed by Grierson as "Elegie XVI. On His Mistris") the speaker calls it "flatterye, / That absent lovers one in th'other bee."

28. See lines 33-36 of "To the Countesse of Huntingdon."

29. The interpretation of "endure not yet" as "nevertheless do not suffer" is given by Theodore Redpath, ed., *The Songs and Sonets of John Donne* (London, 1956), p. 85.

30. This is the argument in lines 13-14 of "Loves Growth."

31. Distinctions among kinds of analogies in this poem are made by Hunt, *Donne's Poetry*, p. 190.

32. A summary of some attitudes toward decorum in selection of images is given by Tuve, *Elizabethan and Metaphysical Imagery*, pp. 196-205. The possibility, noted by Gardner, "Commentary," pp. 189-190, that Donne may have borrowed the compass image from a madrigal by Guarini does not make the comparison more literary in character, although it may be in derivation.

33. This interpretation is in disagreement with a statement by Hunt, *Donne's Poetry*, p. 164: " 'Refine,' for instance, always carries a reference to alchemic distillation: Donne never uses it, as it was coming to be used in his time, to refer to purification of some general sort." For evidence that he did use it in both senses see line 21 of "The Exstasie"; line 81 of "Loves Progress" (printed by Grierson as "Elegie XVIII. Loves Progress"); line 28 of "Satyre I"; line 2 of "To the Countesse of Bedford" ("Honour is so sublime"); line 32 of "To Mr. Tilman After He Had Taken Orders."

34. These physical properties of gold provide imagery in lines 11-12 of "Loves Progress" (printed by Grierson as "Elegie XVIII. Loves Progress"); lines 25-28 of "To the Countesse of Huntingdon."

35. This makes them like the sun in stanza two of "Song" ("Sweetest love").

36. Among Donne's many uses of the figure of the circle, see line 31 of "To the Lady Bedford" and lines 46-48 of "To the Countesse of Bedford" ("Honour is so sublime"). A full discussion of this figure is given by Marjorie Nicolson, *The Breaking of the Circle* (Evanston, Ill., 1950).

37. The opening simile unites the lovers by implying a likeness between them both and "virtuous men," but it may simultaneously separate them by making one lover like the dying person and the other like the departing soul. The plural form seems to make the first possibility the primary meaning, especially since in line 21 both lovers are identified as "soules." "Though I must goe" in line 22 marks the beginning of their separation.

38. These conceits are discussed by Guss, *John Donne, Petrarchist*, p. 17.

39. In addition to "Song" ("Sweetest love"), "A Valediction: of Weeping" and "The Canonization," whose uses of similar language are referred to in this chapter, see also lines 6-7 of "[Tutelage]" (printed by Grierson as Elegie VII"); lines 14-15 of "The Expostulation" (printed by Gardner as doubtful but by Grierson as "Elegie XV. The Expostulation"); the third sonnet from "Holy Sonnets (added in 1635) Divine Meditations" ("O might those sighes and teares returne againe").

40. See "The Expiration."

41. The first two lines are a parody of the traditional categories of earthly glory lamented in such elegiac poems as Thomas Nashe's song from "Svmmers Last Will and Testament," usually entitled "A Litany in Time of Plague," *The Works of Thomas Nashe*, ed. Ronald McKerrow (London, 1905), III, 282-284.

42. The Book of Common Prayer as it was read in churches in Donne's lifetime, reprinted in *Liturgiae Britannicae*, ed. William Keeling (London, 1842), contains many such formulas: "As it was in the beginning, is now, and ever shall be, world without end"; "For the Lord is gracious, his mercy is everlasting: and his truth endureth from generation to generation"; "and bring you to everlasting life"; "hath restored to us everlasting life"; "that we may evermore dwell in him"; "all honor and glory, world without end"; "in thy eternal and everlasting glory."

43. The wording of line 3 allows "they passe" to refer at once to the categories listed in lines 1-2 and also to "times."

44. Another exception is the opening of "To Mrs. M. H."

45. Although Donne's phrase "this paper" is matter-of-fact rather than elevated, his speaker does not adopt the conventional tone of apology for his poetry such as Shakespeare's poet-lover uses in Sonnet 17: "So should my papers (yellowed with their age) / Be scorn'd, like old men of lesse truth then tongue."

46. See Matthew xii: 38-39.

47. Mary Magdalen's conversion is playfully woven into compliment in Donne's sonnet "To Mrs Magdalen Herbert: of St. Mary Magdalen."

48. For comments on this and other possible readings see Gardner, "Commentary," p. 222; Redpath, *The Songs and Sonets of John Donne*, pp. 109-110.

49. The speaker's tone may be measured by contrast with the much fiercer feeling toward such "idolatrie" in the third stanza of "The Funerall."

50. Ovid's *Metamorphoses* X, 329-331, is cited by Gardner, "Commentary," p. 223.

51. This reading obviously denies the possibility that "The Relique" is a "death elegy," the argument of, for example, N. J. C. Andreasen, *John Donne Conservative Revolutionary* (Princeton, N.J., 1967), p. 201.

52. In lines 15-16 of "The Primrose" the speaker points out the disadvantages of loving a celestial lady who "would get above / All thought of sexe."

53. For a similar attitude toward publishing private feelings see "A Valediction: Forbidding Mourning," "The Undertaking," and especially "The Canonization."

54. Line 19 of "[Image and Dream]" (printed by Grierson as "Elegie X. The Dreame"). Other "lovers Sonnets" are mocked in lines 3-7 of "To the Countesse of Salisbury. August. 1614."

55. For examples of such pastoral uses of "pretty" see Marlowe, "The Passionate Shepherd to His Love," line 14; Jonson, *The Vnder-wood* XXXV, line 2 and LXXV, line 174; Andrew Marvell, "The Nymph Complaining for the Death of Her Faun," line 65, and "Young Love," line 5 in *The Poems and Letters of Andrew Marvell*, ed. H. M. Margoliouth, rev. P. Legouis and E. E. Duncan-Jones (Oxford, Clarendon Press, 1971), I, 24 and 26. All quotations from Marvell's poetry are taken from this edition. Most readers would be more likely to describe Donne's poetry by such adjectives as "masculine" and "stout" in the sense of "tough" or "strong," used by Thomas Carew in lines 39 and 52 of "An Elegie Upon the Death of the Deane of Pauls, Dr. Iohn Donne," *The*

Poems of Thomas Carew, ed. Rhodes Dunlap (Oxford, Clarendon Press, 1949), pp. 72-73.

56. See, for example, "The Relique," "The Apparition," and especially "The Computation," which jokes about the "Immortall" liveliness of "ghosts."

57. See, for example, Hunt, *Donne's Poetry,* p. 92; Gardner, "General Introduction," p. liii; J. B. Leishman, *The Monarch of Wit* (London, 1951), p. 175.

58. For differing discussions of "The Canonization" see, for example, Andreasen, *John Donne Conservative Revolutionary,* pp. 161-168; Cleanth Brooks, *The Well Wrought Urn* (New York, 1947), pp. 10-17; Hunt, *Donne's Poetry,* pp. 72-93; Doniphan Louthan, *The Poetry of John Donne* (New York, 1951), pp. 112-118; Wilbur Sanders, *John Donne's Poetry* (Cambridge, England, 1971), pp. 50-56.

59. See Ovid, *Amores* I, xiii, and II, x.

60. The resemblance of the opening stanzas to verse satire is noticed by Hunt, *Donne's Poetry,* p. 74.

61. The pattern of angry and insolent dismissal turning to playful invitation and pretended acceptance makes "The Canonization" initially seem very similar in the shape of its argument to "The Sunne Rising." This similarity does not preclude the more essential difference argued in the remainder of this chapter.

62. The bawdy suggestions of "one neutrall thing" are further supported by Donne's use of "thing" to refer to female sex organs in line 10 of "Loves Progress" (printed by Grierson as "Elgie XVIII. Loves Progress").

63. For Donne's jokes elsewhere about this anatomical detail see line 24 of "To His Mistris Going to Bed" (printed by Grierson as "Elegie XIX. Going to Bed") and line 16 of "The Bracelet" (printed by Grierson as "Elegie XI. The Bracelet"), where "rise" may possibly mean "from the bed" and "in the flesh."

64. This appears to be the view of Hunt, *Donne's Poetry,* p. 87, and Sanders, *John Donne's Poetry,* pp. 54-55.

65. Donne jokes about "Loves riddles" in line 29 of "Loves Infiniteness" and speaks contemptuously about how poetry catches men "Ridlingly" in line 8 of "Satyre II."

66. This letter is quoted by Grierson, "Commentary," II, 16.

67. The interpretation given here is not fundamentally altered whether in line 40 Grierson is correct in following the 1633 printing of "contract" or Gardner in preferring "extract" appearing in manuscripts.

68. The speaker in Ovid, *Amores*, II, x, boasts of wasting his powers in continual love-making and eventually dying in the act, "and may one, dropping tears at my funeral, say: 'Thine was a death accorded with thy life!' "

69. For uses of "Myne" with sexual implications see also line 49 of "The Will" and line 29 of "To His Mistris Going to Bed" (printed by Grierson as "Elegie XIX. Going to Bed").

70. A slight variation of this satiric formula, "Court, Citie, Church," occurs in line 16 of "To the Countesse of Salisbury. August. 1614."

71. For some examples of such use of "spies," see "Breake of Day," line 8; "The Relique," line 5; lines 41 and 45 of "His Parting from Her" (printed by Gardner as doubtful but by Grierson as "Elegie XII. His Parting from Her"); lines 6 and 29 of "On His Mistris" (printed by Grierson as "Elegie XVI. On His Mistris"); "Satyre II," line 79; "Satyre IIII," line 119; "To Mrs. M. H.," line 49; "An Epithalamion . . . on St. Valentines Day," line 78; "A Litanie," line 152.

72. The Petrarchan convention of answering advice to renounce love is noted by Andreasen, *John Donne Conservative Revolutionary*, p. 163; Guss, *John Donne, Petrarchist*, p. 155.

73. This is the judgment of Sanders, *John Donne's Poetry*, p. 52. Similar reservations are expressed by Hunt, *Donne's Poetry*, pp. 87-88.

3. Jonson

1. "To the Great Example of Honor and Vertve, The Most Noble William Earle of Pembroke," VIII, 25-26.

2. For examples from Greek and Roman poetry see Leishman, *Themes and Variations in Shakespeare's Sonnets*, pp. 27-44; Earl Miner, *The Cavalier Mode from Jonson to Cotton* (Princeton, N. J., 1971), pp. 143-148.

3. *Epigrammes* LX, XCI, LXXXIX.

4. *Epigrammes* CIIII, LX, LXXXIX, CIX.

5. The group of ten poems comprises *The Vnder-wood* II. The last two stanzas of part four and some of the fifth had been used in *The Divill is an Asse* (II, vi, 94-113) and the first stanza in *The Haddington Masque*, suggesting that the group was not designed or composed as a whole. See Hereford and Simpson, "Commentary," XI, 49. The poems as a group are discussed at length by Paul Cubeta, " 'A Celebration of Charis': An Evaluation of Jonsonian Poetic Strategy," *ELH* XXV (Sep-

tember 1958), 163-180; Richard Peterson, "Virtue Reconciled to Pleasure: Jonson's 'A Celebration of Charis,' " *Studies in the Literary Imagination* VI (April 1973), 219-268; Wesley Trimpi, *Ben Jonson's Poems* (Stanford, Cal., 1962), pp. 209-227.

6. The speaker's avoidance of even the most playful assumption of the servant's role is in contrast with the lover in Ovid, *Amores* I, ii, where the description of Cupid riding in triumph suggested details for Jonson's poem.

7. Jonson makes this joke in line 101 of "Ode" ("Who saith our Times"), *Ungathered Verse* VI.

8. The relation in Jonson's poetry of the actual and ideal or mythological worlds is discussed in a variety of terms by F. W. Bradbook, "Ben Jonson's Poetry," *From Donne to Marvell*, ed. Boris Ford (London, 1960), p. 136; F. R. Leavis, "The Line of Wit," *Revaluation* (New York, 1947), pp. 10-36; William Spanos, "The Real Toad in the Jonsonian Garden," *Journal of English and Germanic Philology* LXVIII (January 1969), 1-23.

9. The importance of this sonnet is noted by O. B. Hardison, *The Enduring Monument* (Chapel Hill, N.C., 1962), p. 98.

10. For a summary of some long-recognized resemblances between Donne and Jonson see Douglas Bush, *English Literature in the Earlier Seventeenth Century* (Oxford, Clarendon Press, 1962), p. 107. The traditional ways of contrasting them have recently been perpetuated by Earl Miner, *The Cavalier Mode from Jonson to Cotton* and *The Metaphysical Mode from Donne to Cowley* (Princeton, N.J., 1969); Joseph Summers, *The Heirs of Donne and Jonson* (London, 1970), p. 15.

11. Jonson is reported to have "cursed Petrarch for redacting Verses to Sonnets, which he said were like that Tirrants bed, wher some who were too short were racked, other too long cut short," *Conversations with William Drummond of Hawthornden* (London, 1923), p. 5. See also *The Vnder-wood* XLII, line 67.

12. "A Sonnet, To the Noble Lady, the Lady Mary Worth," *The Vnder-wood* XXVIII.

13. The relation of Jonson's poetry to the tradition of the "plain" style is discussed in greatest detail by Trimpi, *Ben Jonson's Poems*; Yvor Winters, "The 16th Century Lyric In England," *Poetry* LIII (February, March 1939), LIV (April 1939), 258-272, 320-335; 35-51.

14. It is true that in such sonnets as *Astrophil and Stella* 24, 35, and 37 Sidney not only names his lady by the metaphorical title "Stella," but plays on "Rich," the family name of the husband of Penelope

Devereux, thought to be the original of the lady in the sequence. Yet he turns that historical name itself into a kind of metaphor (as Donne uses his own last name and also "More," his wife's maiden name, in "A Hymne to God the Father"), whereas the family names in Jonson's poems do not usually allow such meanings. An exception is *Epigrammes* XCI, in which he plays with the Latin origin of his subject's family name, "Vere," meaning "truly." For differing arguments about the significance of names in Jonson's poems, see especially Edward Partridge, "Jonson's *Epigrammes:* The Named and the Nameless," *Studies in the Literary Imagination* VI (April 1973), 153-198; David Wykes, "Ben Jonson's 'Chast Book'—The *Epigrammes,*" *Renaissance and Modern Studies* XIII (1969), 76-87.

15. Line 14 of "To Penshvrst," *The Forrest* II.

16. See Isaiah vi: 6-7: "Then flew one of the seraphims unto me, having a live coal in his hand, which he had taken with the tongs from off the altar: And he laid it upon my mouth, and said, Lo, this hath touched thy lips; and thine iniquity is taken away, and thy sin purged."

17. Howard Babb, "The 'Epitaph on Elizabeth, L. H.' and Ben Jonson's Style," *Journal of English and Germanic Philology* LXII (October 1963), 743, describes the tone in which Jonson speaks in *Epigrammes* CXXIV of the lady's beauty, virtue, and name as sounding "so literal, and he so refuses to adorn them in their development, that they affect us as nearer facts than figures of speech." In this epitaph Jonson again points to the family name as a way of placing a person in the physical, historical world, but uncharacteristically argues that his poem should concern itself only with what survives when the person has departed that world.

18. For a relevant discussion of *Astrophil and Stella* 1 see David Kalstone, *Sidney's Poetry* (Cambridge, Mass., 1965), pp. 124-132. The resemblance of Jonson's poem to sonnets of the period is noticed by George Johnston, *Ben Jonson: Poet* (New York, 1945), p. 121.

19. For other references by Jonson to the tradition of poets "rapt" with divine inspiration see lines 63 and 89-90 of *The Forrest* XII; line 12 of "Proludium," *The Forrest* X.

20. William Hunter, ed., *The Complete Poetry of Ben Jonson* (New York, 1968), p. 49, n. 3. This meaning of "Mary," the name of Jonson's first daughter, also seems to provide the metaphors in lines 7-9 of *Epigrammes* XXII.

21. See, for example, *Epigrammes* LXV; LXXXIIII, lines 5-8; CI, lines 28-30; CXXI, lines 1-4; *The Vnder-wood* LVI.

22. Jonson uses "becomming" in this sense in line 31 of *The Vnder-wood* VII.

23. Jonson was himself responsible for the arrangement of his *Epi-grammes* and *The Forrest,* but he did not live to see *The Vnder-wood,* first printed in the Folio of 1640-41, through the press. See Hereford and Simpson, "The Text," VIII, 17.

24. For discussions of earlier poets whose concerns resembled Jonson's, see Douglas Peterson, *The English Lyric from Wyatt to Donne* (Princeton, N.J., 1967); Trimpi, *Ben Jonson's Poems;* Winters, "The 16th Century Lyric in England."

25. In *Timber: or, Discoveries,* VIII, 639, he speaks satirically of the naïve student of poetry who thinks "hee can leape forth suddainely a *Poet,* by dreaming he hath been in *Parnassus,* or, having washt his lipps (as they say) in *Helicon.*"

26. *The Greek Anthology,* trans. George Burgess (London, 1852), p. 144.

27. The editor of the *Variorum* edition of Shakespeare's sonnets, I, 63, notes under Sonnet 22 references to the poet's old age also in 62, 73, and 138, as well as in sonnets of Petrarch, DuBellay, Daniel, Barnfield, and Drayton. Ronsard's *Sonnets Pour Hélène* are suggested as another source for the figure of the aging poet-lover by Peterson, "Virtue Reconciled to Pleasure," p. 221. In line 5 of "A Satyrical Shrub," *The Vnder-wood* XX, Jonson's speaker apologizes for foolishly valuing a woman's friendship "At fifty yeares."

28. See Jonson's joking about his "weight" also in *The Vnder-wood* LIV.

29. *Epigrammes* XIIII, line 9; XCV, lines 4 and 29-30. See also line 1 of *Epigrammes* LXXIIII and line 11 of "To the Worthy Author on the Husband," *Ungathered Verse* XX.

30. *Ungathered Verse* II.

31. *Timber: or, Discoveries,* VIII, 625-627.

32. Jonson also refers to himself as "Ben" in *Epigrammes* XLV, line 10; *The Vnder-wood* XLVII, line 78, and LXX, line 84.

33. *Amores* I, ix. The account of the episode in Book VIII of the *Odyssey* was also familiar to Jonson.

34. "Complaint of a Lover Rebuked" is actually the title of a sonnet by Henry Howard, Earl of Surrey, *Tottel's Miscellany,* ed. H. E. Rollins (Cambridge, Mass., 1965), I, 8.

35. This effect is observed by J. G. Nichols, *The Poetry of Ben Jonson* (New York, 1969), p. 145.

36. In contrast to romantic notions of grand, mountainous scenery, the most common seventeenth-century descriptive terms for such land-scapes were "Wens, Warts, Pimples, Blisters, and Imposthumes" according to Marjorie Nicholson, *Mountain Gloom and Mountain Glory* (New York, 1959), p. 42. This vocabulary resembles Thomas Dekker's description of Jonson's face, "full of pockey-holes and pimples," in *Satiro-mastix*, cited in Hereford and Simpson, "Commentary," XI, 54.

37. For a more traditional interpretation of this poem, with references to other such discussions, see W. David Kay, "The Christian Wisdom of Ben Jonson's 'On My First Sonne,' "*Studies in English Literature* XI (Winter 1971), 125-136.

38. This shift in tone is also heard and given a similar explanation by William Kerrigan, "Ben Jonson Full of Shame and Scorn," *Studies in the Literary Imagination* VI (April 1973), p. 216.

39. See *Timber: or, Discoveries* VIII, 635.

40. *Epigrammes* CXX is discussed in Chapter 4.

4. Marvell

1. The relation of "To His Coy Mistress" to a rich literary inheritance has often been pointed out, for example by T. S. Eliot, "Andrew Marvell," *Selected Essays* (New York, 1932), pp. 253-254; J. B. Leishman, *The Art of Marvell's Poetry* (New York, 1968), pp. 70-78; Joseph Summers, "Introduction," *Marvell* (New York, 1961), p. 13.

2. Margoliouth, "Commentary," I, 252, cites a parallel with stanza three of Cowley's "My Dyet," itself closely related to Donne's "Loves Diet."

3. The word "languish" is used this way in line 39 of "The Unfortunate Lover." See also Donne's "The Message," line 21. The conventional meaning may have derived from Latin love poetry—for example, Ovid, *Amores* II, x, line 35.

4. A possible source for this metaphor is lines 19-20 of Ovid, *Amores* I, ix, part of an extended comparison of the lover and the soldier: "The one besieges mighty towns, the other the threshold of an unyielding mistress; the other breaks in doors, the one, gates."

5. The syllogistic structure of the poem was observed by Eliot, "Andrew Marvell," p. 254, and is discussed at length by Cunningham, *Tradition and Poetic Structure*, pp. 41-49.

6. *The Poetical Works of Robert Herrick*, ed. L. C. Martin (Oxford, Clarendon Press, 1956), p. 84. The similarity between the two poems in

theme is observed by Joan Bennett, *Five Metaphysical Poets* (Cambridge, England, 1966), p. 125. Marvell was certainly aware of Herrick as a poet since they both contributed to *Lachrymae Musarem*, the volume of elegies published on the death of Lord Hastings in 1649. "To the Virgins to Make Much of Time" was published in 1648 in *Hesperides*, and was perhaps the most popular poem of the second half of the seventeenth century, appearing in ten miscellanies and eleven song books (set to music by William Lawes), according to Norman Ault, ed., *Seventeenth Century Lyrics* (London, 1950), p. 501.

7. This is a critical argument to consider in addition to the textual reasons for accepting "glew" in line 34 rather than the more conventionally pretty "dew." For textual arguments see Margoliouth, "Commentary," I, 253-254, where the editors give reasons why they print "dew" in the text but "make Marvell responsible for 'glew,' at least in an earlier version." Marvell uses the verb "glews" metaphorically in "Daphnis ànd Chloe," line 16.

8. A connection between Marvell's "am'rous birds" and Donne's in "The Canonization" is argued by John Carroll, "The Sun and the Lovers in 'To His Coy Mistress,' " *Modern Language Notes* LXXIV (January 1959), 4-7.

9. This connection with Donne's "The Anniversarie" is mentioned by Lawrence Hyman, *Andrew Marvell* (New York, 1964), p. 61.

10. The comparison with Donne's "The Sunne Rising" is noted by M. C. Bradbrook and M. G. Lloyd Thomas, *Andrew Marvell* (Cambridge, England, 1961), p. 44.

11. This impression of exhausting a "type" of poem is attributed to "The Mower Against Gardens" and "The Definition of Love" as well as "To His Coy Mistress" by Rosalie Colie in *"My ecchoing Song,"* (Princeton, N.J., 1970), p. 21.

12. While we can date most of Marvell's poems on literary and political figures by the events to which they refer and in some instances by their publication, these do not provide any clear pattern of development into which the love poems can be fitted. The poems discussed in this chapter make no references by which they could be chronologically arranged, and none appeared until the posthumous *Miscellaneous Poems* of 1681.

13. This distinction between Marvell and Donne has often been made—for example, by A. Alvarez, *The School of Donne* (London, 1961), p. 119; Joseph Summers, "Marvell's 'Nature,' " *Andrew Marvell*, ed. John Carey (Harmondsworth, 1969), p. 138.

14. *Epigrammes* CXX. Whether or not "Little T. C." has been cor-

rectly identified to be Theophila Cornewall, as in Margoliouth, "Commentary," I, 260, the relevant point here is that the title is in a form used to refer to an actual rather than an invented subject.

15. Jonson's "On My First Sonne" is discussed in Chapter 3.

16. The "child's alienation from and superiority to nature" in the first stanza are discussed by Summers, "Marvell's 'Nature,' " p. 147; Donald Friedman, *Marvell's Pastoral Art* (Berkeley, Cal., 1970), p. 176.

17. Genesis ii: 19-20; *Paradise Lost*, XI, 277. This likeness of the child to Adam is observed by Frank Warnke, "Play and Metamorphosis in Marvell's Poetry," *Studies in English Literature* V (Winter 1965), 27.

18. This argument is close to that of Summers, "Marvell's 'Nature,' " p. 147.

19. The difficulty in defining the final attitude in the poems is felt by Harold Toliver, *Marvell's Ironic Vision* (New Haven, Conn., 1965), p. 171.

20. Discussions of "The Garden" appear in each of the books about Marvell cited in the notes to this chapter, in most of the books on seventeenth-century poetry noted in other chapters, as well as in many other books and articles. These are so numerous that no attempt will be made to list them here or to indicate all the disagreements between them and the argument of this essay. For welcome criticism of the many discussions which ignore the relevance of the contexts in which the poem has been placed, see Colie, *"My ecchoing Song,"* pp. 142-143, n. 2.

21. The use of witty metamorphoses by the libertine poets—specifically, Lovelace, St. Amant, Stanley and Carew—is noted by Frank Kermode, "The Argument of Marvell's Garden,' " *Seventeenth-Century English Poetry*, ed. William Keast (New York, 1962), p. 298.

22. Shakespeare, Sonnet 130. Marvell refers to these symbolic colors also in "Eyes and Tears," line 18.

23. This connection between Adam and the speaker is made by Hyman, *Andrew Marvell*, p. 66.

24. In line 29 of Marvell's Latin poem *"Hortus,"* from which he appears to have borrowed many passages in "The Garden," his speaker cites these as examples of names he will not carve on the trees. For comments on the relation between the two poems, see Margoliouth, "Commentary," I, 243, 271. Marvell imagines Fairfax inflicting "Wounds" on "Okes" by inscribing them with the name of his beloved in stanza six of "Upon the Hill and Grove at Billborow. To the Lord Fairfax."

25. In line 48 of *"Hortus"* the reed is described as *"Sonorum."*

26. A gloss on this stanza from Sir Thomas Browne's discussion of

the vulgar error "That all Animals of the Land, are in their kind in the Sea" in *Pseudodoxia Epidemica*, III, xxiv, is given by Margoliouth, "Commentary," I, 268.

27. The possible meaning of "green" and its conventional uses are discussed by Leishman, *The Art of Marvell's Poetry*, pp. 313-315. Marvell more explicitly calls attention to the deceiving possibilities of metaphor in "Upon Appleton House, to My Lord Fairfax," where he describes the "Mowers" in the "Meadows" "Walking on foot through a green Sea" in line 390 and then in lines 467-468 describes the same scene when an actual flood "makes the Meadow truly be / (What it but seem'd before) a Sea."

28. A source in Virgil, *Eclogue IX*, lines 19-20, is suggested by Leishman, *The Art of Marvell's Poetry*, p. 314. For comparison of the poet to a bird see "Upon Appleton House," stanzas fifty-five to fifty-six; *Paradise Lost*, III, 37-40.

29. The explicit nature of the pun on *"thymo"* in line 56 of *"Hortus"* suggests it was intended also in "The Garden." For discussion of the numerous puns in the poem, including "Toyles," "upbraid," "close," "heat," "retreat," "race," "Mate," and many others, see Colie, *"My ecchoing Song,"* pp. 147-152.

30. Horace, *Odes* IV, ii, 27-29, on the bee's fondness for thyme is cited by Margoliouth, "Commentary," I, 271.

31. This poem was brought to my attention in an excellent discussion of it, to which mine is indebted, in Kalstone, *Sidney's Poetry*, pp. 87-89.

32. Kalstone, *Sidney's Poetry*, p. 88: "In the background of the poem, the four elements are in play: the lover's fire unsolaced by the water, air, or earth around him."

33. Here is one of the most obvious of many connections between this poem and "Damon the Mower," especially lines 3-4. In that poem the mower's preposterous claims to sympathetic oneness with nature are also expressed by exaggerated images of being served by it, as in stanza six. These resemble stanza six of "The Garden" (itself a parody of the convention of willing nature used by Jonson in lines 29-38 of "To Penshvrst"), and also "Bermudas," especially lines 21-22.

34. This reading is in disagreement with those which interpret the refrain as "an invariant motto," such as Geoffrey Hartman, "Marvell, St. Paul, and the Body of Hope," *Andrew Marvell*, ed. George Lord (Englewood Cliffs, N.J., 1968), p. 116.

35. In addition to meaning "to express" or "to inflict," the verb "wrought" carried many of the connotations it still retains as an adjec-

tive, suggesting elaborate or artificial fashioning or creating. Donne uses it with such meanings as a verb in line 22 of "The Relique" and as an adjective in line 33 of "The Canonization."

36. The "fall" in the poem is seen as the mower's "alienation from the 'true survey' of Nature that he formerly enjoyed" by E. W. Tayler, "Marvell's Garden of the Mind," *Marvell Modern Judgments*, ed. Michael Wilding (London, 1969), p. 263. Similar interpretations are given by H. R. Swardson, *Poetry and the Fountain of Light* (London, 1962), pp. 98-99; Friedman, *Marvell's Pastoral Art*, pp. 138-140. The description in stanza ten of how "Damon the Mower" accidentally "among the Grass fell down" is even louder burlesque, whereas the reading of "The Garden" in this essay would see the pleasurable "fall on Grass" of the poet in line 40 as altogether different in effect. For an opposite interpretation see, for example, William Empson, *Some Versions of Pastoral* (London, 1950), p. 132.

37. Words written in sand are actually a conventional metaphor for impermanence as in Spenser, *Amoretti* 75.

38. The "extraordinary and unprecedented" character of the poem is discussed by Leishman, *The Art of Marvell's Poetry*, p. 33.

39. For the use of "relish" in all three senses see Jonson, *The Vnderwood* XXVII, line 30.

40. This reading was suggested to me by David Ferry. Parallels are to be found in the grotesque comparisons to eating in stanzas eighteen and twenty of "Daphnis and Chloe."

41. "An Horatian Ode Upon Cromwel's Return From Ireland," lines 33-34. Resemblance between the descriptions of Cromwell's birth in lines 13-16 and the birth of the "Unfortunate Lover" is pointed out by Ann Berthoff, *The Resolved Soul* (Princeton, N.J., 1970), p. 85; Toliver, *Marvell's Ironic Vision*, p. 165.

42. Empson, *Seven Types of Ambiguity*, p. 167; "*Impression* meant an assault, a *meteor*, and the noxious effects of the night air, as well as the modern meaning which gives 'to make time take some notice of them and be respectful.' "

43. This connection with "The Mower's Song" is made by Berthoff in *The Resolved Soul*, p. 82; Barbara Everett, "Marvell's 'The Mower's Song,' " *Critical Quarterly* IV (Autumn 1962), 223.

44. A source for this myth in *Aeneid* I, 39ff, is cited by Berthoff, *The Resolved Soul*, p. 81.

45. In line 8 of *Epigrammes* XCI Jonson praises the deeds of Sir Horace Vere "Whose rellish to eternitie shall last."

46. This reading argues against an "immediate, rhetorical audience," either a lady or the "Resolved Soul," such as is postulated by Summers, *The Heirs of Donne and Jonson*, p. 158.

47. This discrepancy is discussed by Frank Kermode, "Definitions of Love," *Review of English Studies* N. S. VII (April 1956), 183-185.

48. For a similar use of "object" see "Eyes and Tears," line 3.

49. The connection with "A Valediction: Forbidding Mourning" has often been noticed. For discussions of this among other possible sources for Marvell's poem, see Dennis Davison, "Marvell's 'The Definition of Love,'" *Review of English Studies*, N.S. VI (April 1955), 141-146, and Dean Schmitter and Pierre Legouis, "The Cartography of 'The Definition of Love'" ibid., N.S. XII (February 1961), 49-54. Marvell burlesques the opening stanza of Donne's "Valediction" in stanza X of "Daphnis and Chloe." For a discussion of "A Valediction: Forbidding Mourning," see Chapter 2.

50. Marvell's use of this convention is identified by Leishman, *The Art of Marvell's Poetry*, p. 70.

51. Margoliouth, "Commentary," I, 260.

52. Something like this effect may be implied by the contrast of Marvell's stanza with Donne's comparison of the lovers to compasses described by Bennett, *Five Metaphysical Poets*, p. 124: Marvell's "is (to use Coleridge's terminology) fanciful where Donne's is imaginative. Only linguistic accident enables Marvell to get the effects he wants. Donne's image gathers up and concentrates the idea and emotion that precedes it." It is the argument of this essay that such "linguistic accident" is a calculated device for exposing Marvell's radical, anti-traditional view of the arbitrary nature of poetic language itself.

53. The lover's claim to "rare" feeling for "an object strange and high" burlesques the distinction made by Donne's lover in stanzas four and five between the "refin'd" love which he and his mistress share and "sublunary" passion.

54. This argument is in fundamental disagreement with the current estimate of Marvell's place in literary history, argued, for example by Colie: *"My ecchoing Song,"* p. 4: Marvell "does *not* break new ground in his lyric poetry" but rather "ends a great tradition . . . . He looks back at it, studies it, criticizes it, but he neither questions its absoluteness nor offers radically different expressive alternatives"; Leishman, *The Art of Marvell's Poetry*, p. 70: "This is one of the great differences between Donne and Marvell: while Donne, one might say, devised entirely new ways of saying entirely new things, Marvell assimilated, re-combined

and perfected from his contemporaries various new ways of saying old ones."

5. Conclusion

1. Although the poet's promise to immortalize his "loue" is spoken with varying degrees of confidence, there seems to be some decline of assurance so that 60, 63, and 65 sound less energetic in their assertions than 15, 18, 19, or 55.

2. This common concern of the plays and the sonnets with various forms of power is explored in detail in an essay on Sonnet 94 by Empson, *Some Versions of Pastoral*, pp. 89-115.

3. It is perhaps because they are unique among love poems of the period in their hints of such partially disclosed private material that Shakespeare's sonnets were apparently not thought of as autobiographical until the first quarter of the nineteenth century, when such a view was spread especially by the influence of Wordsworth. See *Variorum* II, 133-134.

4. For uses of "authoritie" in Jonson's poems see, for example, *Epigrammes* XIIII, line 9; LXVII, line 3; XCVI, line 6; *The Vnder-wood* XXXVIII, line 26; XLVI, line 10.

5. "To the Immortall Memorie, and Friendship of That Noble Paire, Sir Lvcivs Cary, and Sir H. Morison," *The Vnder-wood* LXX, lines 65-66. The phrase "lines of life" is part of a metaphor on "Life" as a poem expanded in lines 59-64.

6. Although none of Marvell's love poems can be dated, we know by their topical references that much of his verse satire, very different from his lyrics, was written after 1660, a fact which has led many readers to assume that the love poems were composed earlier.

Index

Index 287